To: Ethan
Fr: Dr Phil

"Safely Through on Broken Pieces!"

'.... Some on broken pieces...' (Act 27: 44)

*Thanks for your support,
May you be motivated,
inspired, challenged &
empowered!*

Dr. Phillip J. O'Connor

University Lecturer, Teacher, Preacher, International Conference & Inspirational Speaker, Author, Broadcaster, Youth Minister, Musician, Academic and Life Mentor.

15/12/23

Safely Through on Broken Pieces

Copyright © 2022 Dr. Phillip J. O'Connor

Published in the United Kingdom by Listening To Your Voice Publishing

The moral right of the author has been asserted.

All rights reserved. No part of this book may be reproduced, stored in a retrieval system, or transmitted in any form or by any means, electronic, mechanical, photocopying, recording, public performances or otherwise, without the written permission of Dr. Phillip J. O'Connor except for brief quotations embodied in critical articles or reviews.

Front Book Cover Image by George Elliott
Back Book Cover Image by Mavis Gibbs

The right of Dr. Phillip J. O'Connor to be identified as the author of this work has been asserted in accordance with sections 77 and 78 of the Copyright Designs and Patents Act 1988.

Because of the dynamic nature of the Internet, any web addresses or links contained in this book may have changed since publication and may no longer be valid. The views expressed in this work are solely those of the author and do not necessarily reflect the views of the publisher, and the publisher hereby disclaims any responsibility for them.

ISBN: 9781915327147

Book Cover Design: Listening To Your Voice Publishing and Dr. Phillip J. O'Connor

Editor: Annette Pearson

Typesetter: Annette Pearson

Proof-reader: Joy Braithwaite

Unless otherwise noted, Scripture quotations are taken from the *Holy Bible:* **(KJV)** are taken from The Holy Bible, King James Version, Public Domain.

Scripture quotations marked **(CSB)** are taken from the Christian Standard Bible®, Copyright © 2017 by Holman Bible Publishers. Used by permission. Christian Standard Bible• and CSB® are federally registered trademarks of Holman Bible Publishers.

Scripture quotations marked **(ESV)** are taken from The Holy Bible, English Standard Version®, Copyright© 2001 by Crossway, a publishing ministry of Good News Publishers. Used by permission.

Scripture quotations marked **(NIV)** are taken from the *Holy Bible, New International Version®, NIV®.* Copyright 1973, 1978, 1984 by International Bible Society. Used by permission of Zondervan. All rights reserved.

Scripture quotations marked **(NKJV)** are taken from the New King James Version. Copyright © 1982 by Thomas Nelson, Inc. Used by permission. All rights reserved.

Scripture quotations marked **(NLT**) are taken from the *Holy Bible: New Living Translation,* copyright © 1996. Used by permission of Tyndale House Publishers, Inc., Wheaton, IL 60189 USA. All rights reserved.

Dedication

I would like to dedicate this work to my wife Rhona O'Connor (Registered Nurse), who made tremendous sacrifices over the last 26 years to weather some difficult storms. I am thinking particularly of our journey and story as we relocated from the Cayman Islands to England in 2001. This transition required resilience, flexibility, humility and grave sacrifices as we 'stooped to conquer', established and carved out a new life and set a firm foundation on which we continued to build.

Additionally, to my parents Lamech and Thelma-Leta O'Connor, and the family in general for their hard work, and tremendous sacrifices they have made to see me through some challenging times during my early formation and beyond. Through their guidance, prayerful support, resilience and perseverance, I developed, the attitudes, values, principles, skills and personal faith necessary to make it through hard times and made it safely through even on my own 'broken pieces.'

> 'Through many dangers toil and snares,
> I have already come.
> T'is grace that brought me safe thus far
> and grace will lead me home,'

"Amazing Grace" is a Christian hymn published in 1779, with words written in 1772 by the English poet and Anglican clergyman John Newton (1725–1807).

Contents

Dedication i

Foreword by Dr. Floyd Antonio i

Endorsements vi

Introduction 1

PART 1

Context to the Story: Setting the Scene

1. Context to the Story Acts 27: Setting the Scene 11
2. Setting Sail to Rome 31

PART 2

Life Lessons and Analysis

3. Life Lessons and Analysis 39
4. Divine Illumination, Revelation and Visitation Despite Hopeless Drifting 66
5. Strength Under Control 122
6. So Near and Yet So Far! 182

7. The Swimmers, the Planks and the Broken Pieces 205

8. Rescued on Malta 251

PART 3

Impact, Relevance and Application: Bitten, Better, Not Bitter but Believing

9. Bitten, Better, Not Bitter but Believing 283

10. Personal Brokenness 294

11. Recapping Some Important Life Lessons 315

12. Parting Words – You will Make it Safely Through, Even on Broken Pieces! 335

References 370

Websites 375

Foreword by Dr. Floyd Antonio

Who is the man behind this book?

I am truly elated with the honour that my long-time friend would consider asking me to pen the Foreword for this literary milestone. I am satisfied that my honoured friend could have found many others who would likely do as good a job (if not better). I theorize that perhaps one reason for his request is that we both hail from the same rural part of Jamaica where there was barely a distinction between rich and poor or even black and white. Inherent dignity and decency were hallmarks of the day and people truly embraced each other in an atmosphere pregnant with genuine love and ambition. I am confident that understanding a bit about the author will make for an even greater appreciation of '*Safely Through on Broken Pieces*'.

I, therefore, invite readers of this book, to allow me to reveal some interesting and relevant drama, the type that the late Rt. Hon. Dr. Louise Bennett-Coverley (1919 - 2006) of Jamaica (Poet) would eloquently describe as, "pop story gi' me". People in general, regardless of our station in life, love a good story about the experiences of others. My presentation might not have you on the edge of your chair like a well-dramatized scene in a soap opera or a sensational headline from a gossip magazine, but it will surely highlight some of the crucial qualities that comprise real men and women. May I, therefore, present to you a snapshot of Dr. Phillip O'Connor?

I was fresh out of college and returned to teach Music at my alma mater where I met the young Phillip O'Connor. He was one of three students who stood tall because of their obvious gifts and talents in the area of music. (Junior Palmer and Cleveland Stanberry were the other young men). Deniz Tarik Önaç, a former high school homeroom (form) teacher of mine, was still teaching Physics on my return to the Frankfield High School Comprehensive (now Edwin Allen High School Comprehensive). His girlfriend Joan Tomlinson (now his wife) was also teaching there. The young student Phillip, who was then Head boy, soon became a dedicated guitarist with the school's cultural club, which became the talk of the town performing in concerts and winning for the school a number of awards and medals. Phillip also knew how to turn a tune. He earned the pleasant nickname 'Brother Moody' because of his special talent when it came to presenting the 'Nine-night Sankey' (a type of Jamaican 'Wake' singing). Phillip would later become a guitarist in The Sonic Salvation Gospel Band (headed by Deniz and Joan Önaç). I, therefore, present to you Phillip the singer and musician.

The trio (mentioned earlier) soon became my friends. They were more like my younger brothers with Phillip being the chief of the three. If they were too early going, or too late coming from a music event, their parents knew that they would be safe at my nearby place of abode. I had learned from Deniz Önaç (affectionately called 'Skip') who was but a few years older than I was, that a teacher and a student could be friends without blurring the line of demarcation or betraying a position of trust. This was now the case with my young musicians and myself. I can therefore present to you Phillip, the respectful, dedicated, polite and hard-working student!

During those high-school years, the young Mr O'Connor easily gained the respect of his peers. Other teachers also recognised some of his outstanding qualities and he soon became a leader among the students serving as Head boy

(School Captain) of the school Prefect body. Please help me to recognise Phillip, the student leader.

After High School, Mr O'Connor became a teacher. He graduated from The Mico Teachers' College (University of the West Indies), in Kingston, Jamaica. It is perhaps not a secret that he is truly a great teacher. I was privileged to be in Kent, England at a ceremony held in his honour for climbing to the apex of the academic ladder. Many of his past students were there to present glowing tributes in his honour. He has taught in numerous schools in Jamaica, Grand Cayman and in the United Kingdom (UK). As he pours into their lives, he has always been able to convince students that there is fun in learning the educational value that extends beyond the covers of the typical textbook. Selected by students and parents alike, he not only received the sole Gold Olympic and Paralympic award for personal excellence, respect, friendship, determination, courage, equality and inspiration of over a hundred staff; but also, was nominated for the Kent Messenger Teacher of the Year Award 2018 out of a thousand teachers. Let us hear it for Phillip the teacher and University lecturer!

Yes, Mr. Phillip O'Connor has always been a musician who devotes his time and talent to the church, but do you know that he has been a student of the Bible from a fairly young age? I know Minister Phillip O'Connor can boldly preach a sermon that would stir the sleeper and perhaps wake the dead. In any event, his message can cause the living to expand their spiritual horizon. Let us hear it for Phillip the preacher!

Mr. O'Connor is also an experienced radio announcer who served on radio in Grand Cayman (ICCI FM 101.1), producing and presenting his own 4-hour show *'Times of Refreshing'* every Saturday from 10am - 2pm. Smooth and eloquent lyrics would tame the beastly inclinations of a restless soul resulting in a sense of serenity. If you have any concerns in this regard, please ask his dear wife Nurse Rhona O'Connor about this claim.

However, just when you may be tempted to think that Phillip was super-talented and there was nothing left in the bag, the world meets Dr. Phillip O'Connor. The grown man not only discovered that he had the gift of speaking eloquently but he took it a step further, by immersing himself even further into the hall of academia and emerging as a giant of a man. Such a feat can only be achieved with diligence, consistency and determination. I therefore applaud and present to you Dr. Phillip O'Connor!

There is more! You are reading the foreword to a fulfilment of a prophecy that my mouth was allowed to speak at the doctoral celebration ceremony (alluded to earlier) and I quote:

'Let me, therefore, use this medium to prophesy that this man will soon further delve with courage and boldness into the writing of books! *His words of wisdom and insight shall go into offices, homes and libraries across national borders. Let us seal this prophecy in honour of Dr. Phillip O'Connor, the author'*. (Dr. F. Antonio)

Dr. Phillip did not get to this point without overcoming many obstacles, some of which I am fairly conversant with but I will not attempt to steal his thunder. I am fully satisfied that when you read this book or listen to Dr. O'Connor, you will be fully convinced of your power and capabilities. *'Safely through on broken pieces'* is a necessary read. Yes, you are encouraged to read and share this book but I also implore you to hear Dr.

Phillip live and in person. You will be glad that you issued the invitation.

On behalf of my wife Rosalie and myself, I want to congratulate you my dear past student, brother and friend Dr. O'Connor. Your marvellous success spans many fronts, the latest of which is this powerful, interesting and encouraging addition to the body of literary works. I am truly proud of you, so much so that I have to declare my joy and conviction in true Jamaican style: "Mi proud a you so tell, mi glad bag bus." (Meaning-' I am proud of you to the highest possible extent.')

I close with the words from an unknown Irish writer:

May the road rise up to meet you.
May the wind be always at your back.
May the sun shine warm upon your face;
The rains fall soft upon your fields and until
we meet again,
May God hold you in the palm of His hand.

Floyd Antonio PhD
Founder, President and Pastor of the CITADEL INC
P.O. Box 26774. Tamarac. Florida-33320
Email: thecitadel4real@gmail.com

Endorsements

Dr. Phillip O'Connor thanks for sharing this encouraging presentation. I have read this passage in Acts 27 in the Bible and heard messages on this account about Paul; but not quite like this, really informative and inspirational. There are lots to think about as we travel the journey of life. What will I do with the broken pieces in my life? One thing I know, I do not need to sit here and allow the broken pieces to hinder me from pursuing the opportunities that God has for me. Thanks for sharing.

Miss Marcella Freeman, Teacher and Former Colleague, Canada

The title of the book is a very intriguing one. It invites the reader to discover what is in store for capturing one's spiritual appetite. The writer's imagination will lead us to an understanding of what it means to be broken yet not to be discarded as worthless and unusable.

Think of the 'potter, the clay', and the question: 'Can any good come out of Nazareth?' This book will enlighten and enrich one's perspective of how one's life can be mended if one is experiencing brokenness and uselessness. The song says, 'All that I have to offer was brokenness and strife, but He made something beautiful of my life' which seems totally broken. A truly inspiring book to read.

Rev. E. Harvey JP, MA.

This literary work is a labour of love from Dr. Phillip O'Connor. It focuses a powerful lens on the vicissitudes of life and gives us an open doorway to grapple with the common human experiences of struggles, failures, disappointments, rejection, betrayal and loss. It reminds us that God has an ultimate plan for our lives that 'all things work together for good'. In addition, that He is able to use what we have left to give us the victory. The themes and life lessons presented in this work transcend age, race, religion and even the confines of time itself. This quintessential book, in its scope and thoughtfulness, is 'a must' read for all. When life rains down its torrents of perceived unfairness, leaving us in a storm of splintered dreams, it is reassuring to know that we can make it safely through on broken pieces!

Dr Fiona A. Blair, M.D. (Paediatrician and Cousin, USA)

****

During our lifetime here on earth, we have been through many trials, namely; sickness, disappointments, sorrow, griefs and pain. In my travelling years, I have had many frightening experiences. Some have been in motor vehicles on the roads and once on a ship returning from England with my husband and three children. After landing safely in Jamaica, we were told that the ship almost caught fire because there were problems in the engine room. As a family, we have endured many storms but by God's grace, mercy and favour, we have overcome and today we give Him the glory for His goodness.

In this book, *'Safely Through on Broken Pieces'* we read about Paul's voyage in Acts 27. 'The winds were contrary and the storm was very fierce. Even though Paul advised that there would be hurt and much damage to the ship and cargo, his advice was ignored. An angel of the Lord appeared to Paul and told him that no life would be lost; however, the ship would be broken and its cargo would be lost. Some swam to shore while others took hold of the broken pieces to float or paddle safely to shore.

Dr. Phillip O'Connor, you have made many sacrifices and I give God thanks for your achievements. '*Safely Through on Broken Pieces*' reminds us that we can be successful if only we use what we have left, and not focus on what we have lost.

Mrs. Thelma O'Connor (Mother)

****

Warmest congratulations to Dr. Phillip O'Connor for writing this masterpiece, '*Safely Through on Broken Pieces!*' This book is spiritual in that it draws on the vicissitudes of life of the Apostle Paul, and is practical in that we can apply the lessons to our lives: 'Focus on what you have left, not on what you have lost.'

Running throughout this book is a strong theme of the Overcoming Life: Overcoming obstacles, sufferings and pain. The author quotes our Lord Jesus Christ in John 16:33b (TLB) and reminds us that "…here on earth you will have many trials and sorrows; but cheer up, for I have overcome the world."

Particularly, Dr. Phillip O'Connor's book will inspire, motivate, challenge, encourage and equip its readers to overcome your own vicissitudes of life! Thank you, my brother and friend, for giving this body of work to the world.

Sutton L. Brown BA (Open);
School Business Leader and Church Minister

****

Relevant, revolutionary and saturated with resurrection power is the apt description of Dr. Phillip O'Connor's work, *Safely Through on Broken Pieces.* In an era devastated by the Covid-19 Pandemic, where fear, anxiety, isolation and uncertainty reign, the author demonstrates how the Apostle Paul chose faith when other persons would flee, freeze or faint. "Are you troubled by many minor difficulties or seemingly insurmountable challenges?" – Then read this book and be prepared to get a Christ-like mindset, one that thrives on "Broken pieces."

Kevin Bailey – Licensed Associate Counselling Psychologist/Co-Host: "The Male Box" on Love FM 101.1, Jamaica.

****

In today's world, we are continually exposed to disagreement, discrimination, negativity, violence, disasters and death. People facing one or more of these trials frequently look for solutions to their problems from books, in the media, through aid agencies, or by resorting to medical therapy. But what happens when all these 'solutions' fail, as they almost always will? Are we to give up by focusing on our negative circumstances, lose hope and become despondent or desperate?

This book, by Dr. Phillip O'Connor, argues to the contrary. Rather than wallowing in self-pity, readers are encouraged to deepen their faith in God, focusing on the positive and embracing optimism despite the prevailing difficulties. Using the challenges faced by the Apostle Paul on his missionary journeys as a basis for his arguments, Phillip shows convincingly that by embracing a strong faith in God, in spite of any personal pain or adverse circumstances, we can not only overcome our own problems but also inspire and encourage others.

As Paul demonstrated during his shipwreck, we must adopt the mindset that good can come from bad, whatever the situation. It is encouraging and uplifting to read a book characterized by HOPE. It will lift your spirits and in turn, will help to solve your problems. It is my prayer that it will find the wide readership that it amply deserves and I heartily congratulate Phillip for authoring this vital and timely literary work.

Mr Deniz (Skip) and Joan Önaç
(Former High School Teachers)

****

I thank God for giving my husband the inspiration to write this book. I strongly believe that this book came at the right time in my life after I went through the death of my mother, father and brother. 'Safely Through on Broken Pieces' will help you discover and fullfil your God-ordained destiny. I highly recommend this book to individuals who are going through hard times, especially during this Covid-19 pandemic. Hold on to your faith in God and He will take you through safely. God bless you all as you enjoy reading this book. If you focus on what you have left and not on what you have lost, surely you will come through on broken pieces!

Rhona O'Connor (Registered Nurse, Wife)

****

This book by Dr. Phillip O'Connor is indeed a marvellous and inspiring one. It provides insights on what to do in the midst of a 'storm' whether it be sickness, trouble, imprisonment or even death of loved ones. There is a way to shake off the poisonous elements that may cleave to you, in a manner similar to Paul's experience with the serpent (in the Bible and referenced in this work). He was not harmed in any way.

Dr. O'Connor notes that the hand on which the serpent cleaved, God caused to become a healing instrument of deliverance. The broken parts of the ship of life can become the part to success. God can use what you have left to bring success into your life, he assures us.

This book by Dr. O'Connor is a must read and a must have! It will inspire you to have courage even on broken pieces!

**Bishop Trevor Baxter, Dip, S.S. (Distinction) and
Evangelist D. R. Baxter,
Certificate in Theology (Distinction),
Church of God World Fellowship Int'l.**

Introduction

Trouble is one common denominator that brings all human beings to a level place. Absolutely no one regardless of class, creed, status, belief, education, wealth or race is exempt. Inevitably, difficulties, challenges, problems, troubles or 'storms' though different in scope, scale, magnitude or type, will visit us all in one form or another at different times in our lives. We may have different abilities, resources, support or strategies to cope but none is immune. These can cause tremendous pain, suffering and major disruptions to our lives. Nevertheless, our attitudes and mindset can make the difference to how we not only perceive our 'storms' but also how we eventually handle and navigate a path through them. Jesus, in John 16:33b (TLB) reminds us that '...here on earth you will have many trials and sorrows; but cheer up, for I have overcome the world.'

As I reflect on my own personal journey and the process of ridicule, rejection, failure, a brief period of homelessness, broken dreams, transitions and tremendous sacrifices, I am thankful for my early formation and values of faith, discipline, resilience, perseverance and a positive mindset that embrace problems as challenges and obstacles as opportunities. These values were incubated in the 'furnace of affliction' and through the 'school of hard knocks.' Nevertheless, they culminated in tremendous success academically, professionally, spiritually and otherwise. Furthermore, through my experiences, processes and storms, I am now able to minister to others with passion, compassion, power and purpose. I can now 'comfort those in any trouble with the comfort we ourselves receive from God' (2 Corinthians 1:4 NIV).

With this in mind, I thought that another title I had been reflecting and preaching on for many years would have been my first inspirational book! Instead, I contributed Chapter 5 in the book *'Being Christian in Education'* (2015) edited by Dr. Howard Worsley and Dr. Hazel Bryan, as part of my Doctoral studies. This work, *'Safely through on Broken Pieces'* is my first complete inspirational book.

After speaking on the topic, *'Safely Through on Broken Pieces'* in England, Jamaica and the Cayman Islands, I felt moved to start writing this book with urgency. This was in part, due to the impact, positive feedback and the requests I occasionally received for my sermon notes after speaking; as well as to provide encouragement and hope during the Covid-19 Pandemic and beyond. Requests for my sermon notes are not unusual I must admit. However, somehow this time was different when the secretary of a London church emailed me after my delivery and wrote:

> *'I dare not lose any point so may I use your entire sermon notes as an extra folded flyer inside the bulletin as this is so precious?'*

Whether delivered as a sermon or inspirational speech it was so moving to see and experience the response afterwards. Various aspects of the message touched the lives of my listeners whether young or old, as I analysed and demonstrated the context, relevance, usefulness and application of the lesson to their lives. On occasions after my presentations, the challenge seemed to be how to get through the number of people who wanted to give a word of encouragement or simply tell me how the message influenced them.

For instance, some of the comments were:

> *'Thanks for the message', 'That Word was for me', 'Many people were blessed by your excellent, inspiring and anointed message', 'I appreciate you sharing Phillip, very good insights…I like how you bring out the contrasts and the various analogies' or 'I want to thank you from the depth of my heart for your powerful, wonderful and timely message…we will never be the same again after that message!'*

As powerful, compelling and encouraging as these comments and feedbacks are; they do not reflect the sum total of my reason for writing this book. I tackled this challenge during the first five months of the Covid-19 pandemic lockdown. I too have my fair share of challenges and setbacks from the 'University of Hard Knocks!' These demanded firm resolve, resilience, determination, preservation and much fervent prayer to pull through. Having a sense of purpose, a powerful prayer life and a positive mindset are crucial in achieving my goals.

In 1984 as a final year teacher-trainee, I wrote in my Mico College, University of the West Indies magazine article, '*Meet Yourself*' and penned these words:

> *'Realistic goals may be achieved provided one has a dynamic sense of purpose that is far superior to all forces that constitute the odds' (O'Connor, 1984).*

This work is inspired by some of my own life experiences as well as the aforementioned sermon of the same name that I delivered. However, it is not meant to be 'sermon notes' but a much deeper, analytical exploration which borrows some inspiration from philosophy, theology, education and psychology.

I write this book primarily from a faith perspective, based on and underpinned by Paul's experience in Acts 27 and part of chapter 28 in the Bible, with many references drawn therefrom, and elsewhere. However, I hope that this work will be insightful, inspirational, motivational, encouraging and challenging to both those of faith and none. It is not my intention to provide a descriptive account of Paul's journey from Jerusalem to Rome to face Caesar for a trial in his defence of his Christian Faith. Instead, I will use that account as a context in Part 1, to help me glean some important and relevant life lessons, emerging themes, insights and strategies on how to cope with and handle the setbacks, incidents, accidents, traumas, failures and vicissitudes of life which will have a broad inspirational appeal.

We might be tempted to simply give up and just walk away or to lose focus, direction and purpose, hence not achieving or realise our God-given potential. Through the chapters of this book, I will suggest some insights, life lessons and strategies to handle life's circumstances on the blustery stormy sea of life of hurts, pain, disappointments, failures and rejection and reversals to find hope, meaning purpose and new direction. Nevertheless, how is this possible you might ask? Well, that is exactly what I will share!

It is important that we understand how to cope when the decisions of others affect us, acknowledging 'that all things work for good…' (Romans 8:28). Perhaps, you are terrified and traumatised by life's circumstances; it could be a financial, relational, medical or a domestic storm that test your resilience to the core. Yet, 'if you believe in the sovereignty of God, you will know that He can make even a bad decision or situation turn out for good. He can make a miracle out of a mistake,' (Jakes 1996, p52). Not all things are good; however, they can be used for good.

He (God) does not necessarily need what you have lost to bless you, but can use what you have left from the broken pieces of your life's experiences to propel you into your purpose and destiny. Even if you feel like you have absolutely nothing left after your storms, the truth is that you do have something there. You may not feel that way but life will never leave you completely destitute. Scripture reminds us 'I will never leave you not forsake you!' (Hebrews 13:5).

Reflection: How do you handle your personal storms? Do you worry, panic, and become stressed out or afraid? Do you feel the fear and go through your storms anyway or do you allow your fears, cares and tears to intimidate and overpower you, so that you abort your God-given potential and destiny?

I will demonstrate how the Apostle Paul exercised tremendous faith, courage and confidence in God as he defended the faith, endured grave trials, tests, persecutions and life-threatening circumstances in firm defence of his personal faith in God and his calling in Christ Jesus. Unquestionable, as Saul of Tarsus, he persecuted the Church but as Paul the Apostle, he made a tremendous difference and impact to our understanding of Faith and the Gospel of Christ to this day through his life examples and profound Epistles. Once converted, he remained steadfast to the very end. It is not really how you start; it is how you finish, and equally important, is the process in between! Paul maintained his firm faith to the very end, leaving behind these powerful words for us to contemplate in light of our own mortality:

> *I have fought a good fight, I have finished my course, I have kept the faith: Henceforth there is laid up for me a crown of righteousness, which the Lord, the righteous judge, shall give me at that day: and not to me only, but unto all them also that love his appearing (2 Timothy 4:7-8).*

For clarity, I divide this book into three distinct sections.

Part 1:

- ❖ Valuing the power of your personal story
- ❖ Context and descriptive accounts on some aspects of Paul's early life, conversion, trials and perilous journey when sailing to Rome

Part 2

- ❖ Life lessons and analysis of the process, extracting useful, relevant and applicable life lessons from the story
- ❖ Divine illumination and visitation despite hopeless drifting
- ❖ The power of the unseen: Strength under control
- ❖ So near and yet so far
- ❖ Unaided swimmers, the planks and the broken pieces
- ❖ Rescued on Malta

Part 3

- ❖ A personal word of encouragement, Further applications
- ❖ Coping while bitten: Being better, not bitter but believing
- ❖ Personal brokenness: Process, pain-passion, purpose and power
- ❖ Recapping some important life lessons
- ❖ Parting words

Do not worry about what you have lost, God can and will use what you have left! Indeed, you can make it even on the broken pieces of your shattered life!

(Dr. Phillip O'Connor 2022)

PART 1

Context to the Story: Setting the Scene

1. Context to the Story Acts 27: Setting the Scene

And do not be conformed to this world, but be transformed by the renewing of your mind, that you may prove what is that good and acceptable and perfect will of God.
(Romans 12:2, NKJV)

Value the Power of Your Personal Story
How do you handle the tough times in your life? How do you cope when things might have started out well whether in your professional, relational, financial, mental, emotional, spiritual or physical life then take a turn for the worse? Do you respond by succumbing to stress, discouragement, depression, grief, resentment, regrets, unforgiveness, bitterness, helplessness or lack of direction? How do you feel about the things (fair or unfair), that have happened to you in life; and do you believe in the value of your personal story?

Dealing with the vicissitudes of life is not easy. The truth is that it can be daunting when you have worked hard to put safeguards in place for a smooth, happy relationship, financially stable future or healthy life and things unexpectedly take a turn for the worse, especially if it is outside your control. You may feel helpless, sad, and lonely; discouraged and even question your faith in life, love, humanity or God. Regardless of what you have been through in life, you can take the broken pieces of your shattered life and broken dreams and move on to overwhelming success to fulfil your God-given potential and purpose!

Here is a thought for your consideration: Your personal story has tremendous value and significance! Every one of us has a story and we are all still in the process of living that narrative through the different chapters, seasons and experiences of life.

'Your story is what you have, what you will always have. It is something to own' (Michelle Obama, 2018). The tendency and temptation might be to rush, ignore or despise our journeys and processes. However, we should value our stories and processes. The experiences you might have had, or those you are going through now could also be a tremendous source of help or even be the answers to someone else' dilemmas.

A seemingly simple act of sharing your story through whatever platform or media could serve as a source of inspiration, motivation, hope, comfort and faith for someone across the nations of the world. Your story could also save the life of someone who feels isolated, abandoned, hopeless and alone. Your very own personal story could make all the difference to show that such a one is not alone; rather, that someone else had been through what he or she is now experiencing and truly understands and empathises. Consequently, never underestimate the value of your personal story!

Do not worry about what you have lost, God can and will use what you have left! Indeed, you can make it even on the broken pieces of your shattered life! It is all part of your compelling narrative, and whilst much may be beyond your control, you decide how your story ends! You may not be able to change the actual situation but you can change your response to it. Attitude is everything.

Consider with me the following:

Put in prison repeatedly
Flogged an uncounted number of times
Faced death on numerous occasions
Received 39 lashes from the Jews on five separate occasions
Beaten three times with rods
Stoned one time
Shipwrecked 3 times
Stuck at sea one day and a night
Exposed continually to danger from rivers and robbers
Exposed to danger from one's own countrymen, as well as the Gentiles
Exposed to danger in the city, in the country, at sea, and from false brothers
Was weary, gone without sleep and often in pain
Was often hungry, thirsty, cold and naked
And continually concerned about the growth and development of a number of churches.

This was the account summary of the Apostle Paul as recorded in 2 Corinthians 11:23-28 in the Bible as he recounted some of the trials he faced. Undoubtedly, this almost seems too much for one person to bear. What is interesting here, I believe is the attitude with which Paul bore and recounted these trials, which he actually referred to as 'light afflictions' (2 Corinthians 4:17). No doubt, it was stressful and painful as he went through these experiences. Vernon Law reminds us that 'experience is a hard teacher. He gives the test first then the lesson later.' Often, as we go through our trials and challenges, we sometimes complain, murmur, get stressed, develop a sense of helplessness, loss of direction, guilt, fear, mistrust, anger and lack of confidence.

For some, these might seem the natural and even expected human responses to our trials and challenging circumstances in life. However, our attitude it is said can determine our altitude in life. In other words, your perspective to your challenges can directly affect how your story ends. Even in the toughest situation, you can purpose to stand firm, hold on to your faith, trust in God and not be swayed by the negative influences or circumstances. You can also see the opportunities that those situations hold, though they might initially be obscured by grief and seem too painful to endure.

Reflection: How do we see your trials and challenges? Is there a way to learn from the terrible experiences you encounter in life? Can you develop a positive attitude and learn from them to be better, not bitter and to make a difference in the lives of others from your personal story and life experiences?

Life Lessons from Paul's Experiences
I believe that the experiences of Paul and his responses to them, especially as he and 275 others sailed from Jerusalem to Italy, can teach us some valuable life lessons on how to cope as we experience our personal 'storms' (trials, difficulties, change, loss, hurts, pains, reversals, disappointments or even death of our dreams or loved ones). I could have used other individuals or experiences, however, as mentioned in my introduction, after preaching on this text under the title of *'Safely through on broken pieces'* I thought what better title to give this book! There is so much to glean from Paul's story. Undoubtedly, these life lessons will help us navigate the tumultuous storms of our life experiences. Some

of the life lessons and applications I will highlight may not be new to you at all, neither will my analysis and application be exhaustive; but I will present them in a manner that will 'Motivate, inspire, challenge and encourage' and hopefully effect a shift in paradigm that will help you to see your:

Crosses as crowns

Stumbling blocks as stepping stones

Impediments as implements

Obstacles as opportunities

Messes as messages

Muddles as miracles

Trials as triumphs

Tests as testimonies

This seems so idealistic, unrealistic or even unreasonable you might say, and surely, it is not easy. As the saying goes, 'He or she, who feels it, knows it!' In other words, our trials and setbacks, hurts and pains in life are deeply personal and painful. You may feel that no one has the right to tell you how to deal with your hurts or to lecture you on how to cope. You might still be angry, bitter or filled with unforgiveness over the manner in which you were treated.

Perhaps you feel like no one really understands. Possibly, you were mistreated, overlooked, ostracised, deprived or even abused in some way. You might have already gotten spiritual or professional help to cope. You might have shared with a friend in confidence or have bottled things up, suffered in silence all these years and have been bearing your griefs all alone with no one to trust or confide in. This can cause a sense of burnout and deep isolation, as you minister to others even in your pain and simply cannot find anyone to open up to in your moment of desperate need.

As we go through these processes it can be very difficult and even seemingly impossible to see a 'light at the end of the tunnel' let alone to see how personal crosses, stumbling blocks, impediments, obstacles, messes, muddles, trials and tests can remotely be viewed through the lens of crowns, stepping stones, implements, opportunities, messages, miracles, triumphs and testimonies. These potential outcomes in no wise negate the grieving process! We must embrace our humanity and respond authentically to life's challenges. Faith does not necessarily negate fear. Courage is not the absence of fear but the conquering of fear. Sometimes we have to step out afraid! We '…do not grieve like the rest of mankind, who have no hope' (1 Thessalonians 4:13 NIV). In a strange way, we grieve while being confident in hope, afraid, yet full of courage.

Although this text specifically addresses the resurrection, yet it is applicable in this context. 'Jesus wept' (John 11:35) at the tomb of Lazarus after purposefully delaying his trip by four days to see him alive, knowing that He would raise him from the dead! Grieving our deeply painful experiences is only human. It is part of the process. However, there can be a time when grieving, how we grieve and for how long we grieve, can become unhealthy. There is the need for closure.

Reflection: After reading this, how do you deal with the trials, deeply painful experiences and storms in your life? What is your attitude to your storms, be they relational, financial, professional, medical or otherwise? How can you develop a positive mindset that will see you through these circumstances so that you too can use them for God's glory and the benefit of others?

A Closer Look at Paul's Life
As we look initially at a descriptive account of Paul's life, let us remember that we cannot make it in our own strength but indeed, 'I can do all things through Christ which strengtheneth me' (Philippians 4:13). It is also very important to remember that 'we have this treasure in earthen vessel that the excellency of the power may be of God and not of us' (2 Corinthians 4:7). This bodily (earthen) vessel of clay holds the precious treasure of the Holy Spirit and it is through Him that we are empowered, made secure and comforted. This realisation should embolden us to face life with confidence. Furthermore, it should help us to place a high value on ourselves: knowing who we are, whose we are and what we embody: our identity, position in Christ and our condition. Thus, this realisation should inspire us to understand and embrace our purpose by virtue of this understanding of our position in Christ, which transcends and supersedes our conditions and circumstances.

The analyses and applications from this story reflecting some experiences of Paul could be difficult to apply in our lives. However, we can make it through. This is possible because of the strength that God gives. With a firm realisation that we have His Holy Spirit within us to guide us into all truth, bring all things back to our remembrance, empowers us for service and to seal us unto the day of redemption (Ephesians 4:30), we can confront life's challenges with confidence.

The Book of Acts describes Paul as a Roman citizen (Acts 16:37, 22:25-29) although he was from a Jewish family based in the city of Tarsus, which was a trading city on the Mediterranean. In Acts 23:6, Paul was described as a Pharisee, and this corroborates with his own account as recorded in Philippians 3:5-6. Being a 'Pharisee' meant that Paul was a member of an ancient Jewish religious group (Sanhedrin), who followed the Oral Law in addition to the Torah and attempted to live in a constant state of purity. The 'Torah', refers to the Jewish Pentateuch, or a parchment scroll on which the Pentateuch is written for use in services in synagogues. The Torah (or Pentateuch, as Biblical scholars sometimes call it), is the collective name for the first five Books of the Bible: Genesis, Exodus, Leviticus, Numbers and Deuteronomy.

Paul was highly educated and studied 'under one of the most respected teaching lineages.' He seems to have been educated beyond the Torah expertise. Dr Floyd Antonio in his book, *'Leadership by the Book – Scriptural Leadership Principles for Contemporary Application'* noted that, Paul

> *'Studied under the famed Gamaliel (Acts 22:3); and after his education would naturally be expected to return to Tarsus and learn the trade of his father…he had leadership characteristics such as determination, knowledge, zeal and focus even while he was meeting out harsh treatment to early Christians' (2016, p127).*

This advanced scholarship no doubt included a deep understanding of the Prophets, Classical Literature and Philosophy. His exchange with King Agrippa and Festus on one of the defences of his faith reflects not only Paul's intense academic rigour but also his verbal virtuoso:

> *At this point, Festus interrupted Paul's defence. "You are out of your mind, Paul!" he shouted. "Your great*

> *learning is driving you insane. I am not insane, most excellent Festus," Paul replied. "What I am saying is true and reasonable. The king is familiar with these things, and I can speak freely to him. I am convinced that none of this has escaped his notice, because it was not done in a corner. King Agrippa, do you believe the prophets? I know you do. Then Agrippa said to Paul, Do you think that in such a short time you can persuade me to be a Christian?" (Acts 26:24-28 NIV).*

Despite this academic learning, rigour, and tremendous persuasive ability, his primary vocation was as a tent-maker (Acts18:1-3). He worked with Priscilla and Aquila who in the Book of Romans 16:3-4 were mentioned as "co-workers."

Paul the Persecutor Transformed

Before his transformation, Paul was actually Saul of Tarsus. He had a dramatic conversion experience on the road to Damascus that changed his life, message, destiny and purpose completely. In the Book of the Acts of the Apostles in the Bible, Saul was depicted as a persecutor of the early 'Jesus movement' that started in Jerusalem. In the times of the early Christians, he was indeed one to fear. In Acts 7:58 and Acts 8:1, Saul is named among those who gave approval of the stoning to death of Stephen, a faithful follower of Jesus Christ. Saul was deeply convicted that he was doing God service by persecuting Christians. In his words:

> *'I too was convinced that I ought to do all that was possible to oppose the name of Jesus of Nazareth. And that is just what I did in Jerusalem. On the authority of the chief priests, I put many of the Lord's people in prison, and when they were put to death, I cast my vote*

> *against them. Many a time I went from one synagogue to another to have them punished, and I tried to force them to blaspheme. I was so obsessed with persecuting them that I even hunted them down in foreign cities.' (Acts 26:9-11 NIV)*

Saul was not only threatening the Lord's disciples with murder, but as we just saw was complicit in Stephen's death by stoning. He was on his way to Damascus on such a mission (as recorded in Acts 9). There we find the account of Paul having a personal encounter with the resurrected Jesus. He had approached the High Priest and requested letters to the synagogues in Damascus, anticipating locating Believers there who he would take as prisoners to Jerusalem. However, as he neared Damascus, a bright light from Heaven flashed around him and he fell, struck from his beast and blinded by a bright light he heard Jesus say, "Saul, Saul, why do you persecute me?" (Acts 9:4, NIV).

He recounted this account in his defence before King Agrippa:

> *About noon, King Agrippa, as I was on the road, I saw a light from heaven, brighter than the sun, blazing around me, and my companions. We all fell to the ground, and I heard a voice saying to me in Aramaic, 'Saul, Saul, why do you persecute me? It is hard for you to kick against the goads.' (Act 26 Berean Study Bible).*

> *"Who are you, Lord?" Saul asked. Then came the reply, "I am Jesus, whom you are persecuting," He replied. "Now get up and go into the city, and you will be told what you must do" (Acts 9:5 NIV)*

What a powerful and dramatic encounter with the Risen Christ! Can you imagine how the men traveling with Saul stood there speechless, having heard the sound but not seeing anyone? As the light blinded Saul, they led him by the hand into Damascus. There Saul remained three days, yes, blind, and refusing to eat or drink anything.

There in Damascus in a strange twist of events, the Lord prepared a disciple called Ananias in a vision to minister to Saul. The instructions were clear:

> *"Go to the house of Judas on Straight Street and ask for a man from Tarsus named Saul, for he is praying. In a vision he has seen a man named Ananias come and place his hands on him to restore his sight" (Acts 9:12).*

Can you imagine how frightened Ananias must have felt! Surely, he knew too well the reputation of Saul when it came to believers in Christ. This fear and concern were reflected in his response to the Lord,

> *"I have heard many reports about this man and all the harm he has done to your holy people in Jerusalem. And he has come here with authority from the chief priests to arrest all who call on your name" (Acts 9:13 NIV).*

This concern was well founded. When Paul came to Jerusalem, he tried to join the disciples, but they were all afraid of him, not believing that he really was a disciple. Nevertheless, Barnabas took him and brought him to the apostles. Nonetheless, the Lord re-assured Ananias, with these words,

> *'Go! This man is my chosen instrument to proclaim my name to the Gentiles and their kings and to the people of Israel. I will show him how much he must suffer for my name' (Acts 9:15 &16 NIV)*

This gave him the courage and confidence he needed to obey the Lord, so he went to the house where Saul was and having placed his hands on Saul's head, prayed for him. The account of this experience is equally dramatic and compelling. The Scriptures declared:

> *'Then Ananias went to the house and entered it. Placing his hands on Saul, he said, "Brother Saul, the Lord Jesus, who appeared to you on the road as you were coming here, has sent me so that you may see again and be filled with the Holy Spirit. Immediately, something like scales fell from Saul's eyes, and he could see again. He got up and was baptized, and after taking some food, he regained his strength' (Acts 9:17-19, NIV).*

A New Man, Message, Ministry and Mission

This sequence of events as recorded in the Book of Acts, led to Saul's conversion to Paul who then trusted Jesus as the Messiah. This 'conversion experience' meant that he embraced Jesus of Nazareth as Israel's Messiah and Lord. In a strange twist of events, Paul then devoted all of his energy, passion and life to proclaiming the message of Jesus Christ to not only to his fellow Jews but also to the nations (often referred to as "Gentiles"). What a transformation! What a new mission! It brings to mind when the disciples (in Matthew 4), were called to be 'fishers of men', instead of 'fishermen' (verse19). Oh, the power of God to transform lives, and to 'make the foulest clean'!

There is something very powerful about when one is converted from a life of sin, shame and evil. When the woman in the New Testament anointed Jesus' feet with expensive perfume and was rebuked for so doing, Jesus made a profound statement: 'She who has been forgiven much, love much!' (Luke 7:47). This does not mean that if you have had a relatively uneventful life before you came to Christ, that you are any less impactful and valuable to the kingdom. Notwithstanding, there is a measure of authenticity, authority, passion and credibility that someone brings to the kingdom when he or she comes from a background where hardly anyone believes there is room, hope or scope for repentance, renewal or redemption!

The Lord has encountered and transformed many from lives of crime, prostitution, drug-addiction, pride, unforgiveness and abuse, to name a few. He then gave them ministries, voluntary platforms and other opportunities to reach out to those still struggling in ways they used to struggle. Changed persons somehow often minister with such power, passion and credibility that in some cases, others without those background experiences would arguably not be as effective. The Lord always uses one from among them. No wonder to redeem us, Jesus came as one of us to be our 'Kingsman redeemer'. There is a powerful ministry of showing care and empathy and to sit where others sit; basically, to 'walk a mile in their shoes.'

For Paul however, it would surely stir up the religious leaders (Pharisees and Sadducees) as well as create mistrust and suspicion among followers of Jesus. How could he on the one hand was such a violent killer of Christians and now claiming to be a follower of Jesus! Galatians 1 tells of Paul's autobiographical account of this transformation to being a Jew who follows Jesus as Lord. Paul noted that Jesus also appeared to him as he recounted this dramatic experience briefly in 1 Corinthians 15: 8.

After this experience, he went to Arabia, Damascus, Jerusalem, Syria and Cilicia. He preached the death, resurrection, and lordship of Jesus Christ and further proclaimed that a share in the life of Christ is only guaranteed through faith. For example, Paul declared that all he knew was 'Jesus Christ and Him crucified' (1 Corinthians 2:2). He preached believers were freed from sin and guilt through the substitutionary death of Jesus Christ; Believers therefore died with Christ and consequently live with him. Thus, he advocates that the death of Jesus did not reflect defeat rather a victory for the benefit of Believers. Here great emphasis is placed on the resurrection of Christ and its significance for the believer, in the salvation promised. This theological approach undoubtedly paved the way for his positive attitude to life and life's painful circumstances when applied thereto.

Paul taught the resurrection of the living Christ, the return of Christ to receive believers and the final judgement. He also taught the resurrection of the dead who will be raised at the return of Christ and be 'caught up in the clouds to meet the Lord in the air (1 Thessalonians 4:14-18). Paul also taught a practical aspect to his theology. Here, he advocates the highest moral standard in daily life.

He writes,

> *'May your spirit and soul and body be kept sound and blameless at the coming of our Lord Jesus Christ' (1 Thessalonians 5:23).*

Paul's Missionary Journeys

Paul's theology understandably caused much controversy, from Antioch as his launching, to various regions of the Mediterranean where he founded many churches. Such journeys and the churches formed reflected his letters in the New Testament from which we so greatly benefit today. Some confirmed 1 Thessalonians, Galatians, 1 Corinthians, Philippians, Philemon, 2 Corinthians and Romans; whilst others are contested: Thessalonians, Colossians, Ephesians, 1 Timothy, 2 Timothy and Titus.

Paul's doctrine and theology as reflected in his confirmed or contested letters caused much controversy, possibly because of the accusation of an 'anti-law' agenda, or that the Gentiles did not have to obey the Torah in its entirety. This led to his arrest and Jewish plots to have him killed. He was eventually transferred to Caesarea where he remained a prisoner for two years. When his case was finally revisited, Paul appealed to Caesar as a Roman citizen for his trial. It was on this trip, as Paul and other prisoners were en route to Rome, Italy that he was shipwrecked as recorded in Acts 27 and 28.

The Rationale for and Relevance of Paul's Story

I chose to outline this context and reflect on aspects of Paul's life and some of his experiences as the lens through which I will address the themes and life lessons in this book. I will do so because I believe that Paul is a very good example to us of someone who although faced with continual storms, hardships, trials and struggles he continued to serve God faithfully with a positive attitude. In Romans 7:15-25 for example, he speaks of his continual struggle. He speaks of his inability to do the right but instead does what he hated. He mentions in 2 Corinthians 12:7 how he was given a thorn in the flesh to keep him humble and grounded because of the 'abundance of revelation given to him.' He further outlined how he prayed fervently on three occasions for it to be removed but was assured of the sufficiency of God's amazing grace to sustain him through this process.

The experiences of Paul and his amazing response to them through God's grace is beautifully summarised thus in 2 Corinthians 4:9-11:

> *'Persecuted, but not forsaken; cast down, but not destroyed; Always bearing about in the body the dying of the Lord Jesus, that the life also of Jesus might be made manifest in our body. For we which live are always delivered unto death for Jesus' sake that the life also of Jesus might be made manifest in our mortal flesh'.*

This is a powerful way to perceive the challenges of life as they befall us. Often, we tend to focus on the negatives or the bad things that happen to us without acknowledging the hope that we have or the good things that also happened. Paul's transformation, trial process and tumultuous journeys by sea can teach us many invaluable life lessons along the path of life.

More than two years had passed after the arrest of Paul by Roman soldiers. In Jerusalem, the Jewish leaders falsely accused him of inciting riots and disrespecting the Jewish temple. His death was demanded; however, Paul's Roman citizenship meant that Roman officials had to carefully follow due process of Roman law, provide protection for him as well as ensure a fair hearing. It was Paul's nephew who uncovered a plot that was hatched to kill Paul. He was subsequently transported under Roman guard from Jerusalem to Caesarea, where Roman Officials would try him. The plot to kill Paul and his dramatic escape are recorded in Acts 23: 23-25:

> *After many days had gone by, there was a conspiracy among the Jews to kill him, but Saul learned of their plan. Day and night, they kept close watch on the city gates in order to kill him. But his followers took him by night and lowered him in a basket through an opening in the wall.*

What a dramatic deliverance and rescue! Indeed, Paul's doctrine and theology were undeniably controversial to the religious leaders. He was very passionate about it as he had a first-hand direct experience with Jesus. Despite that fact, he had appeared on numerous occasions over a two-year period; however, the accusations made by the Jews could not be substantiated. As mentioned, Paul invoked his right as a Roman Citizen and made a request to appear in Rome before Caesar's highest court. He could confidently do this as,

> *'The following night the Lord stood near Paul and said, "Take courage! As you have testified about me in Jerusalem, so you must also testify in Rome." (Acts 23:11, NIV).*

On their way to Italy, Paul was under the direct supervision and guard of Julius, the Roman centurion. However, Paul found favour with him to the extent that he not only treated Paul with kindness but also allowed him to socialise with friends at their first Port of call.

The Mediterranean Sea was very rough. In Myra, Paul and the other prisoners were transferred unto another ship. However due to the stormy blasts and the tempestuous seas, a direct route could not be taken. Thus, the captain decided to sail on the eastern and southern sides of Crete and sought refuge in the port of Fair Havens.

It was here that Paul strongly admonished the centurion not to set sail from Fair Haven. Julius chose however, to side with the captain to sail further along the southern end towards Phoenix. They never made it. So fierce were the winds and waves from the choppy seas that in desperation they had to toss cargo over board to lighten the ship as it drifted aimlessly off course. Navigation was simply impossible, as for days on end, the light from neither stars nor sun was visible! The fear, the desperation and absolute hopelessness gave way to a glimmer of hope as an island called Malta came into view.

Paul, during this time of deep distress and fear, remained steadfast in his faith and hope in God. He had divine angelic revelation and could bring 'a Word' of hope and cheer to the other 275 souls on board. All lives would be saved although property would be destroyed. The ship hit a sandbar and began to break into pieces. There was fear that the prisoners would escape so a plan was hatched to kill them; however, for Paul's sake they were all spared. Orders were given to swim unaided, on planks or broken pieces of the ship (Acts 27:44).

Having all made it safely to shore on Malta, Paul gained respect among the crew, as well as the locals who were greatly impressed by him when he survived a snake-bite. This venomous snake emerged as Paul gathered firewood to make a fire to warm themselves. The local leader, Publius showed Paul and the others much hospitality and this was rewarded when Publius' father became sick as Paul prayed for him and he was healed. Others also came and were healed. Paul spent three months on Malta and waited for the fierce winter to pass before boarding another ship to Rome. The locals on

Malta provided all their necessary provisions for the trip. On arrival in Rome, with a guard Paul lived in his own quarters. In all this God's hands of protection, provision and favour were on Paul. He no doubt developed that firm sense of faith and trust in God that would see him through the trying situation he was about to face!

Contending for the Faith
No doubt as society becomes more secular and liberal, Christians like Paul are called to stand in defence of their Faith. For instance, among many is Dr Scott who attended Medical School at Cambridge University and University College London before training in Paediatrics and subsequently Clinical Genetics in London. The General Medical Council investigated him after a complaint was made about the use of his Christian faith at the surgery in Palm Bay Avenue. However, Margate GP Dr Richard Scott of Bethesda Medical Centre, at risk of losing his job was eventually cleared after the investigation into use of prayer with patients.

Dr Richard Scott (2013), a surgeon and evangelist in his book *'Christians in the Firing Line'* highlights, illuminates and exposes some cases of 'marginalisation and discrimination of the Christian faith. He also specifically shed light on legal cases of those warned, blacklisted, suspended or dismissed for refusing to compromise their Biblical principles in the face of an officialdom seemingly hell-bent on bowing down to the "god" of political correctness and secularism.' He concluded with this warning:

> *'Be prepared to stand in whatever situation God calls you into. Many more of us will be faced in the future with what I might term "Esther" and "Daniel" situations'* (p.200).

(See Esther 3 and Daniel 6 in the Bible). 1 Peter 3:15 (NIV) declares

> *But in your hearts revere Christ as Lord. Always be prepared to give an answer to everyone who asks you to give the reason for the hope that you have. But do this with gentleness and respect.*

I had the pleasure of meeting Dr Scott at the Men's breakfast at our church a few years ago. Not only did I acquire a signed copy of his book but I also had the opportunity to discuss with him aspects of my Doctoral Thesis (O'Connor, 2017). My thesis focused on the controversial nature and tension of combining Christian faith in professional life, the marginalisation of faith and the promotion of a secular and liberal agenda, which are often projected and imposed as neutral positions, which they are not.

Paul had to defend his faith on many occasions. The next chapter looks at his perilous journey by sea to Rome after he demanded a hearing from Caesar. He had the opportunity to minister to Julius, the Centurion and the ship's owner and share his revelation with them. He re-assured all 275 souls on board in times of grave distress and demonstrated tremendous faith and leadership even when all hope was seemingly lost.

2. Setting Sail to Rome

'When you get into a tight place and everything goes against you, till it seems as though you could not hang on a minute longer, never give up then, for that is just the place and time that the tide will turn'

(Harriet Beecher Shower, 1811-1896, American writer and social reformer)

Paul Sails for Rome - The Process Through the Storm
I summarised Paul's journey earlier to give a background to the story. I will now reiterate some points and go in a bit more detail.

The journey by sea to Italy turned out to be anything but a smooth easy passage. The prisoners including Paul were placed in the custody of Julius, a Roman Officer. Overall, there were 276 souls on board and this journey was scheduled to make numerous stops at ports along the coast of the province. Julius showed Paul much kindness and allowed him to even go ashore to visit friends. They had an opportunity to provide for his needs.

As Paul and the others set sail, however, they encountered very strong headwinds that made it extremely difficult to sustain a steady course. Consequently, they sailed north of Cyprus between the island and the mainland. This led them along the coast of Cilicia and Pamphylia, landing at Myra, in the province of Lycia, travelling along the open sea. When the commanding officer found an Egyptian ship from Alexandria destined for Italy, Paul and the others were transferred on board. This was a slow process of sailing for several days and it was after tremendous difficulties that they reached Cnidus. Still, there was no respite; rather, the wind was gravely contrary that they sailed to Crete seeking some refuge along the sheltered coast of the island. This was supposed to be a smoother alternative however; it turned out to be anything but. Furthermore, the journey would take much longer.

So much time was lost as they struggled and struggled relentlessly until finally, they arrived at Fair Havens, near the town of Lasea. The situation was becoming increasingly dangerous for continued sailing. At this point, Paul spoke to the centurion and the ship's owners, in Acts 27:10

>'Men' Paul said,

>*'I believe there is trouble ahead if we go on: shipwreck loss of cargo, and danger to our lives as well.'*

Despite this intervention, the Officer who was in charge of the prisoners paid more attention to both the captain and owner. Thus, Paul's words of admonition were over-ruled.

There was a slight improvement in the weather conditions in the form of a light southerly wind so the sailors thought they could proceed. Pulling up anchor, they sailed close to the shore of Crete. However quite unexpectedly the weather changed abruptly, and a strong typhoon-like wind emerged and pushed the ship further out to sea and this made it impossible for the sailors to turn the ship into the wind. They had no choice but to simply let it drift before the tempest, seeking some refuge along the shielded side of a small island, then hoisting aboard the lifeboat being towed.

At this point, the sailors attempted to strengthen the ship by tying ropes around the hull. This strengthening was necessary in order to avoid the sandbars off the coasts of Africa. In an attempt to slow the ship, they lowered the sea anchor. Notwithstanding, the savage winds continued into the next day to batter the ship relentlessly. The decision and a very difficult one indeed was then taken to throw cargo overboard. This continued the following day, with some of the ship's gear being included in this activity.

Nevertheless, despite all this effort, 'The terrible storm raged for many days, blotting out the sun and the stars, until at last all hope was gone' (Acts 27:20). This sense of hopelessness removed all appetite for food. It was at this point that Paul took leadership. He assembled the crew together.

> *'After they had gone a long time without food, Paul stood up before them and said: "Men, you should have taken my advice not to sail from Crete; then you would have spared yourselves this damage and loss. But now I urge you to keep up your courage, because not one of you will be lost; only the ship will be destroyed. Last night an angel of the God to whom I belong and whom I serve stood beside me and said, 'Do not be afraid, Paul. You must stand trial before Caesar; and God has graciously given you the lives of all who sail with you.' So, keep up your courage, men, for I have faith in God that it will happen just as he told me. Nevertheless, we must run aground on some island' (Acts 27: 21-26 NIV).*

This is a powerful Word of assurance from the Lord though one righteous person on the ship. Mike Murdock notes that 'the Word of God enables you to make wise decisions' (p 11). Two weeks into the storm, about midnight, being tossed across the Sea of Adria the sailors sensed that land was in close proximity. Their test of the water depth confirmed a distance of 120 feet. This was still too deep so they continued sailing and later tested again at 90 feet. However, even at this depth they feared being driven too close to shore unto rocks. Their only option was to let down four anchors from the rear of the ship and earnestly hoped and prayed for daylight.

So great was the fear that the sailors attempted to abandon the ship using the lifeboats. However, Paul realised what was happening and again intervened, saying to the soldiers and commanding officers: *"You will all die unless the sailors remain aboard!" (NLT)*

The lifeboats were then cut and they drifted away. What a night! As the new day dawned, again Paul took control of the situation. He showed leadership and encouraged everyone to eat something. The journey was so scary, demanding and life threatening that all appetite was gone and for a whole fortnight they fasted. Paul implored them to eat and re-assured them that they would all be safe to the extent that 'not even a strand of hair would perish.' He then took the bread, gave thanks to God publicly, and ate a piece, which he had broken off. This somehow restored their confidence and soon they all partook, all 276 souls. This strengthened them, once all had eaten and they tossed the cargo of wheat overboard to further lighten the ship.

With dawn approaching the coastline was difficult to recognise, however they identified a bay with a beach. Their plan was to get to shore by running the ship aground. They severed the anchors and left them behind in the sea. Furthermore, the rudders were lowered and the foresail raised as they made their way to shore. Unfortunately, this was done prematurely and, in the process, they hit a shoal and ran the ship aground too soon. While the bow of the ship remained intact the stern was smashed repeatedly by the fierce and boisterous waves and began to rip apart.

At this point, the soldiers were fearful that the prisoners would escape and wanted to kill them. However, the commanding officer desired to spare Paul's life and as a result, prevented this action. Instead, he ordered all who could swim to jump overboard and swim to shore. The others held on to planks or broken pieces of the ship. In this manner they all made it safely to shore!

Safe Landing at Malta: Hospitality and Healing Ministry

What an ordeal! Thankfully, they were all safe and well just as Paul had said. The natives were extremely hospitable and because of the grave discomfort from the rain and cold weather, kindled a fire to keep them warm. However, as Paul gathered a bundle of sticks and laid them on the fire, a viper emerged, attracted by the heat. It fastened itself on Paul's hand. The natives were alarmed at this and surmised that Paul must be a murderer for such a fate to have befallen him. Although he has been saved from the sea, they thought, the snakebite was justice catching up with him. Astonishingly, Paul simply shook the creature off into the fire and was not harmed. The expectation, no doubt from the experiences of the locals was that Paul would simply swell up and die.

However, this failed to materialise despite their long wait. At this point, they concluded that Paul was a god!

Paul and the others received much hospitality not only from the natives but in particular from Publius, the local leader on the island. He welcomed them and hosted them generously and courteously for three days. Sadly, Publius' father became gravely ill with a recurrent fever and dysentery. Paul went to visit him. He prayed for him, laying his hands on him. He was healed! News of this miracle soon spread throughout the island and shortly thereafter, others who had diseases came to Paul and they too were cured. Consequently, Paul was honoured and greatly respected and when it was time to depart, was supplied with necessities for the journey.

There are many life lessons we can learn from an analysis of Paul's experiences, which we will discuss in Part 2.

PART 2

Life Lessons and Analysis

3. Life Lessons and Analysis

'You must never conclude, even if everything goes wrong, that you cannot succeed. Even at the worst, there is a way out; a hidden secret that can turn failure into success and despair into happiness. No situation is so dark that there is not a ray of light.'

(Norman Vincent Peale 1898-1993, American Writer and Minister)

We often hear people ask the question, 'Why do bad things happen to good people?' This question is frequently asked as they, loved ones or even total strangers go through terrible experiences that might be considered grossly unfair, unreasonable or undeserving. You may not be able to give an answer to this question that is satisfactory to all, especially when you are going through your 'storms'. Nevertheless, we can all be confident in the knowledge that God is sovereign and will always cause 'all things to work out for good to those who are called according to His purpose' (Romans 8:28).

This can indeed be 'cold comfort' in our distress; but as we reflect on Paul and the horrendous things he suffered in defence of the gospel and his faith, some may argue that he deserved such pain and payback based on the seeds he sowed; he previously persecuted the Christians.

We could also choose to look at the tremendous contribution he later made to the writings in the New Testament. We, like Paul, are frail and flawed mortals who have fallen short of

God's glory and hardly can be called 'good'. No wonder the scriptures say:

> *As it is written, 'there is none righteous, no, not one: All have turned aside; together they have become worthless; no one does good, not even one' (Romans 3:10).*

Only through God's grace, favour and mercy can we stand. We can agree that He does not treat us as our sins deserve. Whilst there are consequences for our decisions and choices, Psalm 103:10 (NIV) reminds us that, 'He does not treat us as our sins deserve or repay us according to our iniquities. 'Regardless of the cause, none of your problems could happen without God's permission' (Warren, 2002, p.194).

I do understand and appreciate that this is a 'heavily' theological position to hold and even those of faith could struggle with this stance from time to time. Whether of faith or none, we all have to, at some point in our lives reconcile the matter of how we will deal with those fierce storms and fiery darts that assail us in life. True, some may be of our own making in terms of poor planning, lack of organisation, carelessness, poor choices or risk-taking behaviours, whilst others may have absolutely nothing to do with us at all. Therefore, it is critical to our health, well-being and faith position to find strategies to deal with these inevitable life moments.

Reflection: Will your faith still hold in times of trouble? Will you maintain a position of hope, resilience and purpose, or will you simply surrender to fear?

Confront and Conquer

In the face of life's storms howsoever caused, we have choices to make: fight or flight, fear or courage and faith or freeze. Life however is far more complex than seeing these in a simple linear fashion. By this, I mean that it is possible and human to have resilience, resolve, faith and a fight and still experience flight, fear or freezing! Great men and women of faith and none have demonstrated that they have made tremendous achievements amidst great fear and self-doubt. In fact, Joyce Meyer encourages us to 'Do it afraid!' Often, we wait for the perfect time to move on as if there is ever such a time. Courage as documented is 'not the absence of fear, but the conquering of it!'

> *'Courage faces fear and thereby masters it. Cowardice represses fear and is thereby mastered by it' (Martin Luther King, 1929-1968)*

Reflection: Is there a goal, dream, or aspiration that you desire to pursue but feel afraid to start? How might you address this fear and move on purposefully and prayerfully to achieve your God-given potential?

We have the opportunity of seeing Paul's life opened up to us in a transparent way. We recall his evil deeds prior to conversion and transformation as well as his humility, vulnerabilities and sufferings. Imprisonment, being beaten, left for dead, stoned, shipwrecked repeatedly, tossed mercilessly on the stormy sea's night and day, exposed to dangers of all types from all quarters, betrayals, sleep deprivation, hunger and thirst, not to mention carrying the burden of Christian ministry are some to note. How much can one person take?

We also see his successes in ministry: in leadership, defending the faith, planting and supporting churches, mentoring and training leaders, writing, anointing sermons, divine revelations and illuminations. His successes are also manifested in powerful, inspired and impactful writings that still benefit us today. Paul despite all the difficult experiences and successes resolutely declared,

> *We are troubled on every side, yet not distressed; we are perplexed, but not in despair; Persecuted, but not forsaken; cast down, but not destroyed;*
>
> *Always bearing about in the body the dying of the Lord Jesus. that the life also of Jesus might be made manifest in our body. For we which live are always delivered unto death for Jesus' sake, that the life also of Jesus might be made manifest in our mortal flesh (2 Corinthians 4:8-11).*

This approach to life and its traumatic circumstances takes and demands far more than will power or mere positive thinking. It demands a strong sense of faith in God, borne out of deep fellowship, trust, reliance of His Word, promises and a mature understanding of our part in the sacrifice. We too are called upon to have similar experiences as followers of Jesus Christ. We are also part-takers of His suffering as we manifest the life of Christ. For whosoever decides to follow me (Jesus) must take up his cross and follow me (Matthew 16:24). Furthermore, Christ said in Matthew 10:38, 'anyone who does not take up his cross and follow me is not worthy of me.' The 'cross is an instrument of death, and the person carrying it has no alternative but to submit to the death that awaits him' (Scott 2013, p. 23).

You have a unique and specially designed cross that only you can bear. The sacrifices you have to make may result in death of your dream, desires and expectations. 'No one else can really know how sad or happy you are. Your joy is your own; your bitterness is your own. No one can share them with you'.

'The heart knows its own bitterness, and no outsider shares in its joy' the book of Proverbs reminds us (Proverbs 14:10); and while we 'bear one another's burden', each man must carry his own load (Galatians 6:2, 5-7). In the words of an English proverb, 'Everyone must row with the oars he has.' Does this mean that we should be uncaring and selfish and each person looks out for him or herself only? Of course not! Remenber, you have your cross to bear, your storms to weather, your battles to fight albeit, prayerfully and with help, guidance and prayerful support from significant others.

I remember when I was a child growing up in the rural areas of Jamaica, we used to have 'Rallies' and Gospel concerts which were major and well-anticipated items on our church calendar. There we would have an array of items including gospel songs, stories, recitations, short Bible plays and music. Both these rallies and gospel concerts had a fund-raising element for the church and other local charities. I will never forget Josh, the Deacon's son who almost every time as a child would repeat his favourite recitation. He stood on a chair, as he was too small to be seen by the congregation even though he would be on the platform. Josh spoke thus:

> *"Must Jesus bear the cross alone and all the world go free? No, there is a cross for everyone and there is a cross for me!"*

Even as a child, this harsh realisation was heralded abroad and to this day its truths still bellows from the sacred pages of

Scripture, songs and hymns and is made manifest in our daily lives. One of the most powerful statements Paul makes which I believe we need to hold on to, is the fact although we might be troubled, perplexed, cast down or even persecuted, we can stand strong in God and realise that we need not be distressed, in despair, feel forsaken or be destroyed. This is powerful! How can we go through so much and maintain such a positive attitude?

It is so easy to internalise, reflect and embrace all the negative things life throws at us and feel stressed, depressed, worried, and anxious or even question or abandon our faith. However, my word of encouragement to you today is to hold fast to your faith and 'cast not away your confidence, for it is great recompense of reward!' (Hebrews 10:35).

Life maybe unfair but God is faithful and as harsh as it sounds, 'to live is Christ and to die is great gain' (Philippians 1:21). No wonder Paul says in 2 Corinthians 4:11, 'For we which live are always delivered unto death for Jesus' sake, that the life also of Jesus might be made manifest in our mortal flesh' because He lives, we also shall be raised to newness of life and in the end to eternal life. This is our ultimate hope. This hope gives comfort especially if you are battling an incurable illness, mourning the loss of a precious loved one or contemplating your own mortality. We have a hope that is bright and fair and surmounts the fragility of this transient life. David cried out, 'Lord help me to number my days that I may apply my heart unto wisdom or know how frail I am (Psalm 90:12).

In the midst of our trials and storms, we need to have not just the right attitude to life and suffering but also the correct perspective on life in terms of our own mortality. On numerous occasions on the ship on the raging sea, the sailors, owners, centurions and prisoners all feared for their lives! Storms and struggles can indeed be a great leveller. When we are in extremely difficult situations, often wealth, status, class, race or education, do not seem to matter. Even now with the Covid-19 pandemic, it is no respecter of persons: political leaders, royalty, celebrities, medical staffs, educationalists etcetera. Regardless of all our plans for life, love, pleasure, leisure, investments and legacy, death humbles us and reduces us to one common but harsh denominator and reality: we are frail and flawed mortals.

When we peek into the chapters ahead in Acts 28 we see how the story ends. We can conclude, the counsel of God determined even before the counsel of Festus, Paul should go to Rome because God had work for him to do there. Through the trial process and beyond, Paul's presence made such a difference on the ship through the stormy gale. This did not stop there. His words of assurance and faith, and the letters and epistles later penned have been a source of healing to many.

The Lord orders your steps: your purpose, process and your promise. The challenge therefore, is to ascertain God's purpose for your life and believe you are worthy through Him to achieve and accomplish such feat by His grace. Purposefully, you can then move forward by faith through the process to realise His wonderful promises. Henry Ford (1863-1947) on *believing* wrote, 'whether you believe you can do a thing or believe you can't, you are right.'

One of the biggest challenges we face in life as we journey along its path is that rarely does God specify the path way or the process after a promise is given. Let us look at the example of Joseph in the Old Testament. He knew through a dream that he would be great and that he would be an outstanding ruler but little did he know that the process would take him from the promise to the pit, the problems, the persecution and the prison, all before the palace then finally, his promotion and position as Ruler in Egypt! Consider this, the promise, process, problems, pit, persecution, prison then the palace. Likewise, your process may be a lengthy one, taking you through varied processes but rest assured you will win if you maintain a positive mindset amidst your mishaps and simply do not quit. Speaking of 'mishaps' Herman Melville writes,

> *'Mishaps are like knives that either serve us or cut us; as we grasp them by the blade or the handle.'*

Therefore, what will you grasp from your mishaps? We have the promises of God that 'I will guide thee with mine eye' (Psalm 32:8). This brings comfort to us as we rest assured that God himself is always there for us guiding and protecting us every step of the way and is fully conversant with every minute detail of our lives and all seemingly insignificant issue. I think this is a very reassuring and comforting thought to hold onto.

Do you really believe that your times and processes are in His hands? Consider this also, 'Nothing shall separate us from the love of God', (Romans 8:38). We are not just conquerors but also more than conquerors! I will strongly reiterate that we are more than conquerors when like Paul, we can firmly declare that despite the troubles, perplexities, persecutions and life stressors, through Christ we are not distressed, in despair, forsaken, nor destroyed. You might be down temporarily but you are not out. Your process may lead through dark places...of doubt, fear, questioning your faith as you ask 'where is God in all of this?' but that is ok. God can handle those feelings.

There is nothing you can go through of which He is not aware; furthermore, be assured that nothing happens by chance in the life of the believer! Every pain, every process, every tear and every fear can be turned around for God's glory and be used to impact, influence, challenge and inspire others. TD Jakes writes, 'The enemy knows what you can be, and wants to destroy you before you become what God said you will be' (1996, p27). It is necessary therefore, to stand fast and be steadfast as we move through our processes towards our purpose.

Reflection: What will you do with your setbacks in life? How will you respond to the dark places you have been through and the trials you have endured in your faith walk?

Systematic or Flexible

I must admit here that I am a planner! In addition, a good one I may humbly add. I find pleasure in being systematic, structured, organised and analytical. In fact, I am not sure how I would have completed my doctoral studies with all my other obligations and commitments professionally, personally, entrepreneurially, domestically and in ministry, without this level of personal organisation and methodical stance. In fact, my Professor, in a written tribute for my celebration ceremony, a year after the successful completion of my studies wrote:

> *"Phillip's external examiner, Prof J. was one of the leading professors in the area and the final award of the doctoral degree was earned under rigorous interrogation. It is a tribute to Phillip, that he has succeeded at the highest level of academia whilst*

holding down a full-time teaching post. There are few people who manage to do that" (July 2019).

Despite this measure of structure and organisation, I found that a deep level of flexibility is required not only to get through my studies but life as well. For example, on many occasions, I had to reschedule, readjust and even abandon my plans to accomplish a particular task as something of immediate, pressing and of crucial importance or urgency turned up that required my imminent or immediate attention. Being flexible for me could mean completing that previously scheduled task another time in my study timetable.

Flexibility also required that I avoid being stressed out about the fact that I had to change my plans; and yes, depending on the nature of the task or its submission deadline it could be a challenge. Munroe (1991) asserts that 'plans are documented imaginations; if you can document an imagination, you have developed a plan for action' (p. 64). However, while we document and develop, room must be left for some flexibility. In fact, we are reminded that 'Many are the plans in a person's heart, but it is the LORD's purpose that prevails (Proverbs 19:21). This can be comforting as well as alarming. Does this mean that we do not bother to plan because God is going to over-ride them anyway? I would suggest that we plan and be open and submissive to God's sovereignty, yielding our lives to Him in faith that in His infinite wisdom, grace and mercy. He will guide, lead, direct and protect us to ultimate purpose, victory and success. Detours are not denials and man's disappointments could be God's appointments.

Going Around in Circles
In July 2016, my wife, Rhona and I had the pleasure of hosting here in England, our pastors from when we lived and worked

in the Cayman Islands 1995-2001. It was the 50th anniversary of one of the Pastor's conversion experience at Keswick Convention and he was here in England to mark such a glorious occasion. At last, the day arrived when I would drive them there, all the way from Kent in the South east of England to the far-flung corner of the North, a whole five hours or so by car. I programmed my Satellite navigation system (SatNav), and previewed the journey turn by turn, as I have never driven to that destination before and honestly, did not have a clue where I was going! Along with Rhona and myself, were these pastors and a retired Head teacher and Reverend of a local church in London.

As we journeyed, I realised the traffic was very bad. In fact, I kept getting alerts on the SatNav there were traffic situations on my chosen route. Whereas I had set the destination, I honestly did not expect that much traffic enroute. What I do remember quite vividly was the length of time we were being diverted and circling around and going through the heart of London. I would have preferred the motorway experience. Notwithstanding, all routes including the motorways were flagged up as potential traffic hotspots.

I eventually joined the motorway. After travelling a great distance, we finally stopped for a comfort break off the motorway. My car then was a new 7-seater sports utility vehicle (SUV) or 4x4 with quite a few comfort features. After all that time travelling in what seemed like endless, purposeless and aimless roaming, we desperately needed that break! After having refreshed ourselves and having a bite to eat, it was now time to resume what we hoped would be a better travelling experience! As we were about to resume our journey, I reset the SatNav and checked its settings ensuring the destination postcode were all accurately entered. It was only then I realised that in the settings section I had previously inadvertently checked the box that asked if I wanted the car to automatically choose my route once it had detected impending traffic situations enroute!

For the duration of the journey to that point, despite setting my destination before I embarked on the journey, the guidance system not only alerted me of and flagged up changes in the traffic as we journeyed, but automatically chose without prompting what it considered the best route for me. Furthermore, it automatically redirected me to those paths and diversions, which I was taking. So constantly changing from my originally set route, kept leading me in what seemed further and further away from my destination as the car battled the constantly changing traffic situations in an attempt to set me on, what it 'considered' the best routes!

Actually, I realised what was happening after our comfort break. I unchecked the box in the settings section of the car's computer guidance system, to request a prompt as to whether or not I wanted to change route or remain on my chosen path, even after being alerted to the changing traffic situations! That gave me a measure of control despite the readiness of the car to, on each occasion recalibrate my position and set me on another path, albeit to the same destination. That journey and experience, admittedly, was a bit embarrassing for me with my esteemed passengers and the much discomfort I had caused due to the nearly ten hours the journey eventually took! Despite this, they truly did, after being out of the UK for so many years, appreciate and enjoy the unplanned and impromptu tour of London as well as the amazingly stunning scenic views of the Lake District.

Being analytical and philosophical however, helped me to glean many invaluable life lessons from the experience of the SatNav! I firmly believe that no experience is ever wasted, and nothing happens by chance in the life of the Believer. Thankfully, we had departed very early that morning and after more than 10 hours driving, we arrived safely and in time at Keswick for registration and the evening service!! That was indeed a teachable moment! This experience teaches me that despite having a clear sense of purpose and destination, it is possible to encounter unforeseen issues along life's path. This could mean longer journey time than previously planned to accomplish my goals. Always previewing the journey before I set off is necessary and double checking that I have control over whether or not I accept the invitation to re-route after a suggestion of impending traffic is helpful to maintain some measure of control.

Jason Mills also gleans an important life lesson from his Global Positioning System (GPS). He writes, 'Whenever I make a wrong turn the GPS would recalculate my route and take me on a course leading to my ultimate destination' (2017, p. 145). Previewing my trip gives me some control, confidence and peace of mind that despite any rerouting, my destination is pre-determined and pre-set. However, I find that as I yield control to God, I can trust Him to recalibrate my position and redirect my steps despite my flaws, mistakes, weaknesses, detours or deviations to lead me to my final destination and goals regardless.

T. D. Jakes (2017) in his book, 'Soar!' uses the metaphor of aviation to explain this important concept. He puts it this way:

> 'Not only will establishing these goals before you're airborne help you know where you are going, they will

assist you in making the decisions about growth, product, target marketing…knowing your destination is also helpful in identifying when you need to make changes…' (p. 93).

This establishing of goals and knowing my destination as well as the fact that God can and does recalibrate my future from my present location and condition, give me a quiet confidence that underpins my life. No matter what happens or fails to happen in my life, God is in charge and directs, re-directs and orders my steps to fulfil His set, pre-determined purpose. To reiterate, absolutely no experience is ever wasted and absolutely nothing happens by chance in my life as a Believer! My disappointments could be His appointments, delays are not denials; detours and diversions are only temporary distractions. Furthermore, all these form an important part of my personal narrative, which as mentioned, inform an authentic and credible part of my story, testimony, and ministry. Simply sharing our stories has the power to motivate, inspire, challenge and encourage others.

I am sure you have numerous stories of how you had your plans all fixed and figured out when through setbacks, reversals and disappointments you have had to take a different course but later in hindsight, came to be grateful for the disappointments!

Reflection: So, systematic or flexible, analytical or easy-going; how do you cope with life's vicissitudes? Are your plans flexible or too rigid? Do you see the Hand of God in the events in your life? Can you say that, 'It was good that I was afflicted?' (Psalm 119:71), or are you still working through the process?

I am not trying to politely suggest, rather, to emphatically tell you that your end is set from the beginning! God knows the end from the beginning (Isaiah 46:10). He is the 'Alpha and Omega, the beginning and the end.' The fight is fixed! Whatever happens to you in life, you will win and come forth as pure gold. That is a very liberating thought despite your process. Use this fact to develop and enhance your confidence and wellbeing as you move forward. The final chapter is already written and predetermined! Undoubtedly, you will win! The path may not be particularly pleasant but your success is a foregone conclusion. Therefore, you can conclude, 'You have already won!'

'How could you say such a thing?' You may ask.

Well, based on the Scriptures that proclaim:

> 'I declare the end from the beginning and from long ago what is not yet done, saying: my plan will take place, and I will do all my will' (Isaiah 46:10, Christian Standard Bible).

Let us also consider Romans 4:17

> 'That is what the Scriptures mean when God told him, "I have made you the father of many nations. This happened because Abraham believed in the God who brings the dead back to life and who creates new things out of nothing' (NLT).

Let us not forget Revelation 22:13, which states:

> 'I am the Alpha and the Omega, the First and the Last, the Beginning and the end' (NIV)

Decisions and Consequences

During and throughout the violent storm and tempestuous waves, Paul was mostly silent. Do not talk too much when you are going through your storms. This does not mean you should not share your problems; No way, 'a problem shared (with the right person, under the right circumstances) is a problem halved'. Charles Franklin Kettering (1876-1958) puts it this way, 'A problem well stated is a problem half solved' (The Complete Pocket Positives). However, take your tests in silence. Do you remember your days of taking examinations in an academic environment? And don't be too quick to start discussing the answers you recorded in your examinations after the test! This is could be heart breaking if you provided incomplete, inaccurate answers or totally misinterpreted a question, by giving a perfect answer for a question that was never asked!

After Paul's silent, prayerful contemplations and his divine encounters, he emerged; sometimes with comforting words of affirmation but also with words of admonition and firm rebuke. Paul said,

> *'Men, you should have listened to me in the first place and not left Crete. You would have avoided all this damage and loss. But take courage! None of you will lose your lives, even though the ship will go down. For last night an angel of the God to whom I belong and whom I serve stood beside me, and he said, 'Don't be afraid, Paul, for you will surely stand trial before Caesar! What's more, God in his goodness has granted safety to everyone sailing with you.' So, take courage! For I believe God. It will be just as he said. But we will be shipwrecked on an island' (NLT).*

Whilst we largely have control over our lives and some might argue, are 'masters of our own destiny', it is true to say that sometimes the decisions of others can have a tremendous impact on our lives and how they turn out. With all our planning and goal setting and strategizing, our lives can be influenced, affected or be turned completely upside down subsequently by the choices and decisions of others.

Let us look at the experiences of Paul in our story. He had successfully defended his faith and won the right as a Roman citizen to a hearing with Caesar in Rome. Well, it should have been a relatively straightforward journey, but not necessarily a trouble free one from Jerusalem to Rome. However, despite the impending weather conditions and against the firm advice of Paul who was operating under Divine illumination; the ship's owner, putting profit over people and health and safety considerations, decided to still set sail. This would later be a disastrous decision, which resulted in the loss of the ship, and its cargo, just as Paul had prophesied.

Reflection: Do you suffer because of the decisions of others? How do you feel if you are now going through a terrible trial in your life where it was not of your making but through the negligence, disobedience or greed of others whether such one be in a position of influence over you or a subordinate? And furthermore, how do you feel if you had warned such a one repeatedly of the consequences of such poor decision, risk-taking behaviour or the error of their ways and obstinately they ploughed on to yours and others' detriment?

Further Reflection: As you reflect on how you sometime suffer because of others, ask yourself: What risks do you take and for what? Is it worth the risk? Have you ever counselled, advised, suggested something and against better judgement, these are overlooked or categorically rejected? How do you feel especially when you know that, there is merit to your contribution, suggestion, admonition, advice or warning yet it is ignored?

Sometimes you have to be the one to pick up the broken pieces of others' poor choices and 'put out fires' you did not start! For example, it can be so sad when as a mother you might strongly suggest to your teenage daughter to be aware and careful with her choice of a boyfriend she is seeing, only to be ignored, disrespected and challenged. Later however, when things turn out disastrously wrong, like Paul had to say when the ship ran into a fierce storm, you too had to say, 'you should have listened to me!' (Verse 21). Nobody likes to hear, 'I told you so!'

It may not be easy to say. Initially, it may not be appropriate sometimes in times of suffering, loss or even death as words of assurance or affirmation may be required. However, we can and should be opened to wise, evidenced-based, Godly and loving counsel even though this might go against our plans, goals, desires or natural inclinations. Why should we and what are the consequences of not doing so? Each one is entitled to his or her opinions, decisions and choices and responsible for the consequences they may bring. Nevertheless, there is a place for submission, surrendering and compromising especially in the face of convincing evidence, mature spiritual guidance and loving but firm admonition. It is a sign of humility, growth and maturity to do so.

The Tale of Two Past Student
I was shopping in the supermarket for some groceries. As I went to get the milk, I saw an ex-student of mine who had completed his Bachelor's degree and was contemplating starting teacher training through the Postgraduate Teacher-training Certificate in Education route (PGCE). This he told me

as we greeted each other and caught up on his progress to date. I was his Form or Homeroom Teacher from Year 7 through to Year 11.

'It is such a surprise to bump into you, Sir…!'

He remarked joyfully,

'…because (name given of another student) and I just called your name recently.'

I was curious as to what was the content of their discussion. He proceeded to tell me how this other student although being in the same class as he was and having me as form teacher for 5 years yet he made some bad decisions and choices personally, academically and otherwise and was not in a good place. With regret and much remorse, this student said to his friend in their conversation,

'Sir was right. I should have listened to Mr O'Connor!'

I must be honest with you I was touched by this story. That student should have listened to me all those years ago. His mother cried bitterly at Parents' Consultation meetings over his apathy, indifference and lack of aspiration all those years ago. No doubt, he might have even had a good reason or an excuse for his disruptive behaviour, inadequate work and low aspiration; but then that same attitude persisted long after leaving secondary school and continued into his adult life. What a shame. Indeed, he should have listened to me. Yet I told my past student in the supermarket to convey my best wishes to him and reminded him that it is never too late for a turnaround. Surely, his purpose might have been delayed but does not have to be denied. It is up to him. He can make a shift in paradigm and effect the necessary changes to and in his life that will set him back on the right path of success and purpose.

Sometimes we bear the consequences of ours or others' actions, thoughtlessness, decisions and choices. For example, Paul was preaching the glorious gospel of Jesus Christ; yet he suffered while doing so. He was under the divine guidance of the Holy Spirit as he advised the centurion and ship's owner not to set sail because of the weather conditions however, this was rejected and over-ruled.

Reflection: How about you? What have you or are you bearing the consequences of other people's decions? Could it be the carelessness, deliberate malicious, insensitive, immature actions of a child, colleague, spouse, boss, government policies (retirement plans), natural disasters or even the onslaught of the Coronavirus pandemic with its death and devastations in every single area of life as we know it? How do you feel about this so-called 'new normal'? How will it affect and change your life?

As the world stands still, airplanes grounded, cars remained parked up, thousands of lives lost, failed businesses, financial reversals, shattered dreams, broken lives, failed investments, reduced pensions, unplanned involuntary redundancies, job losses, re-skilling and being furloughed with despair on every side. This calls for a fervent crying out to God as is recorded in 2 Chronicles 7:14

> *'If my people, who are called by my name, will humble themselves and pray and seek my face and turn from their wicked ways, then I will hear from heaven, and I will forgive their sin and will heal their land.'*

As churches, charities, governments , businesses, business and commerce all turn to the internet for online community meeting opportunities through Facebook live, Skype, YouTube, Zoom, Microsoft Teams and other platforms, there seems to be a willingness to adjust to a 'new normal.' Governments have requested some organisations and businesses whilst others are forced for expediency financially, to diversify their operation and produce medical supplies like face masks and ventilators. Oh, how the storms of life can force us into changes in our directions. Yet for us of faith we have a common destination in Christ and a hope that despite these challenging and trying times, is brighter than the perfect day.

Life's Unexpected Turns
Paul's journey, like most things in life began with 'smooth seas'. This could seem to nullify his prophetic word of caution and admonition initially. Do you remember he had prophesied that there would be loss of the ship and possessions but not of life? Perhaps all on board expected a smooth sailing for the most part. No doubt, he could feel somewhat embarrassed and questioned whether he had actually heard from the Lord. Perhaps others might even doubted his input and questioned his credibility and authenticity! The truth is, it can be very difficult to intervene with a word of prophesy, warning, admonition, suggestion or evidenced-based intervention and it is proven to be wrong.

This was true of the disobedient prophet, Jonah. He was a prophet sent by God to warn the people of Nineveh of impending doom but the people in this case repented and the destruction was averted, much to his disappointment! (Jonah 4:1-2). This no doubt made him feel like a false prophet or incompetent messenger. Yet, he had an awful lot to learn about his attitude, character and motive for ministry. He learnt the hard way to correct these character and spiritual flaws.

Reflection: This could beg the question, what is your motive when you minister to others? Do you have a heart for people and really want to see then change or simply protect your reputation? What happens when the people repent and God relents?

Have you ever embarked on any project, relationship, enterprise, academic pursuit business venture, starting a family, marriage for example and initially everything started out so well? No doubt, you were in high hopes and spirits as you enjoyed the 'honeymoon period' of your success and rightly so. It could be that you have planned and prepared adequately for this experience and it is only reasonable and fair that you enjoyed the fruit of your labour.

Perhaps you too were advised admonished or warned of the dangers of embarking on a particular paths and you rejected wise counsel. Possibly, it started out so well, with calm seas and smooth sailing and you turned to your advisers and said,

> 'See nothing is happening, things are going so well, you were so wrong. You did not wish me well or were not happy for me!'

But, alas! As you progressed, you noticed an incremental change and it was not for the better. The winds began to blow, and the seas grew increasingly choppy. The tides now turn against you, and you are filled with regret at your decision. Nevertheless, not all is lost.

As Paul's journey with 275 souls on board the vessel continued, sailing conditions gradually started to get progressively worse. The situation steadily grew worse and worse and worse from 'hopelessness and despair (contrary winds), (vs 13-14), to winds not suffering us to imminent danger (Acts 27:7). It was so perilous fighting the sea, bailing the boat, and manhandling the sails, were all demanding; plus of course the difficulty eating and sleeping as the savage, howling winds bashed with force against the hopelessly stricken vessel.

However, this was no time for vindication for Paul. This was quite a different attitude from Jonah. Paul knew from the beginning through divine revelation and illumination exactly what would happen! It really is a pity when people refuse to listen to wise counsel and you are forced and may have to choose to sit back and allow them to make their own mistakes to learn from them. Some people will only learn from their own mistakes or poor choices. Others are repentant, remorseful and learn from theirs or the mistakes of others. Alongside grace, mercy, forgiveness, restoration and rehabilitation is a place on occasion for tough love. Repeatedly bailing out someone who has no regard or respect for the price of redemption is not helping the person. While this might be enabling them, this might not be empowering them to rise and take charge and full responsibility. Thus, truly sometimes we must learn from our mistakes but at what cost especially to others when wise counsel has been rejected?

It is worth noting the gradual progression in the deterioration of the sailing conditions: from smooth seas to contrary winds, to winds not suffering us to imminent danger to life and property. There was hopelessness and despair and now the seriousness and gravity of the situation became apparent. What a progression! Maybe you started out in whatever sphere of life with good intentions and anticipated a 'smooth ride' and expected outcome; however gradually as you progressed with that marriage, degree, business, raising that child or whatever you set to hands to do, you find a gradual change in the 'wind' of your circumstance. You are afraid, apprehensive, nervous, resentful, guilt-ridden and filled with regret.

'I simply did not see this coming', you exclaim.

Truly you might had set sail with good intentions, the conditions were perfect for sailing at the time but alas things, time and circumstances have changed. I know it is hard, but now is not the time to feel sorry for yourself. You need a strategy to get out of this and to move on with your life. As the saying goes, 'things turn out the best for those who make the best of how things turn out.' T.S. Elliot (1888-1965), reminds us that 'success is relative; it is what we can make of the mess we have made of things, (*Little Oxford Dictionary of Quotations*, p352).

I earlier spoke about the need for flexibility even in the midst of sound systematic planning, structure, organisation and a methodical approach to life and its activities. There might be changes in the 'wind, waves and weather' that no one could have anticipated. Sometimes things started well and ended well; other times they began well and ended badly.

This is life. This is a teachable moment. This is no time for regret. You are now in the situation and it requires urgent action as your life and perhaps those of others: colleagues, friends, family, passengers may all depend on your decision. What a burden to carry but on the other hand, what a tremendous opportunity to make a significant difference in the lives of others.

For Paul, while he was not rejoicing at their plight as their disobedience put all 276 souls in imminent danger, yet there was a rebuke for their stubbornness (v21): indeed,

'You should have listened to me!' He warned.

Paul's insight and warning of imminent danger to life and property could have averted all this; however; God's purposes and ways are past finding out. It is all a part of the story and so too, your trials will form part of your invaluable narrative and process. Use it wisely.

The sequence of events that later unfolded even amidst the raging sea, fierce waves, ship-wrecked and serpent bite, only go to show how God can work His purposes out even in the midst of our most challenges circumstances and darkest hour. We too have to deal with those times when God says 'No' or 'Wait.'

Reflection: What are you going through that seems so dark and hopeless? The winds of life are blustery, fierce and contrary. How are you coping amidst the cares, the tears, the pain, the devastation, rejection, loss and hopelessness? Have you acted against better judgement when given sound advice? Can you think of times when you have headed straight into disaster when have been warned in some way?

Maybe there is potential danger, destruction or imminent loss of property or life. Remember as they were on the stormy seas, for days and weeks on end there was no sight of land, moon, stars or the sun...just hopelessly drifting...further and further off course and into the blackness of night...without hope, direction or purpose, battered by savagely angry waves along the tempestuous path to a seemingly elusive destination.

Sometimes in your life, things might get worse before they get better. Your winds are blustery, contrary and fierce. You are worried and downright scared. Your life might be in imminent danger. Your decision and how you handle this crisis might have grave ramifications on the lives of significant others. The comfort of a prophetic word is reassuring. It could be that for you in the midst of your storm, you may not have a word of encouragement, faith or admonition from another.

There are times in life when like David, you will have to encourage yourself in the Lord (1 Samuel 30:6). This requires you building up yourself in the Lord and having the confidence to trust Him completely. You can develop your spiritual muscles by observing the spiritual disciplines of prayer, fasting, reading and mediating on the Word of God, praise and worship, words of your testimony and sharing and fellowshipping with believers of faith. Jude speaks of 'building up yourself on your most holy faith praying in the Holy Ghost' (Jude 1:20). The truth is that you will not always have someone aboard your 'ship' be it your experience, marriage, work, business or experience, to give you that word of illumination and prophesy.

Life requires a deep and personal relationship with Jesus Christ to the extent that whilst you are not independent of others' help, prayers, or fellowship, are so fortified that in the absence of these you can hear God's voice for yourself. Too much depends on hearing His voice. Some people tend to make rash decisions then seek the Lord to 'bail them out'. It is good practice to seek the Lord diligently before making decisions and embarking on any activity however small.

According to Mark and Patti Verkler, 'God's inner voice comes to us as spontaneous thoughts, visions, feelings or impressions' (p. 220). With this in mind and definitely based in the knowledge of His Word, you can then trust God's sovereignty and believe in Him, even when storms develop along the way. However, thoughts, visions, feelings and impressions that are not founded on or in agreement with Scripture can be considered by some as being humanistic.

Remember, God is in the storms with you and He will not suffer you to perish. He will speak to you even in your storms and providing you stay in tune and trust Him, as you go through your trials, He will give a Word of illumination, assurance and faith to sustain you.

4. Divine Illumination, Revelation and Visitation Despite Hopeless Drifting

'Never let the shadow of failure block the sunlight of success.' (Author unknown)

'Things turn out best for the people who make the best of the way things turn out…Make each day your masterpiece…Do not let what you cannot do interfere with what you can do.'

(John Wooden, American basketball player and head coach)

Paul's presence made a significant difference to all lives in that ship on the stormy seas. It is true to say that his intervention contributed greatly to or even resulted in the saving of all the souls on board, including his very own! Paul was in tune with God even in the storm at the peak of desperation, fear and imminent danger. He heard the voice of God through an Angel in the storm. He had the calm assurance, peace and presence of mind and spirit even the midst of the fierce winds and waves. Whilst there was fear, panic, and dread all around as people 'feared for their lives' Paul was receiving divine illumination, revelation and a visitation from God.

Reflection: How do you handle the fierce waves and contrary winds in your life? Do you have a sense of anger, fear or resentment, asking 'why me?'

You may be at a place or have come to a place of quiet resolve and closure perhaps after your initial reaction. It can be quite scary and intimidating to go through the storms and trials that life throws at you, especially when they are unexpected and or not of your making. Sometimes you may have to simply 'flow with the tides' as you go through these unexpected storms as you have nothing to do with them but also there might be nothing you can do about them at the moment. All you have control over is your attitude during the storm.

But, be still...let us hear God's voice even in the midst of your hurts, pains and trauma...He has a Word of calm assurance and peace for you as you go through your painful experiences. He has divine consolation for your situation, even in this present pandemic God speaks comfort in this storm. You may not necessarily feel that way but He is always there for you. You may feel that you have messed up too badly and He wants nothing to do with you, but know that He really cares. It is clear that our actions do have consequences; but even in disobedience (v22), you can find repentance, reconciliation and rehabilitation with remorse and a returning to the right path. Admittedly, this will be a process but it is one worth pursuing.

You may feel that life is unfair as you are bearing the consequences of others' mistakes, stupidity or deliberate actions. You have every right to feel that way. Nevertheless, you can take some comfort that despite the 'loss to possessions there will be no loss of life' This admittedly might be cold comfort as the possessions lost may very well be of great price monetarily or of high sentimental value. It is also true that what is lost may be priceless, like your reputation, respect and sense of self.

Perhaps you have toiled relentlessly and sacrificially for years only to find that for every step forward you make, you slipped back three. Worse yet you may have to start all over again. I think of the hard labour you might have put into your careers or financial planning for retirement and the impact of the pandemic or recessions, partially or completely decimate your plans. You may have been furloughed with no clear sight of your long-term plans; or being made redundant and the bills still keep piling up. If you have to re-skill and take on another job completely unrelated to, or is below your skills, training, expertise and qualification it can be difficult especially when you have to step down considerably in wages, prestige or status. It can be painfully difficult but a temporary and necessary sacrifice.

I saw in the News today, at the time of writing this book that a few people with previously well rewarding, high status and fulfilling careers were made redundant. Some, in order to provide for their families had to work on farms harvesting crops for considerably lower wages. This is by no means demeaning or beneath anyone; however, while some had a positive attitude in such dilemma as it howsoever small, put food on the table, others were less enthused.

Reflections: In the midst of such pain and disappointment, what do you hear? What voices scream at you? Do you have the calm and quiet assurance of peace and divine illumination even and at such a time of dread and great alarm?

You Are Not Alone in Your Struggles
As I ask these searching questions, I reflect on the Old Testament prophet Elijah, who was so discouraged after an intense battle with idol worshippers. Following a direct threat from Jezebel, he ran away after his great victory and became so depressed to the point of being suicidal. Feeling that he was all alone in his plight, he told God how he felt, 'Let me die, I am the only one left' he cried (1Kings 19:10). With a still small

voice, God spoke to him and gave him direction, purpose and a strategy for his future. He was not in the noise of the earthquake or the heat or brilliance of the fire but God spoke in a still small voice (verses11-12). Sometimes we need to get away from the noise, the hustle and bustle of it all even from the negative attitudes of people who might even wish us well but are not on the same positive mindset or spiritual frequency.

You may be hearing words of hope, faith and courage while others around you may be negative and even depressing in their words and attitude. There is a place for 'social distancing' in a philosophical, social and spiritual sense. That is to say, separating yourself from negativity. Indeed, we have heard an awful lot of 'social distancing' as a strategy to fight Covid-19, but we also need 'social distancing' against a negative mind set. I am not suggesting adopting an air of superiority, pride, arrogance or conceit; rather I am simply recognising that there are times when we have to separate ourselves from people who may pollute, contaminate and affect the spirit or environment by their toxic or negative words and attitudes. This can instil fear instead of faith and prevent you from achieving your God-given purpose.

The twelve spies sent out by Moses to scout out the land of Canaan is a good example. All twelve spies saw the same land but two, Caleb and Joshua came back with a good report declaring in Numbers 13:30,

> 'Then Caleb silenced the people before Moses and said, "We should go up and take possession of the land, for we can certainly do it.'

However, the majority, 10 brought back a negative report. They admitted that the land was good with abundance of milk and honey and much fruit. However, there are giants in the land, we are like grasshoppers in their sight, and they stirred up the people!

> 'Their grasshopper mentality kept them from the promises of God...their minds were focused on going back to the old life, not pressing on to the new one' (Treat, 1992, p.29).

Reflection: My question to you is 'who are you listening to?' What is being said to you and by whom?' Furthermore, are you firm enough in your faith to maintain your convictions and trust the words of faith God placed in your spirit?

Associations Matter
It is no surprise that Jesus could do no miracles in some towns because of the 'unbelief of the people' (Matthew 13:58), and he did not do many miracles there because of their lack of faith. In Mark 6:5, He could not do any miracles there, 'except lay his hands on a few sick people and heal them.' Also, for Him to have healed some folks he had to have them physically removed from the crowd having had the door shut! You will have to shut out unbelief sometimes from your life. As with Caleb and Joshua, the majority is not always right! In fact, 'broad is the way that leads to destruction but narrow is the path that leads to life everlasting, and few there be that find it (Matthew 7:13-14). You may have to stand alone some times in your purpose, convictions and mind set when you like Paul hear from the Lord on a matter or in particular situations.
I am not talking about being stubborn or failing to follow sound and Godly counsel or wisdom. Rather, I am talking about having a quiet sense of confidence in God deep in your spirit in any given situation of fear or dread and knowing beyond the shadow of a doubt that somehow, God will come through for

you. As the songwriter says, 'you may not know how, you may not know when, but He will do it again.' Another song encourages us that when you cannot 'trace His hand, trust His heart' A verse of Scripture that means a lot to me personally is found in Isaiah 30:15 which declares that 'In quietness and confidence shall be your strength'

Meekness indeed is not weakness but strength under control. Assuredly, there is a place for encouragement, and you should not suffer in silence for the sake of your mental health and emotional wellbeing. As you go through your storms and your tests, yes there is a place for sharing and opening up to a trusted friend. However, I am talking about having all the negative things and winds of discouragement blowing all around you and you have to sometimes stand alone in faith on a 'Word' you have received from the Lord to see you through.

As I mentioned earlier, academically, you generally take your written tests in silence! Pull out what is within you. Draw on the deep resources God placed inside of you as 'deep calleth unto deep' (Psalm 42:7); for 'strength is born in the deep silence of long-suffering hearts, not amid joy' (Hermans, 1793-1835). Draw on the knowledge you implanted in your studies, learning and research. Draw on the knowledge gained, skills learned, and attitudes forms and values inculcated. Then in the exam or the test of life, you demonstrate what you have inculcated in revision, like a performer who rehearses in private but performs the recital in public. The 'noise' of rehearsal or practice can be irritating to the untrained ear as one goes repeatedly over bars and bars of music and scales for minutes, hours, days, months even years before the recital! Nobody likes the rehearsal but we all enjoy the recital!

We are tempered in the furnace of affliction. Moses practised his craft on the back side of the desert with stubborn sheep long before he confronted Pharaoh or led the children of Israel out of Egypt (Exodus 7:8-13). Likewise, David the shepherd when he faced the giant Goliath, confidently declared 'Thy servant kept his father's sheep and a lion and a bear came and I destroyed them. This uncircumcised Philistine will be like them' (1 Samuel 17:34). Murdock (2001) notes, 'Moses was needed as a leader to the children of Israel. He was their reward. David was needed by the Israelites to defeat Goliath. He was a reward to King Saul when he defeated Goliath and routed the Philistines' (p. 83). The point is your problem, process and story are the answer to someone's dilemma.

The rehearsal was in private but the recital, being before Goliath with a multitude watching was in public! The difficulties you now face could simply be rehearsal for something bigger and better, your recital! Admittedly, both are scary, demanding experiences! They say, hindsight is 20/20 but when you are facing your 'lion and bear' or on the 'backside of your wilderness', it remains your personal experiences and may not come across then and there as useful learning experiences, to develop your character and prepare you for greater experiences in the future. However, be encouraged and know that you have the power within you to develop a positive mind set and attitude through exercising your personal faith in God to prepare you for the storms of life.

Those closest to you may not have heard or had this Word. Like Paul, they could be traveling with you on the same path. Paul knew what he heard and saw. Likewise, you can be with others who fail to see, hear or share your experiences. You may look silly or even conceited to hold your perspective, attitude, mindset or faith position. Nevertheless, you have a personal experience, you have a personal intimate relationship with God and you know beyond the shadow of a doubt that God spoke to you. Does this mean that you will always get it right? Not necessarily, there might be times when your expectations and desires could contaminate God's instructions to you. These can be opportunities for life lessons and teaching opportunities to reflect, re-evaluate motives, purpose and perspectives and reposition yourself.

Be Encouraged, There is Hope
Paul, the prisoners, owners, soldiers and crew were hopelessly drifting without direction with no sight of sun or stars for days, exceedingly tossed by the angry sea. We can only vaguely conceptualise this unimaginable horror! Indeed, all hope was lost. The blackness of night had engulfed them, the angry waves relentlessly buffeted them on all sides, indeed lives were in imminent danger, 'And when neither sun nor stars in many days appeared, and no small tempest lay on us (in the ship), all hope was then taken away' (Acts 27:20). The fear was beyond words. Life for you can sometimes seem that way; hopeless, dark, aimless drifting, lack of direction and vision. You may feel that your situation is hopeless.

After all the time or emotions invested, effort, sacrifices and planning, it is understandable if you feel a sense of desperation in your storm. Hope: your confidence, optimism, expectation, faith, anticipation and courage are crucial to maintain in your storm. 'Now abideth faith, hope and love' (1 Corinthians 13:13) These three are paraded as important values to embrace. Furthermore, we are admonished to 'cast not away our confidence for it has great recompense of reward' (Hebrews 10:35). Our hope is in God, not in material things or even people, even though relationships are important. Things have their places and people can be so precious in terms of productive and nurturing relationships, however, your hope should be in God. Scripture reminds us that 'If it is in this life only, we have hope we will be as men (persons) most miserable and to be pitied' (1 Corinthians 15:19). So, you need to challenge that sense of hopelessness; that sense of impossibility, desperateness, fruitlessness, ineffectiveness, futility and bleakness.

These can lead into a dark place; a place where all may seem empty, lonely, futile and just, dark. You are tempted to isolate yourself from relationships, new experiences and purpose. Your situation may lead to and through a place where the sun, moon and stars are hidden from view by the ferocity of the storm. You hide away in despair having little or no appetite for leisure or pleasure, food, fun or fellowship. Yet in the darkness of your night, God is so near to you. Through your tears, fears and cares, whilst other reel in abject panic and dread, yet you can find some peace because of your unshaken and unmoveable faith in God. Faith that reminds you that God can give you treasures in darkness (Isaiah 45:1-3). You develop the faith and spiritual muscles and strength of character to believe that your best of times can emanate from your worse of times, at the same time. Your scars can indeed lead to your stars as mentioned in chapter one. Your impediments can be used as implements, your stumbling blocks as stepping stones, even your dark messes can be used as messages and your stubborn obstacles be used as opportunities. All this is within you!

There is no need to continue along the path of aimless drifting. You can hear the words of assurance, illumination and faith, and despite the stormy blast, have the faith, courage and confidence to move forward though slow may be the progress. There may even be moments when you are not making sufficient progress or 'gaining ground.' In times like these, you simply stand and firmly maintain the ground you have already covered.

Ephesians 6 advises and encourages us to 'stand and having done all to stand....' This can be so difficult especially if you are purpose-driven and results-oriented. Admittedly there will be times: days, months and even years when you might not see the results in your relationship, career, education, business, health that you expected. You are in a dark place, drifting without aim, direction, or purpose. Life can beat the winds out of your sails. Life's struggles can beat purpose and direction from your desire. Life can seem meaningless because of the things you have suffered. Life stresses can remove its leisure and pleasures.

Your purpose however, beckons you from a life where you lack direction and vision. Without vision, the people perish (Proverbs 29:18). Regardless of what you go through in life, never lose your vision. Helen Keller said, 'the worse thing in life is to be born sighted but lack vision.' You must see yourself rising again. Countless, businesses have failed and then reinvented, rebranded and moved on to even greater success. Many individuals have suffered tragedies, financial reversals and disasters in life only to return stronger and better.

The Power of Vision and Obedience
Samson, in Judges 16 failed to realise his God-given purpose and ended up in captivity to the Philistines. He was tied up, humiliated and tortured after being deceived by Delilah. His tormentors firstly put out his eyes. The enemy's primary goal is to deprive you of your vision. If he can get you to lack purpose, vision and direction then you will meander through life's maze and your mirage and murky path. Your aimless

drifting may carry on into weeks, months, years, even decades, and the epitome of fruitlessness, inefficiency and ineffectiveness glare savagely at you. This results in regrets, bitterness, despair, hopelessness, jealousy and lack of fulfilment as the years roll by and you fail to see the process that your potential demands. This is not the way to live your life. Like the centurion who Paul admonished strongly, you have a decision to make.

The centurion and ship's owner had a crucial decision to make in the face of this imminent danger to life. Paul warned them not to set sail. Desperate situations call for calculated attention and intervention. Whilst you should not act out of fear, desperation or ill-thought-out actions, sometimes doing nothing is not an option. Yet responding purposefully instead of merely reacting to life's trauma might be a better way of dealing with situations.

'Responding' implies that you are in control and have given thought and due consideration to the issue and have decided on a strategic course of action that is commensurate with the challenge being faced. This could mean careful and thoughtful contemplation and deliberation, open and honest sharing with a trusted friend or significant other, seeking professional help be it academic, relational, professional, financial, academic, legal, spiritual or otherwise. Speaking of spiritual, if you are a person of faith then no doubt you would consider and engage with your Saviour and Lord through prayer and meditating on the Word. This book is not going to be all spiritual but also practical and feasible as the case might necessitate adding that additional layer of undergirding, to match the depth of the challenge you face. You need to balance the practical with the spiritual. Some situations require practical solutions others are spiritual. Still others require a response embracing both.

If you do not have a personal faith in God, then surely you too will need to have strategies to handle life's circumstances and traumas in a manner that results in your personal and emotional wellbeing being protected and promoted. Practical strategies of sharing a problem, seeking legal professional, medical, academic or other forms of relevant assistance or intervention are applicable to all, of faith or none. Nevertheless, all embrace various aspects of spirituality although having a personal relationship with Jesus Christ as a Christian may not be the case for all. This depth of fellowship adds not simply a layer, but a firm underpinning of faith, hope, confidence and trust in God who will never leave you nor forsake you.

Like Paul, you can feel the assurance of His abiding presence even in the midst of life's vicissitudes, traumas and stormy seas. This deep and personal relationship with Jesus, that Paul had, arose out of his Damascus Road and other experiences and stood him in good stead to be calm under intense pressure; to trust God, to be resilient and to lean completely on God's unchanging hands even when his and others' lives were in imminent danger. Antonio (2016) puts it this way,

> 'The Damascus Road encounter resulted in a conversion which created a new motivation, Hence the attributes, qualities and principles...which were formerly employed to do evil, were now used for the good of advancing the Kingdom of God' (p. 128).

From this point, Paul received divine revelation and enlightenment through which he could then advise and admonish the powers that be, (Centurion and ship's owners) that there would be loss of the ship and possessions but no loss of life. It is important to note that just because you receive and delivered a prophetic word from the Lord does not necessarily mean that it will be received or embraced gladly and enthusiastically acted upon! In fact, Paul's Word although from the Lord was rejected.

Reflection: How do you feel and respond when you are sure that you have received a prophetic word from the Lord and it is not received with the sense of urgency that you had anticipated? Or when by virtue of your training, education and expertise, or the evidence you provide, people still reject your wise counsel?

Indeed, it can be difficult. You might have admonished someone to change his or her ways, to work harder in school, to refrain from entering into a marriage or ill-advised business deal for example, and your advice, suggestion, evidenced-based strategy or Word from the Lord was rejected. There are times when a bit of encouragement, gentle prompting or firm rebuke may be all that is needed to change a mindset or shift a paradigm. However, like the Prodigal son in Luke's gospel (Luke 15:11-32), sometimes wisdom dictates that you leave people to face the consequences of their own choices and decisions… a kind of 'tough love' you could say.

This could help to develop their character and give them a sense of independence, ownership and direction. On the contrary, it could be to their destruction and downfall. For good or for ill, they would have to own the consequences of their decisions and choices. It is even worse if you have to pick up the pieces from the poor decisions and choices of others, still worse when they are your loved ones. Like the prodigal son who asked for his portion of his father's inheritance prematurely and squandered it, he had to learn the hard way:

the lesson of respect, obeying authority, the fickleness of association; the exploitative nature of his acquaintances that used him for his money but rejected him when he was desolate, deprived, and destitute. Therein he learnt humility, reconciliation, rehabilitation, restoration, repentance and renewal of a broken relationship and fellowship.

Like the Father in this story, you might have to maintain your love, faith in others, prayer life and a right attitude in the midst of being overridden, rejected or disrespected or simply having your wise counsel and anointed Word despised. It takes much to be there for someone who does this to you. Like Paul sometimes you may have to say, 'I told you so...You should have listened to me!' There is a time and place for rebuke and admonition and challenge, as there is a place for motivation, inspiration, encouragement and acceptance. These can also be given as a package and in the spirit of love! This necessitates however, that the recipient be humble and receptive enough to admit the wrong and accept the rebuke. No doubt, it can be rather embarrassing for them to do so but in the face of potential or worse yet, imminent danger to life and property, stubbornness may not really be an option.

Cast Aside the Weight
As mentioned, the urgency of the situation required desperate measures albeit with a Spirit-led response and a critical strategy. Sailing for days and now weeks with absolutely no sight of land, stars, sun or moon and being severely tossed mercilessly on the raging waves and being thrown all around the ship in a time when all the present emphases on health and safety were not in place, would indeed be beyond scary. To look death in the face in this manner is chilling; and all this after having being advised not to set sail could only have compounded the situation. By the way, let us not forget the

other souls on board! Then they were left with no other option but to lighten the ship. In verse 18, the command was given to cast over board the ship's cargo. That which was initially so valuable and a source of profit for the ship's owners now was the first casualty. Casting aside the weight and the sin that doth so easily beset us is a challenge!

'Casting' or causing something to move by throwing off or away; or 'to get rid of' implies an act to be done deliberately. In this case, on the ship on the boisterous waves in this life and death situation, this decision was taken after counting the cost, weighing possibilities and deep reflection as there was so much to lose; all that valuable cargo that potentially bore the profit and livelihood of the ship's owner. The transportation of the prisoners also formed part of the profit to be made. Not only was the cargo to be discarded over board, but later as the storm got even worse, the centurion contemplated killing all the prisoners on board! The decision as to what to keep and what to discard in our lives forms part of the crucial decision we all must make at some point.

Reflection: How do you decide what to keep possession of or to cast aside? How do you come to the conclusion on what is worth keeping? What is the consequence of holding on to toxic relationships or possessions? These are deep and searching questions. Could there be things, experiences, people, mindsets, attitudes and dispositions that you are holding on to, that are simply holding you back and preventing you from achieving your purpose and God-given potential?

Some of these might be so precious to you. They may have been fixed and affirmed in your consciousness as part of your early formation and you have developed a system of coping that now forms part of your support system; one that somehow and perhaps understandably, provide your crutch or comfort to life's storms. It could be that your comfort crutch; that thing that you turn to for affirmation, comfort, succour, and understanding and as a coping mechanism or a 'drug of choice' now becomes a liability and a toxic companion, destroying your relationships, career, livelihood, confidence, hope or vision. You may want to move on but somehow you just cannot see your way out. It could be that what you hold on to was once useful and relevant at a particular time in your life but now you maybe in a different time, season and stage in your life and those things now need to be cast away! Paul later said, '

> 'When I was a child, I spoke as a child, I understood as a child, I thought as a child; but when I became a man, I put away childish things.' (1 Cor 13:11)

Crucially then, timing is very important! There was a time when the cargo was important as potential profit and an asset but then in a storm it became a liability! It is the same cargo, nothing about the cargo has changed but the situation and timing have! On one occasion that cargo held so much promise for wealth and profit but under a different set of circumstances and at a later time it now had to be cast away to save lives.

Reflection: What could you be holding on to, even embracing stubbornly that need now to be cast away as a matter of urgency because your progress, purpose, potential and very life depends on this brutal action?

No doubt, your 'cargo' was important on some occasion under some circumstances, but now you find yourself in a situation howsoever caused and you have a crucial decision to make.

Paul reminds us here that your maturity depends on three important facts. Firstly, how you speak.

Reflection: How do you speak? What do you talk about and with whom? I earlier mentioned the case of the spies in Canaan. Do you see life's challenges as insurmountable problems? Do you see yourself as a grasshopper like the spies of Israel or as 'dead dog' as Mephibosheth did in 2 Samuel 9:8 when the King summoned him?

The Power of The Spoken Word

The point I am making is that your success or defeat in life has a lot to do with how you speak. You need to speak words of life, positivity and faith. You cannot expect to sow seeds of doubt, fear and negativity and reap faith, courage and hope! As a man soweth so shall he reap (Galatians 6:7) Life and death are in the power of the tongue (Proverbs 18:21). Proverbs 6:2 also reminds us that 'you have been trapped by what you said, ensnared by the words of your mouth.' Meyer (2015) concludes that 'a lot of our problems are caused by our own words' (p. 146).

In like manner, Matthew Ashimolowo (2000) asserts that 'your words are either a blessing or a curse' (p. 10). Furthermore, he encourages us to 'speak your intentions to the mountain like Zerubbabel did,

> *'Who art thou O great mountain? before Zerubbabel thou shalt become a plain; and he shall bring forth the headstone thereof with shoutings, crying, grace, grace unto it' (Zechariah 4:7 (p.32).*

Oh, how we empower others to take control of our lives! You need to take back control of the situation and of your life. This does not mean that you will not occasionally feel fear, loneliness, hurt or disappointment. Of course, you will. We all will. I am talking about a strong resolve and passion to trust God, hold on to your integrity and stand firm with purpose and stubborn determination. It starts with your thoughts.

We are the product of our thoughts, so let your thoughts line up with Scripture. Agree with how God thinks and feels about you and resist those distracting voices and influences. Then speak those positive words into your situation and believe that these thoughts and words will manifest into that rich harvest of desired outcomes.

Reflection: Could it be that you are speaking negative and destructive words over your own life and blaming others?

You create your world by the words you speak. Made in the image of God, you have the unique ability to create, and part of that creative process is to use words to construct and carve your world. I agree that like Paul, you can find yourself in positions in life that was not of your making and you say, 'how can I speak my way out of this?' Well, that is a good question. The truth is that speaking words of affirmation, prophesy and faith is not a magic wand out of your situation. What I am advocating here is speaking and coming into agreement with what the Word of God says about you and speaking those words. The Word or Scripture says that you are God's property and made in His image; you are the head and not the tail. The Lord is your keeper, they that dwell in the secret place of the lord shall abide in the shadow of the Almighty (Psalm 91:1); and 'I know the plans I have for you declares the Lord, plans to prosper and not to harm you,' (Jeremiah 29:11).

When you study the Word (Scriptures) and know what God says about you, speak these words in your storms to your situation. It really does not matter how you feel, this is what the Word says. Surely, there might be times when you are so low in spirit and may not necessarily feel like being positive and speaking the Words of faith. Nevertheless, in those moments you can ask someone to pray for you and believe with you. You may even play worship songs based on scripture or have your App on your smart device read the Word for and to you. It is crucially important that you speak the words of life over your situation for life and death, are in your tongue.

Personally, I can recall several times, seasons and occasions in my life when specific songs that accurately reflect my situations formed the basis for my renewed faith, thanksgiving and fellowship with God. These situations could be times of doubt, uncertainty, brokenness, success or celebration. To this day, most worship choruses, spiritual songs or hymns depicting the faithfulness of God, His ability to heal the broken-hearted or those that speak of His sovereignty, might and power still minister to me in a profound way.

On those occasions when you feel low, remember that in Hebrews 4:15 we read, 'For we do not have a high priest who is unable to empathize with our weaknesses, but we have one who has been tempted in every way, just as we are yet He did not sin.' This in and of itself should be comforting to know that you have a High Priest who knows you and feels your pain and comes to you with urgency to heal, bless and do you good. Now, that does not necessarily mean coming to you on your terms as and when you want. However, He understands and empathises.

Remember Lazarus is the Bible when he was sick and eventually died (John 11:14). He was a personal friend of Jesus yet when he was gravely sick and his sisters Mary and

Martha summoned Jesus, He delayed His coming by four days. This has theological significance. However, when He eventually showed up Lazarus was already buried. Can you imagine the anguish, hurt and disappointment? How could you treat your friends like this? Martha in particular spoke plainly, 'If only you were here then my brother would not have died!' she said (verse 21). Jesus wept with them. Maybe, you feel like Martha too and probably have uttered those or similar words in your grief. However, He comes to you in your pain, sorrow, hurt, disappointments, and anger even at Him, for not being there when you called. He weeps with you to show his humanity, that He is touched by the feelings of your infirmity and yes, He weeps at our faithlessness and unbelief.

I am sure you can testify to times when He came through for you in ways that in hindsight you have to admit is nothing short of miraculous. Yet when you face other challenges, you forget His faithfulness and previous deliverances. A powerful sign of maturity and growth is to reflect on and draw on those previous successes you have had in your life and use them as benchmarks and catalysts to face future challenges. Steven Scott (2013) points out how that 'it is easy to miss the opportunity of the moment because we are thinking about the near past or the near future' (p.65). Sure, the new challenges will be more difficult, different and may set a precedent however; you have your experiences of God's favour, faithfulness and grace to draw on to face any future storm you may encounter.

The Power of Your Understanding and Perception
Secondly, how you understand your situation? How do you feel about your storms? How do you perceive the challenging set of circumstances you now find yourself in? Your understanding reflects the truth you stand under; that is how

you see or feel about your situation. This is powerful! You have the wherewithal to choose how you actually perceive the situation you are in and what your response will be. You have heard of the optimist and pessimist 'half empty, half full' perception of the glass of water. Your perception of life and its circumstances will undoubtedly contribute to or even determine the outcome. Don Colbert, MD (2005) in his book, 'Stress Less' argues that,

> *'Perceptions determine whether something is positive or negative. The problem in most highly stressed individuals is this: they are pre-programmed with distorted perceptions to the point that even trivial circumstances or demands can trigger a massive reaction (p33-34).*

Let us take the example of the two sales representatives. The story is told of how they sat in a board meeting with their sales manager and team. One was assigned the task of breaking into a new market in a country where the inhabitants did not wear shoes. After a while there, the first sales representative got frustrated, disillusioned, resentful and angry at his sales manager for even sending him there. In total frustration, he abandoned the mission and returned home very unfruitful, unproductive and a failure at that assigned task. He aggressively challenged his sales manager, 'How do you expect me to succeed there in that environment? You sent me somewhere where nobody wore shoes, what did you expect?'

However, another sales representative courageously offered to take on the same challenge. He went in the same environment and gradually influenced the locals; before long he became highly successful in the same situation and environment where his colleague had so disastrously failed.

What happened? This is a good question. As he returned to base and sat in the board meeting with the sales team, of course his colleague was also present the question was asked, 'How did you succeed where your colleague had failed? With a smile the second sales representative said, 'Well, you sent me somewhere where nobody wore shoes!' Wow, what a mindset, what a perspective! This is powerful. He realised that he had no competition. He had complete monopoly on the market. No one there wore shoes! His challenge was to believe that he could influence people and get them to buy into his vision, passion, perception, purpose and the comfort he was selling.

It was a new paradigm and way of thinking and it worked. It all starts in your thinking. 'I can do all things through Christ who strengthens me' Paul writes (Philippians 4:13). Yes, I can and yes, I will. Christ gives the strength, but we have to do the 'doing'. It may even sound conceited to talk like that. Some might even resent it, or even you for being confident, and see you as being narcissistic, egoistic, or egotistic. There is a balance of course to be struck. To be any of the latter, depends on mind or will power, and purport to be independent of others, or even of God is dangerous territory to tread. Proverbs, 16:18, reminds us that 'Pride goeth before destruction, and a haughty spirit before a fall.' My point is that with a positive outlook on life and life's circumstances even when they are unpleasant, you can rise above them to overwhelming success while maintaining a humble and teachable attitude.

A Change in Perspective and Strategy
A young man from my county in England who had a very good job in the luxurious financial City of London working as a stockbroker in a well-known international bank was made

redundant during the 2008 recession. At first, he was sad, discouraged, and understandably so. He had poured so much of his life into the job that he loved. He just did not see this change coming and did not plan for his career to end that way. One Saturday afternoon, he had a barbeque and invited a few of his friends over to his house. He made the fire and fanned the coals alight. The smoke and sweet aroma from the previously seasoned and well-marinated chicken and ribs filled the air and filtered over to the adjoining homes.

When it was ready and served, his friends could not believe the taste, the presentation and the quality; well-marinated chicken grilled and barbequed on the out grill pan with that real Jamaican smoky flavour was indeed a tempting treat. One of his friends told him he should consider selling this product. Well, before he had only done this as a hobby but now his friend saw things from a different perspective.

After giving the idea some thought, he took on board the suggestion, in fact he had nothing to lose. He was jobless and the redundancy lump sum pay out would not last indefinitely. Faith arose in his heart. His friend believed for him until he could believe in himself. He started small by supplying a few folks in the neighbourhood; then he ventured into the town centre. He realised that there was a demand for his product, soon he had to move the business from his home into a rented space in the town centre, and employed a few staff to help.

After a year or so, he asked, 'Why did I not think of this before?' This shows the power of turning things around and pulling safely through trials and reversals in life. What was seemingly hopeless and discouraging was now transformed into a viable self-sustaining business venture. It is important to recognise the part that his good friend played in his life and this story. Your associations are very important. You need a network of people who are nurturing and uplifting, not discouraging, negative and toxic. You need assets not liabilities. According to Treat (1992) 'Most people build a circle of friendship with people that help them stay where they are in life and not make changes. They endorse each other's complacency and encourage each other to stay in the same place' (p.82). However according to TD Jakes (1996). If you want to climb from the mediocre to the supernatural, find someone who is doing what you want to do and do it with them...people cannot give you what they have not received' (p56-57).

However, 'if you want to be a success in life you need to get around people who have already been where you want to go (Martin, 2000, p. 9). You need people who can have faith in you and believe for you, sometimes until you can believe for yourself. This might mean friends, relatives, saints, or associates who can challenge you and be that critical friend, mentor and coach. 'A friend loveth at all times, and a brother is born for adversity' (Proverbs 17:17). However, while you are going through your storm your perspective might be blurred. An independent person can help to add some perspective to your otherwise distorted vision of your reality and situation.

> *'Sometimes the people closest to us, like parents can be the most detrimental to our future. They subconsciously want to hold you where you are and keep you from growing. Without realising it they feel challenged if you move on so they try to stop you'* (Treat, p.82).

I would add that sometimes those closest to you may try to delay or deny your purpose and destiny out of a well-meaning and intended but sadly misguided effort to care and protect.

All Things Work for Good
In April 2019, after a period of illness my wife's mother, Mrs Richards sadly passed away in Jamaica. We were comforted by the fact that the year before we had visited and had a wonderful family appreciation dinner at an upscale restaurant in Kingston, the capital for our parents on both sides of the family. Even though my mother-in-law was extremely poorly with a weak heart, she attended. It was the last time we saw her alive.

Following her death, Rhona went down a week ahead of me to assist with the funeral arrangements while I held the fort at home. I took care of our business and then joined her a week later for the funeral service as a pall bearer and gave a tribute on behalf of my family. It was good to meet up with friends and our families and to have sweet fellowship and communion with them. I also had to be the main speaker in Sunday services there as well as in the Cayman Islands, when we popped over there too. In both countries I preached on this subject, 'Safely through on broken pieces!'

It was time well spent. We enjoyed the long drive out to the North coast of Jamaica along the newly constructed toll highway with good friends. In addition, we toured the campuses of two universities and enjoyed mangoes and smoothie with one of the local Pastors and his family. We were also fortunate to further enjoy the scrumptious delights of fried fish and festival at Port Royal with another friend and his family; or spending time with other close friends who showed us around the island.

How can I forget the great fellowship with former work colleagues? They not only attended the funeral, both church services and the committal, but also hosted Rhona and I at their homes for a few days. We explored Mandeville, Spaldings and Trelawny in Jamaica. We also had the pleasure of partaking gladly of grilled and fried fish with crackers at Little Ochi. Indeed, we enjoyed the warm fellowship of friends and family. They invited us to their church service and chauffeured us around to quite a few places. Sadly, a few months after our return to England, one of these friends passed away.

Fast forward, a year to April 2020 and we have the Covid-19 pandemic to contend with a lockdown. You may ask, 'What do these two have in common and how are they related?' Well, as Rhona and I reflected, we had to agree that indeed 'all things do work together for good to them that love the Lord who are the called according to His purpose' (Romans 8:28). This is not some random cliché we pulled out to add some comfort in bereavement; no, far from it.

As we reflected, we had to agree and adopt a mind set and perspective that had Miss Lurline passed away, in April 2020, with the pandemic, there was no way we could have gone to Jamaica, let alone have had a proper funeral send off. With self-isolating for two weeks on arrival, social distancing, borders closed, no planes flying and furthermore, even if there were flights, on arrival we would be in 2 weeks' quarantine! This perspective on a sad situation gives hope and some comfort in this period of bereavement. Rhona knew and repeatedly said how happy she was that she had the chance to show respect and gratitude over the years but more so in that final appreciation dinner in 2018 with friends and family before her mom passed. Consequently, the grieving process was much easier. Somehow, it continues to support us in the process of achieving a measure of closure.

While I reflect and relate this incident, I must spare a thought for those who cannot share this experience. Maybe for you it is the exact opposite. Your loved ones may have sadly died from Covid-19 and you are grieving that you did not have the chance to be there at the bedside to hold a hand and bring a word of comfort. You did not have the privilege to have a proper burial with all your friends, family, work colleagues and the general community to share their last respects. Even a later memorial service may not replace those moments in their entirety. However, God will give you comfort to bear it all in sad time of bereavement, sincere condolences.

Your perspective of hope may be that 'God will not give you no more than you are able to bear' but will with the trial make a way of escape' (1 Corinthians 10:13), and that His 'grace is sufficient for thee' (2 Corinthians 12:9). This is in no wise an attempt to trivialise or spiritualise your heart felt grief and suffering; rather it is to acknowledge that even during or after your pain, God is able to give you an immeasurable supply of grace, mercy and favour to cope that will baffle greatly those who observe. You too might be baffled yourself at how you have coped and managed to deal so calmly and effectively with situations, especially if that was not your prior modus operandi.

Turn It Around
I believe that you can turn scars into stars, impediments into implements, obstacles into opportunities and your messes into messages. Many have used extremely sad and heartrending circumstances for good. I am thinking of a person here in the UK whose daughter, while in university studying Medicine,

tragically died after taking illegal substances known as 'legal highs' on a Friday night out. These are substances which are sold for the main purpose of mimicking the effects of real hard drugs but are sold with a caveat that they are not meant 'for human consumption' This is how they get around the law.

After the sad passing of her daughter, a medical student, her mother went around to universities to warn other students about the dangers of taking 'legal highs' (drugs). Out of evil came forth good. Surely, she and family had their period of grieving and will continue to grieve the sad passing of a lovely daughter with so much potential however, as her perspective changed, she saw where she could use her grief to benefit humanity, despite the reality of her tragic loss and great pain. Cormac McCarthy reminds us that, 'scars have the strange power to remind us that our past is real (in 'Little Oxford Dictionary of Quotations' p, 394). Ignoring the pain or living in denial is not helpful, but confronting the painful past helps in the process of closure.

Reflection: How can you use your pain for the benefit of others? Could your passion be in your pain?

Product of Our Thoughts
Thirdly, how you think! We are the product of our thoughts. So, the person you have become today and what you have achieved so far or plan to achieve, is a direct result of your thinking process. 'As a man thinketh, so is he' (Proverbs 23:7) reminds us. Can you imagine that you have the power to determine how you respond to life's trials? Sure, you cannot determine how life may turn out or the things that happen to you but you have the power to decide how you think and what you do about it. Indeed, 'things turn out the best for those who make the best of how things turn out'. Bad and terrible things

do happen to good people, there is no doubt about that; however, what do you think about what has or is happening to you, makes all the difference. You have options and from these options, you can make choices or decisions. Having weighed up your options and explore your possibilities, whether prayerfully and with Godly help, advice and support, you can make informed life choices.

Your ways of thinking might be affected by your early formation, associations and your life's experiences. You may have had a positive mind set and purposeful living modelled for you. Maybe on the contrary, you were surrounded by negativity, dysfunction and purposelessness in your upbringing that later affect your associations. You may think that it is too hard now to change your mind set and create the 'world' you desire to live in. There is one interesting thing about this thinking process: it is 'you've to do it for yourself'. Just like the 'casting over board' those things, which have become liabilities to your destiny.

When the Bible says: 'whatsoever things are just, pure, lovely of good report' (Philippians 4:8) and so on, it specially commands us to 'think on these things!' No one can think for you. They can influence your thinking just as hopefully I am trying to do now in this book: to challenge your mind set and disrupt your thinking patterns and processes and to enable a paradigm shift that will change your life, course and destiny. I want to shift you from a pattern of fear, negativity and "I can't", to one of faith, positivity and "Yes, I can!" You have to take full responsibility for your life. Alvin Day (2003) in his book, *'If Caterpillars can Fly So Can I'* endorses this point, he states that 'as a start, you must take responsibility for your very own welfare and development' (p.3). It is said that 'the highest fences we need to climb are those we have built within our minds' (Author unknown),

True, some bad things might have happened to you that was not your fault and they really hurt. However, after the healthy grieving process and period you have to come to a place where you say, 'that was then but this is now' and then purpose in your thinking that nothing or no one will be given that level of control or power to determine how your story ends. You may have to forgive and pray for some folks who have hurt you or caused your misfortune and predicament deliberately or otherwise. You are the master of your destiny, the author of your script and the director of your movie. William James (1842-1910) puts it this way, 'Believe that life is worth living, and your belief will help create the fact.' Therefore, go ahead and write your script, move the characters around, determine that by the grace of God through tears, cares, scars, fears and brokenness, "I will come through safely even on the broken, splintered pieces of my life!"

We are encouraged in Romans 12:2 to be 'transformed by the renewing of our minds; in contrast to conforming to this world and its mould. In John 15:19 we are reminded we are in the world but not of the world. There is a pattern of thinking in the world system that is contradictory to the Word of God. We guard ourselves from the depressing stories in the News while being aware of our current events locally, nationally, and globally. Yes, we guard our hearts and minds. How do you do this? You will be careful of what penetrates and permeates your eye gate, ear gate and heart gate. Casey Treat (1992) endorses this truth when he writes, 'Jesus said we must be careful of what we hear, because we will soon be controlled by it, whether it is good or bad' (p22). You be careful what you hear, see, entertain, and accommodate. Also be carefully who speaks into your life. You must be careful what you read, the movies watch, your social media activities, your associations, and the influences all these have on you.

Reflection: Are these influences and relationships nurturing or toxic? Do they propel you towards your purpose and God-given potential or lead you further away? Do your relationships, engagements, activities and interactions 'feed' you spiritually, morally, intellectually, emotionally, academically, financially, socially, mentally? Are they assets or liabilities in your life?

Only you can answer these questions. Scripture reminds us the weapons of our warfare are not carnal but mighty through God to the pulling down of strongholds. Casting down imaginations and every high thing that exalts itself against the knowledge of God (2 Corinthians 10:4). Again, we have the responsibility of 'casting down' and 'thinking'. We have to 'capture every thought and bring it into obedience to the word of God.' So, what are you thinking and does it line up with what and who God says you are? Treat (1992) further reminds us that, 'in the process of renewing the mind, we must realize that there are as many thoughts and attitudes that must be taken off, as there are that must be put on' (p.26). You may need to remind yourself that 'you are the righteousness of God in Christ' provided you have accepted Him as your personal Lord and Saviour. You are 'fearfully and wonderfully made' in His image (Psalm 139:14). These Scriptures should help you to have a high value on your life and thus impact your thinking of yourself. You know whose you are (position and fellowship) and who you are in Christ (identity). You know your position in Christ while understanding your condition. You recognise your place spiritually but understand your flawed nature; prone to fear, flight and freeze but having great potential for faith, focus and fruitfulness.

There is a strong relationship between your speech and your thoughts; your level of understanding, the truth you stand under, your perception and your actions. What you cast away, aside or fail to put away reflect your level of thinking which bears significantly on your level of understanding, thought pattern or mind set and ultimately the actions, decisions and choices you make as you deal with life's circumstances (the circle of your standing), which confront you.

Take Personal Responsibility
It is one thing when you can take full and personal responsibility for casting aside the weight or 'lightening the ship'. It is quite something else when the situation requires someone else to do the casting where life and property depend on such a decision. From a personal perspective however, you have to make a decision as you go through your storms what strategies to employ to deal with. A decision to lighten the ship is never taken lightly. You might have personal attachments, emotional, sentimental value or great costs previously incurred, and casting aside a 'weight' might be difficult or in some cases, not even really an option gladly contemplated.

Reflection: So, what 'weight' do you need to cast aside in order to achieve your God-given potential, run your race with patience, achieve your goals, purpose and leave a legacy in the earth?

Could it be fear, doubt, low self-esteem, acquaintances, and toxic relationships, habits and addictions, procrastination, lack of purpose and focus, lack of organisation and structure, laziness, sinful practices or whatever for you is hindering and preventing you from reaching your God-given potential is a weight.

> *"Lay aside the weight and the sin that doth so easily beset us and let us run with patience the race that is set before us" (Hebrews 12:1).*

The sin and the weight are separated because not all weight is a sin, but all sin is a weight. Sometimes you may be filled with fear and doubt, dread, anxiety, distress, panic, and alarm. Your situation may fill you with further doubt: hesitation, uncertainty, low self-esteem, mistrust, misgivings, disbelief, and reservation. These may engender lack of confidence and you long for sureness, self-assurance, self-confidence, poise, assurance, buoyancy, coolness and a departure from low self-esteem, hopelessness and lack or loss of direction. You may have to lay aside some toxic relationships that serve only to contaminate your thinking and lead you further away from your purpose and destiny by negatively influencing your thoughts, perceptions and actions. They could lead to a lack of purpose, drive, determination, resolve, persistence, tenacity and single-mindedness. Thus, your focus, emphasis, attention, effort, concentration and self-application are all adversely affected.

Achieving your goals, target and ultimate purpose could be negatively influenced by your lack of structure, organisation and sense of direction. This direction informs the way, path, route or bearing necessary to achieve your goals. Your thoughts, perception, attitude and actions will serve to provide some guidance or supervision pointing to your motivating purpose.

Another weight to be laid aside could be that of procrastination. Perhaps you have a tendency to put things off, to defer, postpone, stall or delay important tasks that need to be done. This results in a measure of ineffectiveness, incompetence, and inefficiency. Failing to lay aside this weight means that you are not producing the desired or intended effect, and precious time is wasted as energy and life itself are squandered. You may even convince yourself that you are incapable, incompetent, or even counterproductive, unworthy of any wholesome, lofty achievement or success.

All these weights may very well be because of some deficiency in our early formation resulting in insecurities and divers fears especially of failure. However, according Mills (2017),

> *'Our perspectives on failure need to change if we expect to see the greater purpose God has in mind for us. We cannot wallow in self-pity or allow others to define who we are. We must believe in what God has deposited in us despite what happens to us or what doesn't happen for us' (p. 175).*

Not only are we admonished to cast or lay aside the weight but also the sin that doth so easily beset us (Hebrews 12:1). Whatsoever is not of faith is sin (Rom. 14:23). Sinful practices: immoral and unrighteous, wrong thoughts, deeds and actions refer to us missing the mark or God's righteous standard. While we strive for 'decent, ethical, good honest, honourable, just, moral, right, righteous, upright and virtuous' lifes, the sin nature can only be dealt with through the shed blood of Jesus Christ.

The old 'Adamic' sinful nature is removed at conversion when Christ is accepted as Saviour and Lord. This is not merely about religion or spirituality, rather I am talking about a deep and personal relationship with Jesus where you trust God to help you 'cleanse yourself of the filthiness of the flesh and of the spirit (2 Corinthians 7:1). A deep and personal relationship with Jesus where you walk daily in sweet communion and fellowship with Him. This will give you that calm assurance and faith in the midst of life's raging seas and savage storms. No wonder Paul could remain calm in the storm while others panicked and feared greatly. This does not mean that he was not concerned about his life. However, Paul had a word of assurance, revelation and illumination. This prophetic word gave fresh direction and warned of imminent danger along their chosen path. In the end, you have to take personal responsibility for the direction of your life, regardless of the storms howsoever caused.

Divine Rerouting: Satnav Revisited
A very crucial thing in life you must adopt is the ability to be flexible. I earlier explored structured, organised, systematic or flexible working patterns. However, life will demand a measure of flexibility. Sometimes situations require that you change routes even though you might have had a pre-set or pre-determined course and destination in mind. This is exactly what Paul saw in the spirit and warned the ship's owner and the centurion about, but of course, they failed to listen.

I often refer to the metaphor of my SatNav as a useful way to explain this deeply relevant and spiritual concept. When embarking on a journey, especially when I am not familiar with my destination, for example, my interesting experience to Keswick I mentioned earlier; not only do I set the destination from the start of the journey but I also need to be flexible to know to roads taken as I drive may change. It is ill-advised to set out without ascertaining where I am going and then miles later on the motorway, lost and confused, I either pull over to ask for direction or to consult my SatNav, google or road map!

How much better and advisable would it be if I simply take a few minutes before I set out to confirm my address and destination, programme the same into my SatNav then preview the route to ensure that the path really led to, and end with my desired destination all before I even set out.

This is common sense but not necessarily common practice. Previewing my route also gives me the opportunity to select either the fastest route, most eco-friendly route thus saving petrol consumption, the quickest route, whether or not I choose a toll road, the highway or country roads. Additionally, I can also select the points of interests including service stations, hotels, tourist sites etcetera along the route. It makes so much sense just to do this simple task before I set out. It is so important as mentioned, especially if and when I am unfamiliar with my destination.

Despite all this preparation however, there will be times when I will have to change my route and adjust my travel plans. This could be because of detours due to road repairs, closure, accidents, crashes, or simply that I missed my turn. Even if that is the case, I need not worry as the guidance system (SatNav) will automatically recalibrate my position and instructs me to turn back or simply reroute me. In any case, I still reach my destination. Surely, this could mean in some cases additional time to my journey or having to adjust and adapt to situations that I did not necessarily plan for along the path en route to my destination. This is where the openness, flexibility, adaptability, trust, faith and maturity and having a positive attitude to life and circumstances come in. Importantly, there is absolutely no need to panic or be afraid.

I think this is a powerful life lesson to learn. Regardless of how fearful you may be or concerned that you are off course, God can take seemingly insignificant events in your life and turn them around for your good and His glory. Eleanor Roosevelt (1884-1962) states that,

> *I believe that anyone can conquer fear by doing the thing he fears to do, provided he keeps on doing them until he gets a record of successful experiences behind him.*

This is not easy. As you face your fears and then to move on to repeating that thing that cause you dread. However, this 'record of successful experiences' will develop your confidence. I normally say, 'areas of competence lead to areas of confidence.' Life requires a re-positioning. Be flexible and open to be re-routed from time to time. Conversely, you can be confident that detours are not necessarily denials; you will still reach your final destination. Mills (2017) reassures us thus, 'In making wrong moves, God still has a purpose to get us from one stage of development to another' (p. 157).

These can be difficult concepts to grasp and embrace especially if you are more systematic, structured, fixed, inflexible and well organised in your approach to life. That is to say if you are more a rigid planner, organised and a 'to-do-list' person. These qualities are very important however, life does require a degree of flexibility as circumstances will undoubtedly pop up in life to challenge you; some of your making and some of the making of others.

Hearing the Word, Recognising the Voice
Flexibility also requires you to know not only the Word of God (logos) but also to recognise the voice of God (Rhema Word). It was quite interesting that in one instance Paul instructed the men on the ship to remain on board as their very lives depended on obedience to that word. Acts 27:31says 'unless

these men remain on the ship they will not be saved'. The storm was so fierce, the ship was so badly battered, and the prisoners wanted to cast themselves over board. In that depth with raging winds and waves, they would not stand a chance of survival. Remember the lifeboat was cut away and they had no life jackets or other safety apparatus. Yet, it is so amazing how calm, confident and reassuring Paul was. Being confident and calm under intense pressure, especially so when life and property were subjected to imminent danger was indeed more than just a personality trait; 'it was the peace of God that passes all understanding' (Philippians 4:7). It was based on a Word from the Lord, underpinned by Paul actually knowing the voice of God.

When Jesus for instance, told his disciples 'Let's go over to the other side of the sea' and the storm struck, Jesus was asleep in the stern! The disciples cried out in fear, 'Carest thou not that we perish!' (Mark 4:38). For Jesus to be sleeping in the storm tells us so much. It tells us that He is the Master of the winds and waves; that He is supreme over the elements; that with him on your ship you have nothing to fear and His destiny leads to a cross not death by drowning! There is therefore no need to panic as Jesus is with you in your ship on your stormy seas of life.

Victor Hugo (1802-1885) French Poet and Writer puts it this way,

> *'Have courage for the greatest sorrows of life and patience for the smallest ones, and when you have laboriously accomplished your daily tasks, go to sleep in peace. God is awake.'*

Rest assured you are safe with Him on board. He gives you a word of calm assurance and hope – speaking to your winds and waves, 'Peace be still!' (Verse 39).

In the same way, however you need to know the Word of God. It is crucial to know the voice of the Lord in each situation in your life. This is not about being legalistic and overly 'religious' but about being in a deep and personal relationship with Jesus so that you can sense His presence and direction through His word, His voice and other ways in which He may choose to speak to you, whether through people or circumstances. Paul was in tune with God. In the midst of this life and death situation on the stormy sea, he had a divine revelation and illumination. He could thus stand with boldness and confidence and declare words of power and of faith. No wonder he found favour with the centurion! Paul's presence on that ship saved them both spiritually and literally.

When the ship had broken apart and the soldiers conspired to kill the prisoners lest they escaped, it was because of Paul's presence why the centurion ordered them not to be killed. Your presence makes a difference wherever you are; whether in your homes, on your jobs, driving, on a plane, in that shopping establishment or simply walking along the path of life. The Holy Spirit is the means which you carry the presence of God with you in each circumstance.

Reflection: Could it be that others have been spared because of your presence in particular situations? How has your presence influenced decisions and outcomes of others?

Indeed, you will find favour because God is with you. I must reinforce that. You will be confident and reassured whilst others are filled with fear and dread. They will marvel at your sense of calm and quiet confidence in potentially troubling times and will wonder how you can be so calm! It is that deep and quiet sense of confidence in God that His Holy Spirit is in you. This makes all the difference. He indwells and comforts you along the path of life, in and through all circumstances. Indeed, the peace of God, which passes all understanding, will sustain you. Having proof of God in your life gives you the confidence to boldly declare and decree a thing; like Paul, 'except these men abide on the ship they will not be saved!' (v31).

On the other hand, however, flexibility and discerning the voice of the Lord and the Word of the Lord (a logos and rhema word) is important. It is important to note although in one instance Paul admonished the men to remain on the ship in order to be saved, in another instance, as they hit two seas and the ship broke apart, the command was given to jump and swim for shore. The level of openness, flexibility, discernment and obedience paved the way for the fulfilment of the word earlier given, 'there will be loss of possession and the ship but no lives will be lost!

Oh, the joy of divine protection by visitation, revelation and illumination through the obedience and spirit-led life of one man – Paul. You too can be confident that your life, presence and personal relationship with Christ is significant. They undoubtedly can and do make a difference in situations as well as in the lives of others. God indeed can, and will use you to accomplish great exploits. Indeed, 'the people who do know their God shall be strong, and do exploits' (Daniel 11:32).

Speaking of knowing the voice of God, I recall the case of Abraham as recorded in the book of Genesis 22. God had instructed Abraham to take his son Isaac and offer him as a sacrifice to test his faith, obedience and loyalty. This was also a 'type and shadow' of Jesus being later offered on the Cross for us. Abraham obeyed and as he journeyed, he separated himself from the servants and those who travelled with them. They of course were not privy to the true nature of the mission.

Life requires discretion and wisdom in the time we choose to or not to disclose any Word we might have received from the Lord. Abraham declared, 'Stay with the ass and I and the lad will go yonder to worship' (Genesis 22:5). It is so profound! The place of separation is crucial – not everyone is called to go with you to the heights of success or to the place God has called you to go. Jason Mills (2017) observes a profound fact when he writes, 'God removes some people from our lives, block some from entering and allow some to enter…for divine reasons' (p. 86). Not everyone has the faith to believe with you for the things that God has called you to do, see, experience or possess. No wonder Jesus had to remove some folks from among others before he could even heal them. Scriptures say because of the unbelief of the people, Jesus could do no miracles or mighty works! (Mark 6:5). Isn't that interesting?

There has to be a place of separation in your life; you simply cannot take everyone with you when God gives you a Word. The higher you climb or go in life the smaller your circle of association becomes. Not that you are better than others but not everyone is called to go with you to the next level or see the move of God in your life and certainly not everyone has the faith to believe with you. Sadly, some people are so negative, jealous and lacking in faith they will kill your dream and cause you to abort God's will and purpose for your life. Motivational speaker Les Brown once said 'some people are so negative they can go into a dark room and begin to develop!' This is all about your associations and relationships: toxic or nurturing. It is about assessing what part they play in your life and how you are being influenced in your thinking, perceptions, understanding, interpretation of life's circumstances and by extension, the course of action you choose to take subsequently.

Abraham and Isaac separated themselves. Isaac asked his father 'We have the fire and the wood but where is the sacrifice? (Genesis 22:7). This life and death situation required every ounce of faith, courage and obedience, Abraham quietly replied, 'God will provide the sacrifice'. This is an amazing level of faith and trust in God despite the potentially deadly situation he was facing; indeed, a crucial test of his faith. To say to the servants, 'I and the lad are going yonder to worship' is also a profound declaration of faith, knowing full well that the true purpose of the mission, unbeknownst even to Isaac that he was the intended offering. Yet he referred to this as 'going to worship'…amazing.

As the wood was gathered and Isaac was tied to the altar and he in obedience yielded to the act, the voice of God came forth, 'Abraham, stay thy hand!' Note that the earlier command was to take that son, thy only son and offer him. Now the voice of God returned, 'Stay thy hand!' This level of openness, flexibility and obedience to the Word and the voice of God are very profound. It is important to know the Word of God, but it is also of crucial importance to discern the voice of God in life's circumstances. Remember God will always provide. As Abraham and Isaac travelled up the mountain, the ram was being prepared, simultaneously. On the other side of your pain is the provision! You have to keep on keeping on, to behold the better that is on before. Keep running on to see what the end is going to be; and the 'silver lining behind your dark clouds' and the 'light that awaits at the end of your tunnel.'

Reflection: Could it be God may have spoken to you prior, but in an updated memo, now asks you to change course or do something differently, but you hold on to the original word and ignore His voice?

This is exactly the point I am making. Here, in one instance Paul declared 'except you remain in the ship you will perish' and then when situations changed, the new and updated command was, 'Jump and swim to safety!' May God grant us the flexibility, discernment and obedience to be so in tune with God we can not only know His Word but also obey his voice in every situation; indeed, so much is at stake and depends on it. 'There will be times when God gives you a command others think (and you may think) is crazy, But He will reward you for your obedience' (Martin 2000, p. 29).

Staying Put
'Remaining on the ship' is also a significant concept and life lesson as well. Jumping too early can also be to your regret, disappointment or demise. Remaining on board to fight through some struggles and challenges is only part of life's circumstances. We sometimes use the phrase 'jumping ship' as a metaphor for giving up too soon or bailing out of a situation prematurely. Perhaps in the face of this Covid-19 pandemic we can spare a thought and even pray for our political leaders globally as they agonise and grapple most fervently as to when and how to start lifting the lockdown restrictions. They have to consider seriously and try to balance both health and economic considerations. Lifting the lockdown too early and it could spark a second wave and new spike of infection potentially worse than the first and damaging confidence. However, lifting it too late and the economic ramifications could be catastrophic. It is a grave decision to make.

Leaders around the world sought scientific, medical, economic and political advice and had to balance all these factors, economic, health including the mental health implications of the lockdown as well as the human factors as relating to the horrific death tolls, providing adequate personal protective equipment (PPE) and lack of support in the final moments of life. No doubt, spiritual guidance could have also played an important role in the advice being sought.

Our circumstances in life require discernment, wisdom, preservation, resilience, and maturity. Through reliance on God, fellowship with spirit-filled believers and wise counsel we can forge a path of resilience and purpose that sustains through the bleakest and darkest moments in our lives. Having personal goals and a purpose cannot be understated or over emphasised. These can serve as guides to encourage along the way and keep you focused when the winds of life are contrary. 'Where there is no vision, the people perish' (Proverbs 29:18). If you do not know where you are going, then any road will take you there.

It is crucial that you have clear focus and a sense of direction in the storms of life. Dr Samuel Johnson (1709-1784) states that 'Our aspirations are our possibilities.' Does that mean that there is always a definitive answer to everything? Of course not, but whilst the process might be blurred or even unknown the destination should be established. There are exceptions to this of course. Let us take Abraham again as an example. God on one occasion told him, then Abram, to pull up root and take his family to 'a land I will show thee!' Where is that? Well, not even Abram knew!

Knowing God's Word as well as His voice remains a crucial part of your Christian walk of faith. Undoubtedly, this can be scary and intimidating however; it does form an integral part of your testimony and builds your faith and trust in God for future challenges and storms. For Paul, it caused faith to arise in the hearts of his fellow travellers on the ship as well as giving him favour with Julius, the centurion.

It is also important to remain on the ship because the timing may not be right to jump. As mentioned above, Paul strongly admonished that the prisoners remained on board for their own protection, safety and life; yet in another scenario supported the centurion's decision they all jumped and swam to shore. In one instance they were further out on the stormy blast at about 120 feet depth and on the other, they were within sight of Malta at 90 feet depth. Testing and gauging the depth in your storm is also very important. This could mean counting the cost and evaluating the situation, making informed life choices and decisions. There is a place for prompt impulsive action but there is also a time for reflective response. Both cases could be intimidating and pose risks to life for most, yet at that point, in time they simply had no option as the ship had struck a sand bank where two seas met and the ship was being torn apart.

Sometimes, life's circumstances will thrust you into making a decision and a life changing one at that time with potential for grave distress, disappointment or demise! When you have no option, you have to act. This can be particularly difficult if you are of a careful risk-averse disposition. It can also be intimidating even if you are confident but the circumstances harbour potential or imminent risk and disaster, or if you are forced into such situation based on the carelessness, insensitivity, and, or deliberate actions of others.

'Remaining on the ship' could also demonstrate your strength, stability, maturity, reliability, resilience and commitment to your cause. This admittedly and even controversially could be hurtful and inconvenient to you; but may be the right thing to do under the given circumstances. You might have no choice when you sum up the alternatives. Staying in an unfulfilling marriage for instance, whether or not for the sake of the children; remaining on a job that is not progressive as far as scope for growth advancement or promotion are concerned; forbearing with a difficult child or an unreasonable family member could all be difficult situations which could challenge your decision to remain or to leave. Your mind set, faith position, perspective on life be it an individualisation thesis where your basic concern is for your own personal wellbeing and happiness or one that seeks and actively pursues the greater good and wellbeing of others even at your expense, could determine your chosen path.

Divine Protection Promised

Even when you remain in 'the ship', some things will be lost. Nevertheless, except ye abide in the ship ye cannot be saved (v31). All 2 hundred, 3 score and 16 souls (v37) were saved eventually. Perhaps, you were previously taught that once saved, it will be smooth sailing. However, 'God is a present help in times of trouble' (Psalm 46:1); 'Whom the Lord loves he chastens and scourges every son he receives' (Proverbs 3:12, Hebrews 12:6); also 'no suffering at the moment is joyous but grievous nevertheless afterwards it yields the peaceable fruit of righteousness (Hebrews 12:11); 'all who live Godly will suffer persecution (2 Timothy 3:12-17).These scripture verses seem to suggest that trials, and storms are all part of the lives of Believers and that being of faith and serving the Lord, does not necessarily exempt you from challenges in life.

Paul writes; 'We are pressed on every side by troubles, but we are not crushed. We are perplexed but not driven to despair' (2 Corinthians 4:8). Your attitude is everything. Yes, your attitude in suffering in life's storms, reversals and vicissitudes. An attitude of gratitude will go a far way and set you in good stead to receive the blessings of the Lord from life's circumstances even though unpleasant, inconvenient, embarrassing or potentially dangerous. It might be financial, relational, professional, emotional, physical, academic, and mental or otherwise. We all have storms. However, a misconception some hold sometimes is that some people are living stress free with perfect lives. What a misconception! Don Colbert (MD), in his book *Stress Less'* writes,

> *'Your perceptions are at the root of a very high percentage of the stress your body experiences. Your perceptions determine how you see the world'* (2005, p. 33).

The wheat and the tares indeed grow together. In Matt 13: 25, we know that both grew side by side and look alike but one is fruitless. When the disciples asked Jesus whether to pluck up the tares from among the wheat, they were admonished to leave them alone so that they can both grow together until the day of harvest. The grass is not necessarily 'greener on the other side'. In fact it still has to be mowed! In addition, the rose on the other side has thorns. No one comes out of life without a cross.

Do you recall the poem Josh recited? When I was a child in Sunday school class, I can remember this poem being recited in concerts and rallies: 'Must Jesus bear the cross alone and all the world go free? No, there is a cross for everyone and there is a cross for me!' I cannot over emphasise how important it is to keep your attitude in check. How do you really feel about the things that life thrust on you? Some people become angry, bitter, and cynical and lose their faith in the midst of life's reversals and storms.

Appreciate and Use What Life Hands You

I find the story of the talents quite interesting. In Matthew 18:21-35, Jesus tells the Parable of the talents. One servant was given five, another two and still another, one talent. Both the five and two talented servants invested their master's money and yielded a return of 100% on their investments. For this they were praised and highly commended. However, the servant with the one talent was worthless. He buried his master's money and returned it just the way he got it. His master was angry and sharply rebuked him thus:

> *'You unprofitable and slothful servant, at least you could have put the money in the bank and there it would have yielded interest' (Matt 25:25 ESV).*

However, the servant accused his Master:

> *'I knew that you are a hard man harvesting where you have not sown and gathering where you have not scattered seed' (Matthew 25:24, NIV).*

What a perception and understanding of God.

Reflection: How about you? Do you see God or life as being 'hard' on you or unreasonable to you? Do you compare yourself with others who may seem more gifted, talented, blessed or more highly favoured than you? Are you making the best of what you have or do you embrace a defeatist, pessimist or fatalist attitude? Helen Keller (1880-1968), deaf and blind American Writer and Scholar noted,

> 'No pessimist ever discovered the secrets of the stars, or sailed to an uncharted land, or opened a new heaven to the horizon of the spirit.'

As difficult as it can and will be, can you see the good side to life's traumas? or in cases where you do not understand, can you 'trust his heart when you cannot trace His hand?

The truth of the matter is that while all situations generally are common to mankind, our 'crosses' or 'storms' are different and sometimes we will have tumultuous, consecutive or concurrent storms. The parable of the tares among the wheat illuminates this concept. It records that whilst men slept the enemy sowed tares among the wheat.

Tares refer to several species of flowering plants commonly called vetches, which grow in an unwanted place. Examples include *Vicia sativa and V. hirsute*. It is worth noting that the enemy seeks to plant or sow these distractions, incidents, accidents, traumas or storms in our lives particularly in but not necessarily only in our formative years, to divert and distract us from our goals, God-given purpose and destination. Tares represent weeds growing in our lives where they are unwanted and counterproductive.

Having weeds among the wheat posed a matter of grave concern for the farmer regarding his yield and ultimate profitability.

> 'Should we pull them up?'

> 'No', replied Jesus, 'Let the wheat and the tares grow together until the day of harvest.'

My point here is that both wheat and tares grew side by side, simultaneously and concurrently. This is how circumstances will be sometimes in your life. The best of times can be the worst of times all at the same time. That is life. For instance, you may have your health intact but then you have financial issues; your health and finances might be going well but you have a, professional, relational or marital problem. Life's storms especially when they come at the same time can be troubling and fervently stressful. Fighting concurrent or simultaneous storms or battles require faith, resilience, trust, a word of assurance and re-affirmation that even if you lose some possession or cargo, or even the ship itself, you personally will make it safely through and over.

Paul and the others faced this situation after weeks of sailing in the dark, tumultuous, stormy and deadly sea. So bad was their situation and fearing destruction they cast down the anchor and had no choice but to ride out the storm, wait for calm and *wish for 'day'* (Acts 27:16). Have you ever had to 'ride out some storms?' Ephesians 6:13 encourages us:

> *'Wherefore take unto you the whole armour of God that ye may be able to withstand in the evil day, and having done all, to stand.'*

Paul and the others could not gain ground or make any progress and the sailing conditions were simply too dangerous to even attempt to advance any further. Life will sometimes throw some deeply disturbing situations your way that require you to simply 'stand ye therefore' and ride out your storms. These can be discouraging moments, when you feel like you are not making any of the required progress in your life towards your goals, destination or purpose. This could be in any area of life: Your marriage, career, family, marriage, goals, finances or ministry. It could be that you have made some progress and life knocks you back. As the saying goes, 'you made one step forward and got knocked back two steps. This can be upsetting, discouraging and frustrating to say the least. It could also deflate your confidence, trust, faith, ego and self-esteem.

I re-iterate that such situations could be of your own making by way of poor decision and choices: poor judgement, wrong associations, poor financial planning and management, marrying the wrong person accepting the wrong job, under-performing, procrastinating, missing opportunities through pride, conceit, fear or laziness. Here the feeling of regret, remorse, disbelief, dumbness, anger, sadness, lack of direction can be overwhelming.

Another problem I find, is when the circumstances you face are not of your making, that is to say, result from without. For instance, at a macro level it could a national or global recession that resulted in redundancy, financial reversal, business going insolvent, bankruptcy, and loss of earnings, interest rate rises, inflation, pension deficit, and health benefits withdrawal, loss of equity in property or even repossessions of assets and property. You may have paid in your pension investment instrument faithfully for years only to be informed of changes in the age at which you can retire. Maybe you are forced to work for another 5 or even 7 years longer than you originally planned. It could also be that you no longer qualify for a guaranteed final payment but are now placed on a variable or average payment with no guarantee of what was promised at the time you took out this investment instrument.

These are fervently difficult situations to sometimes comprehend and deal with especially after you have done everything right in terms of sound financial planning and yet the policies or mismanagement of government finances or financial institutions as in the case of the subprime mortgage and which resulted in the financial crash of 2008 which caused such devastation. So many individuals and families are still struggling over a decade later to recover from such reversal, having lost jobs, being made redundant, and being underemployed. Some lost significant value in property, assets or investments. The economic repercussions of Covid-19 will also acerbate and aggravate an already gravely dire situation as millions globally lost their jobs and only sources of livelihoods.

Wars and displacements, disease outbreaks, epidemics and pandemics, famines, hunger, natural and man-made disasters, exploitations and other international crises can also devastate lives and families. You and your family might have worked hard your entire lives and have been highly successful only to now find yourself refugees in sub-human conditions in tents exposed to the elements with loss and lack of personal dignity; or immigrants in another country having to start all over again. Oh, the sad memories of your previously wonderful life, career, lovely family, friends and beautiful home with all the comforts there-of, now only a distant memory. How sad, as you take on two, three, four menial jobs…swallowing your pride and forgetting all your education, expertise and training as you humble yourself just to stand ye therefore and re-establish yourself. It is even compounded when you have to do all this amidst rejection, prejudice, stereotype, discrimination, racism and negative attitudes towards you.

Reflection: How can you come safely through all of these? How do you cope with these macro-economic, political and global issues that negatively impact, you, your family and investment plans? How do you cope when you have to take on even menial tasks to accomplish your purpose?

God Will Sustain You Through the Storm
I am sure you can think of many situations that you have gone through required you to simply stand. You may be going through a 'stand' now. How long you may have to stand or exactly what 'standing' may look like for you, I cannot say; however, I can only assure you God is with you and will give you the grace, strength, faith and courage to hold your ground. You may think of all you have sacrificed and how much it is taking out of you but you will have to a make decision as to whether or not the 'standing' will be worth it.

Reflection: Do you sense that you are in the centre or the permissive nature of God's divine will and purpose for your life?

Answers to these questions will serve to strengthen your resolve and encourage you in the midst of these storms. Even in the permissive will of God, you can find grace, courage, and strength to maintain your faith. Remember one thing that certainly encouraged Paul was the Word of affirmation and prophesy he received from the Lord. Later, he also mentioned that an angel appeared to him and told him that although the ship and its cargo would be lost, there would be no loss of life.

Praying and seeking the Lord not just when you are in a crisis but as a routine part of our spiritual journey and relationship with Christ will do wonders for our attitudes and practice in our storms. Sadly, we might have to lose some things sometimes to save others and ourselves. This requires having things in perspectives. What is important and what do you prioritise...things or life? True, our 'cargo' or possessions mean a lot, we toil for them, made grave sacrifices to work for them and it is hard to just let them go. They are precious, valuable financially and perhaps of great emotional value, but in the end, lives are saved. As the saying goes, 'where there is life there is hope'; hope to rebuild, restart, and resurrect dashed hopes, broken dreams and aborted plans.

'A man's life consisteth not in the abundance of things he possesseth' (Luke 12:15) and 'What shall a man give in exchange for his soul?' This is really about priorities, 'seek ye first the kingdom of God and His righteousness and all these things will be added unto you' (Matthew 6:33). It is the Father's good pleasure to bless you. However, it is important to note that if 'riches increase, set not your heart upon it' (Psalm 62:10). Probably the Centurion and the owners of the ship had misplaced priorities of esteeming possessions over health, safety and life itself. Nonetheless, life can thrust us into situations where we have to come face to face with these crucial decisions and thus are forced to prioritise. I hope that we will not have to make this decision in sickness or at death's door.

Ride Out Your Storms
This is a very important concept and life lesson that requires revisiting. You 'ride out your storms' by holding your position and dropping anchor and trusting God to see you through. You do this by maintaining your position; by continuing with that job, relationship, situation or perspective although things might not be exactly what you had expected or envisaged. Nevertheless, you hold the fort and stand firm. Indeed, this is not always a pleasant experience. You sometimes feel like walking away but for the greater good you remain. Surely, there is a time to jump ship and we will discuss this idea in later chapter but now the focus is on what to do when you

have to ride out your storm. What are the benefits of doing so? By remaining on the ship in the storm, you show your faith in God's word to preserve you. You show stability and dependency even in tough situations that try you to the core and test your unflinching resilience. You remain for a higher purpose, and a greater good that is beyond your feelings, desires or will.

It could be a job that causes you stress, disappointment a brings you low wages and does not meet your expectations initially. Instead of just walking away and 'jumping ship' you settle yourself and remain on the ship in order to provide for your family. You take what you get until you get what you want in order to be the provider. Yes, it is hard, yes, it can be humiliating but in the end your glory will be revealed, you will reap the fruit of your labour! The Psalmist reminds us

> *'He who continually goes forth weeping, bearing seed for sowing, Shall doubtless come again with rejoicing, bringing his sheaves with him. (Psalm 126:6).*

Sometimes promotion may come later but sometimes, your ability to stay and ride out your storm may have absolutely nothing to do with you but could be for a greater purpose as mentioned. Mills puts it so well, 'the struggles and wounds we face in life have a greater purpose' (Mills 2017, p. 165). You could be the only person of faith on that job or in that situation and God has you exactly where He wants you, there on assignment.

It is always about seeking God in every situation and having the peace of God to discern what He is saying to you: when to remain and ride out the storm or when to leave; when to speak and when to hold your peace. I am talking about knowing and differentiating His Word from His Voice. In any area of life and whatever the circumstance, these are tough choices especially when you have major life changing decisions to make. You will definitely need to pray and seek Divine guidance but you may also require professional help, wise counsel or support from trusted family, friends or saints. Do not suffer in silence, seek the help you need and trust God to see you through. You have the strength to pull through.

5. Strength Under Control

'God designed and predestined you to be a success story'

(Dr Myles Munroe, 1991, p. 57)

In the depth of dark despair and staring disaster in the face, Paul and the others on the ship had to ride out the storm. The sailors had dropped anchor and they had no choice but to remain firm and secure in the Saviour's love based on the promise of spared lives. Your anchor will hold even in the stormy blast. When it is bleak, cold and the fierce winds are raging, 'drop your anchor' and ride out the storm. The weight of your anchors will keep you secure even in the face of the fierce and boisterous thundery gusts. It is comforting to know you can put your faith and confidence in God even in the seemingly hopeless situation you are facing right now. Indeed,

> *'In quietness and confidence will be your strength'* (Isaiah 30:15).

When you hear a word from the Lord, you know His voice. Regardless of how rough the waves might be, that word of assurance and affirmation will serve to sustain you even when others around you are in panic, dread and turmoil. This 'peace that passes all understanding' (Philippians 4:7) can only come through the Holy Spirit. It is not the peace with God that is justification by faith; it is not the peace in God or peace with God, that is fellowship with God, but the peace of God. He apportions His peace to you even in the midst of your storm. This peace acts as the umpire in your life and rules richly in your hearts (Colossians 3:15-17).

Reflection: Have you ever been asked the question: 'How do you do it'? Or how can you be so calm? What was your response?

Well, it is the peace of God. Some years ago, I was driving through Half-way-tree, the capital of Kingston Jamaica when I saw a large sign along the road, which I still remember to this day. It read: 'Know God, Know peace, No God, No peace!'

There is nothing like having strength under control. You are not getting hysterical in the midst of life's storms, instead you have this quiet assurance that it is well and it will be well. This does not mean you do not grieve or care; in fact, you should grieve healthily for the sake of your own health and wellbeing. However, we do not grieve hopelessly. Jesus raised Lazarus from the dead after weeping at his funeral. He wept knowing He would raise him up. You can weep with them that weep and you should. You can weep to empathise. You can weep with hope and you can weep knowing you will come through successfully but you identify with others and with your humanity. This attitude can only come from complete trust in God. It also has to do with your mindset and you having a positive attitude to life and circumstances.

I mentioned Les Brown earlier. He often said in his motivational speeches, and I repeat: 'Some people are so negative they can go into a dark room and begin to develop!' I know we do not develop photographs in the way we used to in dark rooms as in years gone by because of digital and technological advancement; however, the point remains that there is nothing like a positive mind set. To see the good in situations, to accentuate the positive and minimise the negative should be a reasonable target to set. This does not mean you ignore the negative things, over spiritualise or trivialise major issues in your life. It simply means that you face but do not focus unhealthily on them. Indeed, when there is a difficulty or a crisis at hand, it will require your full and undivided attention. Here I am talking about your focus, attitude, paradigm and belief systems in the midst of your difficulty.

It Is Well
About thirty years ago, I remember really struggling with the case of the 'The widow' as recorded in (Kings 4:26) in the Old Testament, whose only son had died. She had previously been very hospitable to the Prophet Elijah. Now her son had passed, she had the quiet faith and assurance God, through the Man of God would come through for her in her moment of desperate need.

On her way however, to find him she encountered many well-wishers along the path. As they inquired of her, how she was, she simply replied, 'It is well!' Really? I struggled with it in years past because, like you no doubt, I was saying 'No, it is not well, your son is dead!' However, as I read into the passage and meditated on it, I realise that on one hand she had such established faith in God through previous miracles from the Elijah that nothing would shake her faith.

Secondly, she had 'sown' into his life, ministry and the work of God through her hospitality when she needed nothing in return. However, now she could make a 'withdrawal' from her previous 'deposits.' She was not using God as an insurance policy or spare parts in her desperation. No, she had made an investment in the life of the prophet, yet in a strange way, she did not do it expecting a return. This is not to say that she was 'buying' or earning salvation or miracles through works but she recognised the principle of sowing and reaping. She had poured unconditionally into the life of the Man of God in his moment of need.

Nothing is as undesirable and even disgusting as using or exploiting people or worse yet your family, friends or acquaintances for selfish ends. Some people never call, write or visit you unless there is something in it for them. There is always an ulterior motive. From such stay away or carefully manage your interactions with them because they simply do not have your interests at heart.

Thirdly, never share your problem with those who cannot help you, those who have no real investment in, respect and appreciation for your pain, circumstances, experiences or success. The widow recognised the difference between a sincere and genuine 'How are you' or 'Is it well'? and a mere casual exchange of pleasantries. The latter can be just a simple polite greeting. You may need someone to sit with you, hear your heart, empathise, nod and groan with you in all the appropriate places and just hear you out. Sometimes or dare I say, most times, a 'How are you?' tends to be a polite act of pleasantry. Only few will really make the time and sacrifice to be there for you in your deep moments of need to relate to you at this deep level of support. No wonder the widow wisely responded, 'It is well' and hastened to the source of her need, comfort and help. 'I will lift up mine eyes unto the hills from whence cometh my help' (Psalm 121).

Reflection: When you ask someone 'Is it well'? Are you genuinely interested in their circumstances and prepared to invest the time into listening, empathising and sharing in the fellowship of their suffering or are you simply or merely exchanging greetings so you can quickly move on with your life?

I must hasten to point out it is possible to make a judgement and assumption some one cannot help you with a problem when the truth is that they could have the answer or part thereof to your pressing dilemma. Admittedly, they may not be able to help you in the entirety of the solution to your problem or in the way you anticipate. Notwithstanding, they could be able to share a word of encouragement or an experience that could hold the key to solving your problem. Sometimes all that is required is a word, a statement or sharing your story. Never underestimate the impact of your contribution on the life of another. A simple word of encouragement could save someone in their deepest need.

However, this requires discernment, wisdom and God's leading to know who, what, when and where to share. The widow in this case knew exactly the source of her help, the focus of her deliverance and the centre of her hope. She pursued that path with unbridled resolve and persistent determination. This kind of focus reminded me of when Jesus set His face 'like flint to Jerusalem.' Having purpose requires you to know the source of your deliverance, provision and destiny then focus on that end, avoiding the distractions along the path. These distractions could be in the form of discouragement, faithlessness or negative words, which could cause you to abandon your faith and consequently abort your mission.

You simply cannot go under when Jesus is in your boat! Surely, you have to weather some storms. Remember that, 'in this life you will have tribulation' (John 16:33), however, with Jesus in your ship, you can smile at the storm. His presence gives re-assurance, faith, confidence and hope. Hope, that you will make it safely over and not under! This undoubtedly will be hard to accept in the face of sickness, financial reversals, disappointments, broken relationships and the death of your dreams. Nevertheless, trust in God's unfailing love and believe that He will see you safely through. Jesus had a purpose and destination in mind even through the storm.

The man with legions of demons at the tomb of Gennesaret was destined to be delivered that day. No wonder there was an un-natural storm. Un-natural storms usually precede great miracles, deliverances and blessings. The enemy sends 'storms' your way, but the gravity of the storm should serve as an indication of the magnitude of the impending blessing! The greater the calling on your life, the more intense the preparation will be. The greater the purpose, the greater the process will be. The hotter the battle the sweeter will be the victory.

In the case of the sinful woman forgiven, Jesus said, "I tell you, her sins, and they are many have been forgiven, so she has shown me much love. But a person who is forgiven little shows only little love." (Luke 7:47). The higher the building the deeper the foundation will need to be. The greater the transgressions pardoned, the greater the love, commitment and passion. Intense trials should serve as confirmation that your life counts for greatness.

No construction company brings in heavy earth-moving equipment to a site without plans to erect a building of substantial structure. The extent of your trials is an indication of the purpose and calling on your life. I know of no powerful, influential and anointed person who has not been through great struggles. Somehow, these struggles are necessary as a crucial part of the process to prepare you for your purpose and mission, and further to refine your character. When you reach the top, the upper echelon, the pinnacle of success, the epitome of your dreams all will be tempered with empathy, care, love for others and unbridled humility.

'Underneath Are Everlasting Arms….'

The dropping of the anchor and riding out the storm as mentioned earlier hold important life lessons. I have established that sometimes you have to ride out some storms. In another context, I will borrow Ephesians 6:13 which describes this process as 'not gaining ground but stand, ye therefore having your loins girded…'. There will be times when your best defence and process will simply be to stand. These are times when you are not making the process you desire or aspire to because of the ferocity of the storm, howsoever caused or in whatever area of life.

 I reiterate that the strength of the anchor maintains the vessel and souls on board because its strength is greater than the winds than assail it. It is a powerful revelation that is simply life changing. You realise your inner hidden strength is greater than the external battles that come against you. You may not realise this or feel like it but your success is always based on what is already in you. 'God has given to us the measure of faith' (Romans 12:3) as you face your storms you may say 'I don't have what it takes' but you do have what it takes. The answer is within you.

The faith required for that trial or test is within you. Moses' 'stick and 'stutter' were sufficient. He really did not need Aaron! God carefully chose, groomed, and prepared Moses all his life to be the deliverer for the children of Israel from Pharaoh's bondage in Egypt. However, Moses made all the excuses he was slow of speech and had a stutter (Exodus 4:10) Moses said to the LORD,

> 'Pardon your servant, LORD; I have never been eloquent, neither in the past nor since you have spoken to your servant. I am slow of speech and tongue.'

Although God allowed Aaron to accompany him, yet Moss did the talking to Pharaoh. Notice also that it was Aaron who caused problems in the wilderness by leading the people to worship idols while Moses was on the mountain with God receiving the commandments (Exodus 32:4) "He (Aaron) took what they handed him and made it into an idol cast in the shape of a calf, fashioning it with a tool. Then he said, "These are your gods, Israel, who brought you up out of Egypt." You do not really need who or what you think you need to accomplish God's purposes in your life. Watch out for the distractions, diversions, detours and detractors. They often parade themselves in your insecurities and try to convince you that you are inadequate.

Abraham had a similar experience with his nephew, Lot. So, Abram said to Lot, 'Let's not have any quarrelling between you and me, or between your herders and mine, for we are close relatives' (Genesis 13:8). There were conflicts over providing grass and water for their herds of cattle.

In another story, Lot's wife was severely judged for her reluctance to freely abandon life in Sodom and flee at God's instruction in the face of imminent doom and destruction. Oft, we feel that we need people who are not called to accompany us to fulfil God's purposes in our lives. Whilst we are not independent of others' help, support and guidance, there are times when God calls and instructs us and that is specific and individualistic. God called you He did not call them.

As you recall the story of the widow in the Old Testament, the cruise of oil, and flour in the house was all that was required to feed the prophet, the widow and her son. In addition, the widow in the New Testament who lost her coin swept relentlessly until it was recovered; but all along, it was in the house! (Luke 15). Consider also David when he slew Goliath. All that he needed were his previously tested, tried, proven rag, and a rock to slay Goliath. He was told to put on Saul's armour but alas, they were too heavy and further they were not tested and tried by him (1 Samuel 17).

You cannot fight your battles in someone else's armour. Use what you have. This does not mean you are closed to exploring appropriate options, possibilities and strategies; however, it simply means you are not depending on others' resources to fight your personal battles. You know who you are and whose you are and the source of your hidden strength based on your deep and personal relationship with Christ. The experiences you have had over time of how He came through for you in your battles, now embolden you to believe that He will do it again, howsoever and whenever. Jason Mills notes that 'total contentment is coming to the realisation of who we are, who we belong to, what our purposes are in this life, and what is truly worthwhile.' (2017, p. 29).

These examples of using what is already within us serve to reinforce the fact more than often the answers we seek are within our reach, grasp and capability. This knowledge by no means negates the need for mentors, coaches, encouragers or prayerful support in your life. However, it does put things in perspective that we do not depend on others or things external to give satisfaction, meaning and purpose to life. Warren (2002), argues that 'Without God, life has no purpose and without purpose, life has no meaning; without meaning, life has no significance or hope' (p. 30). So, the inner strength comes from the inner Christ.

Paul whilst on the stormy sea could find peace, divine revelation, illumination, and a word of knowledge about his situation. This unique relationship was not the case for the other 275 souls on board the doomed ship. Paul had something or better still, someone (The Holy Spirit), within him that the others did not. This made all the difference in how he managed the storm. The Holy Spirit gave comfort and peace, discernment and direction. The Word of God declares:

> 'Greater is He that is in me than he that is in the world' (1 John 4:4)

The Holy Spirit comes within you at the point of your conversion. You therefore possess peace, assurance, comfort, discernment, guidance, confidence and the measure of faith that are all necessary in your storms. You can speak to storms and mountains in your life. You can stand with confidence and give a word, which can speak to the destiny of yourself and others. Your inner strength is far superior to the strength or ferocity of the winds and waves without. Your inner confidence is far superior to the voices of fear, doubt, insecurities, unbelief, helplessness, numbness, anger, disappointment, grief or trauma.

A Quote From my College Magazine

In my introduction, I mentioned I was about 19 years old at the Mico College, University of the West Indies in Jamaica when I penned these words:

> 'Realistic goals maybe achieved provided one has a dynamic sense of purpose that is far superior to the forces that constitute the odds' (O'Connor, 1985)

I was coming to the end of my Teacher Education training as a secondary school teacher and specialist in Music and Physical Education, at the University of the West Indies (Mico

Teachers' College). I wrote and submitted an article for publication in the Magazine for the graduating class of 1985 called *'Meet Yourself'*. I still have a copy to this day, approximately 36 years on! From such an early age, I recognised the power on the unseen, the hidden and the power within. I also realised that these were more powerful and far superior to the external forces; for indeed 'greater is He that is in you than he that is in the world (1 John 4:4). I could speak words of power, of inspiration, encouragement, positivity and hope instead of dwelling on failure or the past. I agree with the Word which states, 'You are not snared by the words of another but by your own words' (Proverbs 6:2).

When you realise the power you have within, you do not assign or delegate your power to others. This however, is quite different from delegating responsibility as a useful management strategy, which every successful leader should employ. I will discuss this concept later. You take control and determine your purpose and destiny. Far too often we empower others to control our lives when we should remain in control even if we delegate, we need to regulate. I usually say to my students: 'Be a great original and not a cheap copy!' Garland (1922-1989) puts it this way, 'Always be a first-rate version of yourself, instead of a second-rate version of somebody else.' Ralph Waldo Trine (1866-1958) who went on to become the father of the Word of Faith Movement, an Evangelical Christian philosophy later embraced the New thought Movement, wrote,

> *'Don't surrender your individuality which is your greatest agent of power, to the customs and conventionalities that have got their life from the great mass…. Do you want to be a power in the world? Then be yourself.'*

This individuality must not be interpreted wholly in a merely humanistic, liberal, secular and philosophical way, but also a religious and theological one. For instance, Scripture assures us that:

> *'I will praise thee; for I am fearfully and wonderfully made: marvellous are thy works; and that my soul knoweth right well' (Psalm 139:14)*

In Jeremiah, we read these words that should guide, inform and even dictate the development of our self-confidence:

> *'Before I formed you in the womb I knew you, before you were born I set you apart; I appointed you as a prophet to the nations' (Jeremiah 1:5, NIV).*

You are an individual, specially created with definitive purpose and destiny. Be prepared to find that purpose and stand alone to fulfil the same. Paul stood up, stood out single-handedly on the ship among 275 unbelievers, and proclaimed his faith, confidence in God and the prophetic word he got in his spirit. That no doubt took courage. Yet you might argue that since he had defended on numerous occasions his faith in front of Felix, Festus, and King Agrippa and was now on his way to Caesar in Rome, he not only had practice in the past but was actually using his current situation to further practice and build his faith. Probably that played a part. I think it was a different situation on the ship to proclaim the words of power, affirmation, faith and challenge in front of the captain, ship's owner, centurion, soldiers and prisoners. There was quite a mix in that audience though we are not sure who heard his pronouncements each time.

The case of David and Goliath earlier mentioned is an interesting case in point also and is relevant to this discussion.

When David confronted Goliath, he did so using what he was accustomed to and what was tested and tried in his life. As a result, Saul's armour was too heavy, untested and uncomfortable. Again, use what you have! But another very important point to note is that, David referred to and used the successes of the past to formulate a battle plan and built his confidence to face Goliath. He said:

> 'Thy servant kept his father's sheep and a lion came, and a bear….this uncircumcised Philistine shall be like them…' (1 Samuel 17:34)

Reflection: How do you face your current struggles and storms? Afraid? In panic, fear or dread? Stressed out or complaining? Do you see the good in life's circumstances even when they may not be pleasant? Do you build on your past successes however small or seemingly insignificant and use them as catalysts to achieve your goals? Your successes begin with what you have left; the seemingly insignificant.

Draw on Past Successes for Future Victories

As mentioned, I usually say 'areas of competence lead to areas of confidence.' The more you do and are good at, the more your confidence will and should develop. You 'prophesy in proportion to your faith!' (Romans 12:6). Take small steps and celebrate each step as you go. 'And the evening and the morning were the first day, and God said, "That was good" (Genesis 1:31). Celebrate your small steps. This ties in so well with the concept of standing and riding out your storms.

> 'Take pride in how far you have come. Have faith in how far you will go. But don't forget to enjoy the journey' (Michael Josephson).

There will be times when you have to draw on past successes to face future challenges. Bishop TD Jakes, often talks about fighting the enemy and not glorying in his 30,000 members at the Potters' House Church Ministry, in Dallas, Texas. Instead, he often goes back to his roots to his storefront church in West Virginia with a handful of saints. He emphasised the things he learnt out of his struggles, deprivation, repossessions, and grave sacrifices through frustrating moments. All of those things form a crucial part of his story and his process. There is something about life's processes and the things we suffer. When you suffer, struggle, and make grave sacrifices for your success, you respect and value what you have more. You will not let it go so easily because you paid the price. There is a saying, 'Easy come, easy go.'

There are times also when you have to celebrate your own successes and say, 'That was good!' Saying 'that was good' does not mean or imply that your goals or final destination is reached. However, it means that you are prepared to celebrate and acknowledge small seemingly insignificant steps and milestones in your life and being prepared to accentuate them during your process.

It is important to remember that celebration does not also attract rejoicing from everyone! You will need to be comfortable in your own skin to know the sacrifices you have made and what it costs you to achieve your goals in the face of jealousies, belittling, lack of recognition or undermining of your success. Yet, there is the need to be measured in celebrations as others could be grieving and over exuberance could be inappropriate in some situations. For example, if someone is suffering a loss or bereavement, there is need for sensitivity and empathy. Nevertheless, being afraid to celebrate for fear of offending others who might have not achieved is not a good thing. I do understand that you might see the need to temper your celebration to protect others who might be in holding patterns in their lives.

The Power of The Unseen
> *'The eternal God is your refuge, and underneath are the everlasting arms. He will drive out your enemies before you, saying, "Destroy them!" (Deuteronomy 33:27 NIV).*

The knowledge of the Eternal God, All-Powerful, All Mighty, All-Sufficient, All Knowing, Being; the One holding it all together in your life, is a sobering and comforting thought. The one 'in whom all things consist' that is, in Colossians 1:17, 'He is before all things, and in him all things hold together.' He is your refuge, your hiding place, your security and foundation. As you build all things in your life on Him; your hopes, dreams, purpose, destiny and eternal salvation, you can have the calm assurance that regardless of your processes and path life takes, His plans will always materialise.

The Eternal God is not only your refuge but underneath are His everlasting, strong, enduring and secure arms. The foundation is unseen yet supports and upholds the structure of the building…your life. This structure provides the underpinning and hence guides your purpose. I am fascinated by the concept and the reality of being undergirded by the auspicious Almighty Hand of an Eternal God! I can rest assured that whatever transpires in my life and yours is within the knowledge, foreknowledge, will, purpose and destiny of His amazing grace. Despite the cares, the tears and the fears you can know that you are upheld and sustained by Eternal Hands that will, and can never fail. This I believe and it gives peace and reassurance in every storm.

He knows your structure and the specifications required to sustain you in every stormy gale. He factored in your construction the specificity of all that is required to keep you safe in every situation. No wonder as mentioned earlier, He has given you 'the measure of faith' and furthermore, 'There hath no temptation taken you that ye cannot bear, He will not allow you to endure more than you are able to bear.' (1 Corinthians 10:13).

No strong winds, storm clouds or gale force winds will destroy you, because you were designed in your specification to withstand them all. You may feel like or even have said or heard others uttered in their distress, 'I cannot bear this' or 'this is too much for me' but the truth is that your trials, storms, temptation, challenges are all accounted for in your design and specification. Truly, we have different abilities, capabilities, gifts and talents; however, God knows exactly how much you can bear and you can rest assured that your load is factored in your design. You will make it safely through. Contemplate the words of Jentezen Franklin:

> *'God created you with the storms of life in mind. In fact, He designed you to be waterproof. You can let the winds blow and the storms rage around you because you are going to make it through with Christ who lives in you' (2013, p.19).*

Isn't that wonderful to know? In fact, your specification was factored in your design. Thus, you are well able to bear anything life throws at you, because it is all in your deliberate design. 'Nothing happens to anybody which he is not fitted by nature to bear, Marcus Aurelius, AD 121-180 (*Little Oxford Dictionary of Quotation*, p394).

If I may compare and use the anchor with the everlasting arms as a metaphor, then the source of your strength is below what is seen. That which sustains and undergirds is greater than that which is visible. Like an iceberg, the greater portion is hidden but is more significant than that which is seen. Your strength and foundation may be hidden but they remain the bedrock of your very existence. Indeed, the Eternal God is your refuge and His everlasting arms sustain you; arms that will never tire. His arms will never grow weary. His arms will never fail. Through the storms, through the stormy blast, through the hurts, pains and disappointments of life you can rely on the unchanging and eternal hand to keep you. Indeed, 'His right hand and His holy arm has gotten him the victory' (Psalm 98:1)

Whilst others see the glory, you know your story. Whilst others see the successes, you know your secrets. The glory and the successes demonstrate the outer manifestations of the story and the secrets. Naturally, the former are the visible manifestations that others tend to notice and applaud. It is these also that they may covet. The grass always seems greener on the other side but the lawn has to be cut. The roses indeed have thorns wherever they grow. Regardless of the glory and the successes, your processes, that is to say, your story will always be the path that will lead to your success. Sadly, this basic truth is often what others overlook.

For me, I must admit that I endure a bit of frustration when people look at my academic achievement and say, 'you are just bright!' and the implication here, whilst harbour some compliments (which I humbly accept and appreciate), tend more to suggest that I am so intellectually endowed that I need not exude much of any effort to succeed. It is true that some people are gifted and talented academically; however, we should never lose sight of the hard work, the sacrifices, deferred gratification, long hours in the library, the late nights of study 'burning the midnight oil', reading of complex journals and other heavily academic literature just to grasp the basic concepts of fervent academic rigour.

When I think of the last 6 months of my doctoral study, I sometimes shudder at the reality of managing the rigours of academic demands, with full time work and, part time ministry (preaching, youth seminars, playing bass guitar in the worship band at church, encouraging and supporting others, hosting and hospitality, coaching and mentoring) plus my entrepreneurial endeavour. Drafting and re-drafting thesis chapters, getting ethical approval, preparing and submitting drafts and final thesis submission to external examiners and preparing for and embarking on Mock and real thesis defence (Viva voce). Let us not forget the amendments that generally follow even a successful defence of the thesis. I was given 6 months to amend however, did so in 2 months. Immediately afterwards, I attended and gave a tribute and was a pallbearer at the funeral of my mother-in-law in Jamaica April 2018. This is only part of the story but what a journey! It is more than just being clever, it costs. To God be the Glory!

A Tribute from the Doctoral Final Review Panel Chairman
No wonder in a tribute for my doctoral thanksgiving celebration the chairman wrote:

> *Phillip O'Connor was a key member of the Jubilee "Christianity and Education" cohort of the Professional Doctorate programme established in 2012 at Christ Church to mark the University's 50th anniversary. Christ Church was founded by the Church of England to train teachers for church schools. It seemed a fitting*

> *gesture to mark the Jubilee with a cohort of doctoral students focusing on the Christian contribution to education.*
>
> *Phillip's thesis tackled one of the most important and challenging topics facing Christian PSHE teachers, namely how do they reconcile their personal Christian commitment with the controversial nature of the subject matter they teach. His extensive empirical study was a mammoth undertaking and was conducted with rigour and resilience.*
>
> *Phillip's external examiner was one of the leading professors in the area and the final award of the degree was earned under rigorous interrogation. It is a tribute to Phillip that he has succeeded at the highest level of academia whilst holding down a teaching post. There are few people who manage to do that. And it is also a tribute to Rhona who has supported him on his long academic journey. For me one of the joys of my time at Christ Church has been sharing a journey with Phillip.*

Furthermore, for my Reviews leading to my Viva voce, my supervisors wrote:

> *'Phillip's seven chapters contain significant signs that it could potentially be a very strong thesis and we are delighted to see how much his thinking and work have developed. The interviews have produced very interesting and important data of a kind that addresses the purpose of the Christianity and education doctoral cohort.' (Professor 1-First Supervisor's comments after Final review)*

> *'Phillip submitted a significant piece of work to the Panel. The work demonstrates that he has made good progress in his analysis and more importantly, his understanding of some really interesting and important issues.' (Professor – Second Supervisor)*

> *Phillip is to be congratulated on producing a substantial draft of his thesis. He has worked incredibly hard on his empirical research, his engagement with the literature and his writing style has made massive improvement since his last review. Particularly impressive is his data collection he has undertaken with the teachers. His analysis of that lays bare the challenges that they experienced in seeking to integrate their personal Christian convictions with the requirements of teaching PSHE. The potential contribution of this thesis lies in the discussion of the strategies that teachers adopted. Potentially, this could be a significant contribution to an important topic.* **Phillip's thesis epitomises the sort of work we had hoped would emerge from the Jubilee Cohort'** *(Final Review Panel Chairman)*

Following the successful defence of my thesis, my External examiners agreed that:

> "The thesis was well-written, thoughtful and original, on a topic of some significance to the teaching profession – and beyond - about the particular experiences of teachers of PSHE who have strong Christian beliefs and convictions, which have various origins and are in transition, and which sometimes present these teachers with dilemmas in their working lives. They adopt a range of strategies for resolution or compromise. It was evident that great care had been

> *taken in the writing of the thesis, which was clear in its presentation of the literature, methodology and, to a large extent, the data and conclusions from the research.*
>
> *"Phillip was thoughtful and articulate throughout the viva. His ability to pinpoint specific arguments and to refer the Examiners to precise page numbers in his thesis was most impressive and indicated that he was extremely well rehearsed in the discussion of his work and prepared for its defence."*

Overall, the External Examiners agreed that the study was of a doctoral standard and wish to commend and congratulate Phillip on his work.

These comments and feedback reflect the hard work dedication, resilience, sacrifices, tears, fears and cares of a process lasting approximately five and a half years. Through the rigorous demands and intense feelings of isolation I have come, even on my broken pieces. One songwriter puts it this way:

> *'Through many dangers, toils and snares, we have already come, Tis grace that brought me safe thus far and grace will lead me home!'*

The glory indeed has a story. It is all about the process and your attitude therein.

Reflection: How do you now handle success, glory and power? Can you stand to be blessed? Will you now demonstrate humility, grace and empathy? Will you use your success for the benefit of others and leave a legacy in the earth for the benefit of humanity or will it all be consumed upon your own self-gratification and aggrandisement?

His eternal hand and His holy arm support the story and the secrets. Through the depth of your pain and your struggles, He is the one who is there with you. When you have come through successfully, folks like to look only at the successes but you know the sacrifices, the costs and the pain to get there. You know and value the process. That process, which remains largely hidden, shapes our character and determines our attitudes, maturity and spiritual growth.

> 'And after you have suffered a little while, the God of all grace, who has called you to His eternal glory in Christ, will himself restore, confirm, strengthen, and establish you' (1 Peter 5:10 ESV).

I wish I could tell you how long 'awhile' is but each one has his or her own path, cross and process to endure. We trust the sovereignty of God to tailor each trial to the specificity of our individuality, calling and purpose.

Muddy Waters
Naaman is an interesting case in point. According to 2 Kings 5:1, he was Captain of the Host of Syria. He had accomplished much and had reached the pinnacle of military success. Decked out in his fine apparel, he was no doubt the enemy of every junior officer and the desire of every available suitor. Highly successful and at the epitome of his military career, he however harboured a deep secret. He had great successes but shielded an embarrassing and deadly secret. He had leprosy! I am sure the public manifestations of his military victories drew the attention of all including the King. However, none would dare fathom that the mighty Naaman, Captain of the Host of Syria extraordinaire was thus afflicted.

I speak of this strange dichotomy. How can your best of times be your worse of time at the same time? On the one hand, life is going so well and yet on the other, in another area, things could not be worse. Moreover, of course, it is all going on simultaneously. Your marriage is perfect, but your finances are in a mess; your finances are going well but your children are going off the rails; your children and finances are going well but your health is failing! You fill in the blanks of things and times that are just so amazingly glorious in your life and then you look around and see that simultaneously, another area or areas are enough to bring you to the edge of dark despair.

Naaman had a maid from Israel who diligently executed her duties. At the realisation of his master's plight, she encouraged and uttered with deep care and sincerity, 'I would to God that my master go to Israel…there is a Prophet in Israel' (2 Kings 5). The mighty military man then made a life-changing decision on the word of a Maid! Ironically, he humbled himself to such a word, yet when the man of God, the Prophet Elijah (who refused to dignify his request for healing with his presence, but sent someone to him), gave orders for him to dip seven times in the muddy river Jordan, that was simply too much for him! Angrily he exclaimed:

> 'Abana and Pharpar, the rivers of Damascus, are better than all the water in Israel. Why can't I wash in those rivers in Damascus and become clean?" He was very angry and turned to leave' (2 Kings 5:12 NIV)

It was the obedience, humility and faith in the words of a maid that led Naaman through the process that led to his ultimate healing. Yet he was argumentative, confrontational, defensive and downright reluctant to follow the words of the Prophet for his healing. Eventually he swallowed his pride, followed closely the words the Man of God, dipped seven times in the muddy river, and was fully healed. Sometimes the demands and requirements of the process can simply seem or actually be too much. The humility, the isolation, the sacrifices can be overwhelming. Yet, it is part of the process: the story and the storm through which we must go in order to reach safely through to the other side…the side of success and victory.

Reflection: What is it you are going through or have to go through that seems too much to bear? Is it a situation that requires humility on your part?

Take What You Get, Until You Get What You Want

I speak with young people and adults all the time. They might have completed their studies and cannot immediately find employment commensurate with their education, expertise and training. This is understandable as they grapple with the tiring process of sending dozens and dozens of job applications only to hear, 'Sorry no vacancy' because 'you lack sufficient and required experience.' How frustrating this can this be!

There are times however when circumstances require desperate actions. For example, you may not have gotten the job of your choice or desire but you have financial obligations and commitments. Sometimes you may have to take what you get until you get what you want. True, there are times when you do not settle or compromise but stand still, hold fast and ride out the storm. Wisdom and discernment again are required. However, circumstances may necessitate that you humble yourself to maybe take on a role for which you are over-qualified, underpaid and over-worked.

I remember when Rhona and I, for a while, stacked supermarket shelves, flipped burgers, carried out janitorial tasks and worked at the till or cashier for £3.50 per hour. It was hard especially while studying and working full time. Sure, some had their opinions but now with our academic and economic achievements in record time, those naysayers are not laughing anymore! Indeed, 'he or she who laughs last, laughs the best!' God smiles upon us and grants His grace, mercy and favour, but we had to pay the price. Now it is part of our story. I learnt this memory gem in primary school and I recite if often and teach it to my students:

> 'Whenever a task is once begun, never leave it till it's done, Be it little, great or small, Do it well or not at all (Author unknown)

Back to Naaman's story: Such a humbling process, like Naaman having to dip seven times in the muddy waters of the Jordon River, will extract every ounce of humility, resilience and sacrifice out of you. Your very pride is on the line and in full glaring view of others. Because it is one thing to have to guard your secret flaws privately, but quite another when your process and storms have to be faced and lived out publicly. We certainly do not mind having our successes and glory manifest publicly but having your secrets and stories aired publicly can be humiliating and painfully embarrassing.

Nevertheless, this level of exposure if harnessed and channelled appropriately, can lead to authentic, credible, effective and genuine ministry. Such experiences and stories shared with empathy, humility and sincerity can serve to edify, encourage, uplift, inspire, motive and challenge others to reach their God-given potential. You also get something out of sharing your story: Your confidence will increase, you will be more authentic, genuine and credible and gain the love, trust and respect of others, in a way that you would not have, had you not been through your process, because others can relate to and identify with you.

Health warning: Indeed, wisdom and discretion are required in fine-tuning the public version of your story as not all chapters maybe appropriate for public consumption despite an attempt to 'keeping it real!' When others are involved in your story and processes it might be appropriate and ethical to get their consent to you sharing at all. Otherwise, you may anonymise personalities by using pseudonyms or changing some of the details and saying so. Furthermore, the ramifications of sharing private details of your story on others and your personal relationships must be factored in.

Treasures in Darkness

Your success and glory lie in the power of the unseen. When I was much younger in primary school, as a rebuke to lazy pupils, some of my teachers would exclaim 'Empty vessels make the most noise!' By this, they meant that the students who failed to achieve academic success were usually those who were most disruptive, lazy and boisterous, with poor attitudes to learning. The assumption was that once the students were quiet, on task and working they were potentially focused learners and ultimately could be high achievers. This could be so but not always the case. However, their point was well taken that there is a place for deep, quiet reflection, contemplation and focus; a quiet place of confidence where and when you know whose you are and who you are. This minimises and ultimately eliminates the need for jealousy, competition or low self-esteem as you flourish in the knowledge of your own identity and potential. You know, accept and embrace your identity: who you are in Christ. 'But ye are a chosen generation, a royal priesthood, a holy nation, a peculiar people' (1 Peter 2:9a). You are 'seated in Heavenly places in Christ Jesus (Ephesians 2:6)

The mighty arms of the Eternal God undergird the strength that comes from within; your hidden 'iceberg' or 'anchor' I mentioned earlier, that supports, sustains and withstands every stormy blast. Underneath the manifestations of success are fervent prayer, fasting, praise and worship, private warfare, deep personal relationship with God, sacrifices, tears, cares, fears; undergirding, faith, resilience, support, structure, network, positive and nurturing relationships.

Deep within in the depth of your inner being often lie the wherewithal to carry on; the preservation, resilience, stick-to-itiveness, hope and faith. However, the deeper within you probe, the darker things seem to become. Like Naaman, the deeper we probe into his success, the darker the secret of his leprosy. Could it be that you struggle with deep secrets that mask your success? Could it be that you have secrets flaws, weaknesses and failures, that mar and ridicule the very nature of your achievements and goals? Maybe you feel so intimated that you are afraid of greater success lest such public success could unearth private flaws and expose you to public scrutiny. There is a proverb that 'the higher the monkey climbs, the more he is exposed.'

Each new stage of success brings a greater level of challenge, interrogation and scrutiny. The present age of social media does not help here at all and whilst it has its powerful and helpful platforms, the negative and dark side of abuse, internet trolls and unkind comments and misuse is never far away. While it is possible that secrets can be the downfall and humiliation of some, still others can turn things around like

Naaman, to his advantage. Many motivational and inspirational speakers, even comedians create a message from their own personal stories and use them as the basis for their presentations. These become part of their mantra, unique selling points and experiences which bonds them to their audiences and enables a deeper sense of authenticity, credibility and genuineness. This ensures that they can relate to their audiences who see them as 'humans' and 'one of us' and as a result, they become very effective. Therefore, this is one aspect of using your dark places and experiences as treasures.

However, there is another aspect that I want to focus on, the nature of valuable things or experiences hidden in dark places. Isaiah 45:3 (NIV) declares,

> *"I will give you hidden treasures, riches stored in secret places, so that you may know that I am the LORD, the God of Israel, who summons you by name."*

We often associate 'treasure' with the word 'buried' and that is very significant. Valuable things are normally buried and disguised in their original states. We often miss great opportunities because of the state in which they initially present themselves to us. The buried states certainly will not be altogether lovely or glamourous. No wonder we sometimes miss our blessings and opportunities because of the raw materials and the seemingly unattractive manner in which our blessings are disguised as problems wrapped in prolonged processes. Just like Naaman and the muddy waters.

Panning for gold or digging for diamonds is not a glamourous process or experience yet these treasures are hidden in dark and muddy places. The typical pan used is circular metal dish, which is light and has with a flat bottom. Its sides are at a gradient of about 45°. The inner surface is free from rust and is smooth. When panning for gold the pan is first filled about halfway with gravel, soil, and rocks. Immersed in the stream, and the mixture is thoroughly soaked and stirred. The unwanted elements like lumps of clays or large stones are discarded. Still under water, the pan is then given a combination shaking and rotating motion. The purpose for this process is to allow the heavy particles to settle while the lighter materials are brought to the surface. From time to time, the pan is tilted, and the surface materials that are lighter are washed off. This process is sustained until only heavy "black sands" and gold remain. The gold is removed after the material is dried. This process of panning is slow and backbreaking work.

Digging for diamonds also has its challenges. Diamonds are not only beautiful and greatly desired but are extremely hard. Understandably, mining for diamonds is not only resource-heavy but also a very time-consuming process. Indeed, such processes require technological advances and engineering tools but diamond mining still incorporates a certain level of Art and Science combined. Even prior to the actual mining process, prospectors must first locate the diamond sources. Once located, ore samples are examined to ascertain suitability and profitability. For efficiency and effectiveness, the raw rock and soil are usually not examined on site. Instead, they are transported to special plants. Here, the ore is processed and the rough diamonds are extracted. Depending on how rich the ore is, it will take a tremendous amount of ore to be sieved just to produce a minute carat of gem quality rough diamonds. Even after this, the rough diamond is still far from being ready to be set in an engagement or anniversary ring.

Rough stones are sorted into various gem-quality categories and industrial-specific grades in heavily secured facilities. Subsequently, the roughs are sold, cut, polished and commercialized. Thus, the process a rough diamond undergoes from its violent formation stage to being exquisitely mounted is a long, laborious, time-consuming, labour-intensive and resource-demanding process.

The Stones Cry Out!
This process of mining for precious stones can be a metaphor for achieving success and coming through the storms in your lives. Consequently, there are life lessons for us to learn and apply:

Firstly, the process of formation 'toughens' us up or equips us with resilience. Similar to the process that the diamonds go through. The thought of being 'toughen' can be a bit unpalatable. However, life is tough and it demands that we have a sense of resilience to bounce back from life's traumas, incidents, accidents, adversities and storms with renewed confidence, rigor, vigour and faith. Robert Schuller says, 'Tough times don't last but tough people do!' The tough times will indeed pass but you should last. 'And it came to pass....' Not to remain.

One student some 12 years ago shared a wise saying with me. I honestly cannot recall whether it was during lesson or at break. He said

'Sir, you are always teaching us wise-sayings, may I share one with you?'

'Yes,' I replied.

Then he said,

'A setback is a set up for a comeback!'

How wise this 12-year-old student was! Life's hurts, however, pains and disappointments could be catalysts for change and personal advancement. I cannot emphasise more the importance of the process. Do not despise your processes.

> *'Do not despise these small beginnings, for the Lord rejoices to see the work begin, to see the plumb line in Zerubbabel's hand.' (Zechariah 4:10).*

The processes of germination or mining are slow time-consuming ones but the end products are simply amazing! Never abort your destiny or forgo your purpose because your genesis is small, chaotic or seemingly insignificant. You may have to creep before you can crawl or climb. You must believe that there is a giant oak tree in the seed, a beautiful butterfly in the caterpillar; lush and amazingly green vegetation and trees in the seemingly lifeless stumps in the middle of a dreary, dark and cold winter. Indeed, 'Things turn out the best for those who make the best of how things turn out' – little is much when God is in it.

My First Review Process

I remember after my First Review on my Doctoral programme. This is where after few months in the programme I was asked to present a chapter (in this case Chapter 3 Methodology) to the Panel of two doctors (now professors), my first and second supervisors and the Panel Chair, a Professor. This process is primarily to ensure that a proper transition is being made from writing at Master's standard to Doctoral level 8 academic writing.

To be honest and mild, it was bruising and I honestly did not find it too nurturing at all! The comments and feedbacks were hard to hear; not that the writing or adjustment was necessarily bad, but the review itself was designed in part as initiation into the world of academia. This means in part being able to produce drafts and redrafts; hear and accept graciously bruising yet constructive and cutting criticisms and feedbacks. These are not personal. Given that academic writings need to be peer reviewed whether for Journals or other publications, this Review was preparation for these and other later post-doctoral processes.

However, the Professor afterwards emailed me and encouraged me to focus on and not despise the process. That made a world of difference. Five years later, I graduated being only the 4th of 5 graduates from a cohort of 22 originally selected from across the United Kingdom. The Professor also stated, 'Phillip's thesis epitomises what we hoped would emerge from the Jubilee cohort!' I am talking here about valuing the process, weathering the storms and not giving up in the face of adversity and difficulties.

Secondly, treasures are indeed hidden in dark places. Regardless of how dark and dismal your circumstances may look, you have to believe that there are treasures buried therein. They have to be located but before that you must believe that they exist.

Reflection: Do you believe in yourself, your capabilities, your God-given potentials and purpose? Do you have the confidence to follow your dreams and purpose? Are you comparing yourself with others and doubting yourself? Are you allowing memories from the past to obstruct and hinder your progress today? Perhaps words of fear, doubt, and condemnation spoken over your life in your formative years, and they still reverberate in your head. Possibly these dilute and pollute your imagination, creativity, and confidence to achieve great things? What 'treasures' do you have buried in your dark places?

These are searching questions I know but they are challenging points for reflection. My mantra is to 'Motivate, inspire, challenge and encourage.' I hope that through my processes I can give something back; and I am learning along the path of life to leave a legacy in the earth. Your passion could be hidden in your pain, your messages in your messes, and your triumphs in your trials!

Little is Much
Thirdly, your process will require great sacrifices for often little returns. Sometimes there will be no returns at all, at least initially. Statistics show that new business start-ups can sometimes take years before they turn a profit! This is a long time to wait to see the fruit of your labour. This is a long time to weather a financial storm when you have financial obligations and commitments.
In 1974 James Dyson (now Sir) released his first invention, the ball barrow. The Ball barrow, was a modified version of a wheelbarrow, which featured a single moulded wheel (or ball), made from moulded plastic. He then had another idea, a bagless vacuum cleaner. This invention took not just 15 years, but 5,127 attempts, different tweaks, making and testing prototypes and modifications between 1979 and 1984 before his bagless cyclonic vacuum first cracked the market. This was indeed a challenging time as the British retailers initially rejected the inventor's idea. However, now, the Dyson Vacuum, the Air blade hand dryer, and the Air blade Tap have been incredibly successful. Thomas Edison (1847-1931), American Inventor and Businessman also similarly said,

> 'We have not failed. We now know a thousand things that won't work, so we're that much closer to finding what will.'

So, we can learn from Thomas Edison who has been described as America's greatest inventor. He developed many devices in fields such as electric power generation, mass communication, sound recording, and motion pictures. We can also learn some valuable life lessons from Sir James Dyson (OM CBE FRS FREng) who founded Dyson Ltd. He is a British inventor, industrial designer, landowner and entrepreneur, in terms of their resilience and stick-to-it-attitude. According to the Sunday Times Rich List 2020, he is Britain's richest person with an estimated net worth of £16.2 billion. He served as the Provost of the Royal College of Art from August 2011 to July 2017, and opened a new University on Dyson's Wiltshire Campus in September 2017.

His story epitomizes how real innovation requires setbacks, and seldom takes hold overnight. According to Mochari (2014), what is important is not merely that Dyson stayed patient and resilient in launching his vacuum cleaner; it's that he built a billion-dollar company whose engineer-friendly culture encourages radical experimentation and the thousands of prototypes and decades of effort that real innovation requires.

Truly, few will reach this level of financial success and I doubt very much that it is the ambition of most. However, the point is that success in whatever sphere and to whatever degree, requires hard work, patience, resilience and great sacrifices in the face of setbacks. Talking about a long, dark, process! Nevertheless, look at his rewards now! You may pour years into your hopes, dreams, family, children, marriage or business venture and there seems to be no evidence of success. Maybe you do not see the process you had envisaged, and you feel discouraged and disillusioned. Maybe you might be ignoring the small steps of success along the way…

> *'I could do nothing without my problems' writes Charles Kettering (1876-1958, American Engineer and Inventor), 'they toughen my mind. In fact, I tell my assistants not to bring me their successes for they weaken me; but rather to bring me their problems for they strengthen me.'*

Indeed, your process will be labour-intensive, extremely time-consuming and undoubtedly resource-heavy. Undoubtedly, it will be worth it all in the end. Your returns may be incremental but hang in there. Maybe your child's progress and behaviour are challenging, the state of your relationships, finances, spiritual growth, professional development and advancement are not as they should be. Notwithstanding, remember the Chinese proverbs which reminds us that 'the journey of a thousand miles begins with a single step!' Sure, there are times when you may need to challenge yourself (and others) and demand greater progress, effectiveness and efficiency. However, do so in a firm but nurturing manner.

A useful proverb to remember is that 'a brother offended is harder to win' whilst it is harder to win and influence those you have offended (we should challenge appropriately), we could also apply this to ourselves. Do not 'offend' yourself by being too critical, judgemental, and self-sabotaging. If you adopt self-confidence, destroying tactics and damage your self-esteem then it will be much more difficult to pull yourself back to a place of hope, confidence, and success. Sometimes you might need someone to believe in you, to motivate, model, coach, inspire and encourage you until you reach that stage for yourself to independently see your way confidently.

I recall the story of Elisha and the servant:

> "Those who are with us are more than those who are with them." And Elisha prayed, "O LORD, open his eyes so he may see." (2 Kings 6:17a)

There is also another story of Elijah and his servant. After months of drought, Elijah had prophesised that it would end. On three separate occasions after Elijah told King Ahab that it would rain, he sent his servant to visualise the physical manifestation. On three occasions, he missed it. Elijah had confidence in God and knew that his prayers were answered. Furthermore, he saw in the spirit realm what his servant did not see. When his servant was asked what did he see to demonstrate or indicate that rain was imminent he said 'I see nothing' When pressed however he finally conceded.

On the seventh time the servant reported, "There is a cloud as small as a man's hand rising from the sea." (1 Kings 18:44). Wow, that was all Elijah needed! The confirmation and answer to his prayer was not a mighty rushing wind or earth-shattering sound but just a speck of cloud the 'size of a man's hand! On another occasion, God spoke to him in a 'still small voice' (1 Kings 19:11).

How often we miss our blessings or opportunities because we are looking for something 'grand' and earth chattering to happen to usher us into our purpose and destiny! True, there are times for those life-changing experiences but on these occasions, it was so different, just a 'still small voice' and 'a cloud the size of a man's hand!' It is these seemingly insignificant moments that can make the difference between opportunities missed or those grasped. These small steps lead to the attainment of our goals. Sometimes you might be tempted to focus on the big steps only and ignore the smaller steps along the process.

Be very careful not to 'despise the day of small beginnings' (Zac 4:10). The fact your plans, hopes and dreams may be in the embryonic or even chaotic stages does not mean they will not flourish. Be patient. Be gentle with yourself. Appreciate your process. Your small beginnings hold the key to your grand revelation. Sometimes you learn more in the formative years and rigorous process than you do when things are fully materialised and realised. Small steps help you to pay attention to details. Value and celebrate each small step because you will most certainly attach worth and significance to them. In addition you will cherish more your outcome(s) after you have paid the price for success because of the small steps and painful processes you have gone through.

In Education, Sports, Business and other spheres, the concept of **marginal gains** is used. It is all about 'small incremental improvements in any process adding up to a significant improvement when they are all added together.' Not everyone agrees with or sees its benefits; however, the general principle of making small steps to achieving bigger goal does have some merit. True, there will be times when a definitive action will be required to achieve a particular goal and the urgency of the situation might necessitate prompt action rather than incremental steps. Notwithstanding,

> *The 'steps of a good man are ordered by the Lord and He delights in his ways!' (Psalm 37:23).*

It is comforting to know and remember that the Lord orders your steps. So, whilst you aspire for the grand and the mighty, remember steps are ordered; though slow, laborious, often repetitive and time-consuming steps. 'Steps' imply process, slow and with just sufficient illumination for the next move. 'Thy Word is a lamp to my feet and a light to my path' (Psalm 119:105). So, while the path is illuminated, the lamp is reserved for the feet.

Reflection: Could it be that your challenging and problematic steps are ordered? Alternatively, do you feel it is only those 'outwardly successful' moments are ordered? Could it be that the Lord ordered Paul's ship journey to Rome although he was shipwrecked? Can the Lord order your steps even in a storm? Can you think of a time or incident when you were in a storm and then it all worked out for good and you said, 'Now I see why I had to go through that!'

Indeed, you too can see the flip side of adversity and boldly exclaim, 'It was good for me to have been afflicted' (Psalm 119:71), because out of evil cometh forth good. This is cold comfort when you are going through your storms. Even in the storm when others were panicking and fearing for their lives Paul was having peace, divine revelation and illumination. Similarly, on the stormy seas with the disciples screaming, Jesus was of all things, sleeping! Indeed, your strength is birthed in quietness and confidence; reduce the volume! Ecclesiastes 8 reminds us that 'in the day of prosperity be joyful, but in the day of adversity reflect.'

The Link in a Chain
Fourthly, your laborious process however labour or emotionally intensive may just be a step in a series of more difficult ones and there may be many channels of challenges

pending before 'ultimate' success is achieved. After all the rigor to get all that is dug to the surface, many more steps are still required in the labour-intensive process of producing finely cut diamonds before they reach your fingers! Far too often, we give up too soon. Life requires that we hold on, ride out some storms and stand ye therefore and see the salvation of the Lord. The kingdom indeed suffers 'violence and the violent taketh it by force' (Matthew 11:12).

There is a place for purpose, proactivity, assertiveness and controlled aggression. Aggression, as in dogged and grim determination, and a fighting spirit that refuses to give up. Here, you take back what the enemy stole from you. I am talking about assertiveness to stand up for your purpose, and aggression to achieve all that God has purposed for you and to leave a legacy in the earth. Les Brown puts it this way and ends his motivational speeches thus:

> *If you want a thing bad enough to go out and fight for it, to work day and night for it, to give up your time, your peace and sleep for it… if all that you dream and scheme is about it, …and life seems useless and worthless without it… if you gladly sweat for it and fret for it and plan for it and lose all your terror of the opposition for it…if you simply go after that thing that you want with all your capacity, strength and sagacity, faith hope and confidence and stern pertinacity…if neither cold, poverty, famine, nor gout, sickness nor pain, of body and brain, can keep you away from the thing that you want…if dogged and grim you beseech and beset it, with the help of God, YOU WILL GET IT!*
> *– Les Brown*

High-Level Security

Fifthly, your process requires you to guard your heart, mind, spirit and your dreams. Scriptures tell us to 'Above all else, guard your heart, for everything you do flows from it, (Proverbs 4:23) and 'out of the abundance of the heart, the mouth speaketh (Luke 6:45). Indeed, our hearts, minds and spirits can be contaminated with unhealthy, unproductive, immoral, unhelpful and toxic thoughts, counterproductive to our hopes, goals, purpose and destiny.

It is important to note that after the earth is exhumed containing diamond in the very raw stage and phase, it is transported to a safe and secure location to be further processed. A great mistake we sometimes make is that we 'mine our treasures' publicly or expose our treasures prematurely. Jesus gives us the perfect approach to this principle when he asked his disciples an interesting question:

> 'Whom do men say that I am?' (Mark 8:27)

Quite an interesting question, isn't it? These were His disciples and He had been with them for over three years feeding, teaching, mentoring, healing and bringing to earth the Kingdom of God. Jesus being very God and very man knows all things, yet He asked this important question; not to get information, but to see if they knew and grasp the magnitude of His mission as well as His true identity. It was necessary also to ascertain before going to the cross that they fully understood and appreciated the gravity of the mission.

They needed to grasp this also as the weight of continuing the formation and growth of the early church would be on their shoulders. Not to be arguing over who will sit on the 'right or left side in his Kingdom' (Matthew 20:21) or whether He was the one to overthrow the Romans and restore all things to the Jews. 'The Son of man came to seek and to save the lost' (Luke 19:10). 'For God so loved the world that He gave His only begotten Son that whosoever believeth on Him should not perish but have everlasting life' (John 3:16). This is the mission, but did they get it? Did they realise that the mission would go by way of the cross? 'Except a grain of wheat falls in the ground and dies, it abideth alone, but if it dies, it bringeth forth much fruit…' (John 12:24).

The answers were equally interesting:

'Some say you are Elijah and some say you are a prophet' yes, said Jesus, 'But who do you say that I am?' When Peter through divine revelation and illumination replied:

> *'Thou are the Christ, Son of the living God' (Matthew 16:16)*

Jesus exclaimed 'Flesh and blood did not reveal this unto you but my father who is in heaven' (Matthew 16:17). Then he hastened to add 'Tell no man!' This is the crucial point I want to make here. Peter's response guided by divine revelation was spot on, even more so as Jesus had not yet revealed himself to them and told them who He was. His hour had not yet come. Jesus knew that if you expose your mission, plans, purpose too soon especially to the wrong audience, they will either do one of two things or both:

Firstly, they will 'crown' you too soon before you are 'crossed' and secondly, get you to pollute, dilute or abort your mission. Giving the crown, accolades, rewards, recognition, acknowledgement, and honour before you have gone through your cross, storms and process is doing you absolutely no favours. Munroe (2003) sums it up well when he wrote,

> *'You can't tell your plan to everyone because some people won't be able to handle it while you're making it'* (p. 107).

There is something special about life's processes. They can humble, teach, train, guide, and prepare us for greater things to come. There is something about growing your way into a position which takes you through the steps of preparation so that when you get to the pinnacle of success, you have been there, paid the price and know and appreciate what it took to get you there. Additionally, you are familiar with the steps necessary to be there, so you can support others to go on a similar journey. In other words, you can do the jobs of most in the company because you have been through the posts from the menial to the mighty. Have you ever been in a workplace or organisation where the person leading it has not gone through the ranks? These managers sometimes are ineffective, incompetent, unfruitful, judgemental, insecure, territorial, and uncaring because they lack emotional intelligence or the understanding of what it takes at each step on the process.

I find the TV programme 'Undercover Boss' to be interesting. It's a programme where owners, bosses or CEOs of companies go under cover for a week or two to get credible authentic first-hand insights into the running of their organisations. Such a one may sit at the helm and formulate policies and plan strategies and programmes for the organisation but might have never actually done them. They might not have the foggiest clue how repressive their policies might be on those at the bottom of the rung who have to actually implement them. In other cases, the converse may be true.

Going undercover and sometimes having to do menial/small step tasks reveal the true depth and difficulty of implementing some of their own policies and directives. Some bosses have been through the process and have worked their way up through the ranks of their organisation to reach the top. Their challenge was not to blow their cover by being 'too perfect' when given seemingly menial tasks! However, others got to the top without having a clue of how to do the simplest task in the organisation because they on the other hand, did not come through the ranks. There is a place for learning on the job and learning by doing. However, it does work to pay the price, go through the process, and bear your cross before wearing the crown, because your qualification to wearing the crown is the cross that you bear. A crown is far too heavy for a head that did not rest on a cross.

The second issue here is that prematurely disclosing your vision can result in others causing you to abandon your dreams and purpose. The strange thing here is that it is possible that you could be forced or encouraged to abandon your dream, cross or destiny, through the jealousy of others. However, an equally challenging situation is when those closest to you: spouses, friends or family encourage you to abandon your destiny. This is so difficult because this encouragement comes from significant others and often from a place of love, care, and concern.

Their words could be of encouragement as they see fit and uttered with the best intention. Nevertheless, it is possible that they do not share your vision or simply did not receive the Word you got from the Lord. In the midst of Job's suffering, having lost all earthly possessions including his children in a 'spiritual attack'. Job's wife said to him, 'Are you still maintaining your integrity? Curse God and die!' (Job 2:9). The book of Job explained fully the fact that he was a righteous man who was very wealthy, yet he was the subject of discussion in the heavens. 'On the day when the sons of God assembled, Satan came and God said, have you considered my servant Job?' This conversation in the heavenlies would be unknown to Job. Job suffered having done nothing wrong.

In other words, he was not suffering or going through such a rough process because of his own making. Yet, 'Despite Job's losses (flocks, possessions, children and health), he praised God and did not become bitter' (p. 87). This does not mean however that he was happy with the process. He had his moments of isolation, questioning and intense pain. Job 3 explains,

> *'After this opened Job his mouth, and cursed his day. And Job spoke, and said, Let the day perish wherein I was born, and the night in which it was said, There is a man child conceived. Let that day be darkness; let not God regard it from above, neither let the light shine upon it. Let darkness and the shadow of death stain it; let a cloud dwell upon it; let the blackness of the day terrify it. (Job 3:1-5).*

He had a lot more to say which were honest and hard things to utter, but God appreciated his honesty. Nevertheless, he concluded:

> *Naked came I out of my mother's womb, and naked shall I return thither: the Lord gave, and the Lord hath taken away; blessed be the name of the Lord (Job 1:21)*

Indeed, there are times when we do suffer because of our own actions. Other times it could be part of the refining process of our character development. 'Those who live godly will suffer persecution' (2 Timothy 3:12) and those who the Lord loveth, He chaseneth' (Hebrews 12:6). We all have a cross to bear and it will be different for each of us but there are lessons we can learn as we bear our crosses.

Another interesting lesson I find was when Jesus said He must 'suffer many things' Peter declared 'Not you Lord, be it far from you". Then Jesus who had earlier referred to Simon as Peter 'the rock' now rebuked him as 'Satan'.

> *'Flesh and blood did not reveal this to you but my father in heaven, and I say you are Peter and upon this rock, I will build my church and the gates of hell will not prevail against it'* (Matthew 16:17).

Like Peter, we all struggle with life's processes and tend to vacillate between doubt, faith, unbelief, anger or helplessness. It is not exactly a linear experience. Some of life's storms and processes will test us to the core. You will find that life takes you through stages, phases and processes where a range of emotions could be encountered. You may be strong in one instance and weak in another; full of faith and confidence one moment and riddled with fear and doubt the next. You could be a person of firm faith until a circumstance of grave consequence hits and you question yourself, your friends, family or even your faith in God.

Remember on the stormy sea, Paul and the others feared for life. It was indeed a life-threatening situation, as 'all hope of life was gone'. Paul was just as exposed to the dangers of the raging sea as all 275 other souls on board. However, he was stable in his faith in God and the Word of faith that illuminated the darkness and the despair, 'No one will be lost' the depth of your personal faith and trust in God will make the difference as you go through your storms.

For Peter it was clear as Jesus referred to him as three distinct 'individual name types' in such a short space of time: 'Simon - Peter- Satan.' In one instance, he was 'Simon' the unstable, unsure one; then Peter (the rock that signifies stability, firmness and certainty). Jesus referred to him as 'Satan' when he tried to abort the purposes of God for Christ. 'Simon, Simon, behold, Satan demanded to have you, that he might sift you like wheat' (Luke 22:31); But then, look at Peter at Pentecost! He spoke with power and passion after the anointing and infilling of the Holy Ghost. 3,000 souls were added to the church that day! What a transformation.

Your enemy is the person or circumstance that seeks to dilute, pollute or abort your mission and purpose. Never mistake your friend for a foe. Just because someone tells you, the words you want to hear that are gentle and warm does not mean that they are the right words for purpose. In addition, simply because someone challenges you with firm but nurturing words to jolt or propel you into destiny does not mean that they despise you or that they are your enemy!

As mentioned, the challenge here is that it is usually people closest to us who can lead us away from our purpose and destiny. Sometimes this may be done out of malice, spite or jealousy. However, it could be done inadvertently because they may be protective of us and really and sincerely mean us no harm. Sometimes we need a 'coach' and not a 'friend.' That half time challenge in the dressing room can be bruising but after the victory the nurture comes and you say, 'it was good for me that I was afflicted' and faced the adversities that I confronted.

We can also learn an awful lot from Joseph sharing his dream too soon. When he had the dream that he would rule over his brothers (Genesis 37:1-44) and had gotten a coat of many colours from his father, it was clear to his brothers that he was favoured. Mike Murdock (2001) commented on this incident thus:

> *'His father rebuked him; His brothers envied him. He knew rejection. But he was rejected because he had a dream! They were intimidated by his dreams, they were angered by his future, they were uncomfortable with his destiny, they were infuriated by his goals, they misunderstood his assignment; their minds were too small for the bigness of his future' (p. 120).*

Not everyone will rejoice at your promotion or purpose of success and victory. I reiterate life requires that you use wisdom, discernment and discretion, when, where and how to share your dreams and with whom as we go through our processes. On one hand, we should 'write the vision and make it plain, so that he who reads it may run with it' (Habbukuk2:2) but on the other, you must consider the timing of the writing and utterance.

Joseph went through the pit, the prison and the palace. Thrown in a pit by his brothers after his clothes were soaked in animal's blood to mislead and deceive his father; then sold into slavery and lied upon by Potiphar's wife and forsaken in prison before his gift to interpret dreams brought him before the king. Indeed his 'gift made room for him and brought him before great men' (Proverbs 18:16). But we can appreciate the terrible process that Joseph had to go through before he came through successfully at the other end!

Mike Murdock argues that 'Someone's anger can put you in the pit; your faith in God can move you into the place' (p. 14). When you are going through your storms, sometimes it seems like it will never end. You may ask 'why me?' or tend to feel that life has done you unfairly. Conversely, you can take comfort and encouragement from these examples cited. They did not have it easy, in fact there were storms, after storms, after storms: of jealousy, rejection, ostracism, isolation, threats of death, imminent dangers, reputational damage, character assassination, defence of faith with life threatening potentials to name a few. However, "In solitude we give passionate attention to our lives, to our memories to the details around us' (Virginia Woolf, 1882-1941).

Your strength is in meekness not weakness, wisdom to discern when, how, when and with whom to share your vision and blessings. Hezekiah displaying his treasures before the enemy learnt this the hard way (2 Kings 20). Being a relatively good King, he had a strange visit from the prophet who admonished him to 'set your house in order for you shall die and not live!' He turned his face to the wall and prayed, offering praise, worship and intense supplication. He was given 15 years more after God heard his cry and instructed the prophet to tell him that news.

However, what did he actually achieve in those additional 15 years? My greatest concern was that he exposed his treasures and disclosed palace secrets to his enemies. He grew so selfish and self-absorbed that he had no issue, care or concern that his future generations would be taken into slavery and his kingdom ruined completely. Indeed, tell no man! In this case, 'Show no man!' You can be 'crowned' before you are 'crossed'! Be wise as a serpent and harmless as a dove.

Delayed Gratification

In a far less dramatic way, I recall my preparations for the oral defence of my Doctoral thesis in March 2018 after its submission to the external examiners in December 2017. I had followed a fervently rigid structure and timetable over six months to complete the thesis. As I did, I considered what would be an appropriate reward for my thirteen years of non-stop study with a full-time job and ministry and voluntary work. After careful thought and yes prayers, I came up with a plan! Well, I pray about everything!

> *'Trust in the Lord with all thine heart and lean not to thine own understanding. In all thy ways, acknowledge Him and he shall direct thy paths (Proverbs 3:6).*

I decided to upgrade my car. I did much research across different ranges and models, based on the features I desired. These included horizontal and perpendicular parking, pilot assist (semi-autonomous driving capability), blind spot monitoring system, heated steering, hot and cold leather seats, to name a few! This is my little 'guilty pleasure' I suppose, since I do not indulge in much leisure otherwise. I settled for a particular make and model, which ticked all the boxes and more for me. I negotiated with the dealers all relevant details and asked the sales representative to make the collection day be three months away given that a number of these features were customised and personalised.

However, what I did not tell him or anyone else for that matter, was that the day, the 17th of March 2018 was the day after my defence of my thesis (viva voce!). I wanted to focus on my studies and preparation, ensuring I knew my thesis inside out as one can never tell what angle of interrogation the examiners will approach.

As I prepared for and after I did a Mock defence in January, the sales rep called me proudly to announce that the car had arrived earlier than expected and was available for collection 2 weeks earlier than previously agreed. Well, great for him and maybe another customer or even myself under a different set of circumstance. However, I was not ready for the car!! The plan was to complete my exam successfully then the day after I would collect the brand new semi-autonomous driving SUV as a reward! Remember my principle of the cross before the crown! I asked the Dealers to keep it there for me.

All this time my exam date remained a well-guarded secret. My faith was rewarded and on the 16th of March 2018. I successfully defended my doctoral thesis and on the 17th my wife Rhona and I went to collect our brand-new SUV and what a pleasure to drive! And yes, my favourite features are self-parking and Pilot-assist (semi-autonomous driving!)

This seems so trivial but there are a few lessons here for me: One of not saying too much too soon as relating to my exam date. I know that this exam was crucial and I did not want a fuss and for others to be too worried or cast doubt in my mind in any way at all. I prayed quietly for months and prepared myself rigorously and thoroughly. I simply wanted to focus on the task at hand and get on with it without alarm, stress or fuss. Remember, 'in quietness and confidence shall be your strength!' Secondly, I knew the value of deferred or delayed gratification. I had already been delaying my gratification over the years with so many years of continuous part time study. I had forgone so much that simply waiting a few weeks to collect a car was doable!

I continued to learn the value of discernment, timing, deferred gratification, and more so, to value the process. The value of the process through this academic storm must also not be understated. It was a challenging, rigorous and isolating process requiring much individual work, often with little support. Hence, I had to believe that in the absence of support, to 'Build yourself up on your most holy faith praying in the Holy Ghost' (Jude 1:20)

It is this silent work; private practice and much reflection that leads to public manifestation of overall success. The years of reading, researching, revising, drafting and redrafting of chapters are all mostly done in private. The critical reflections, bruising and nurturing feedback and peer reviews all play a part in the 'rehearsal' process. Surely, the outer manifestation of success with the glitter and glamour of graduation, the 'recital' are all lovely to behold. However, behind every glory, there is a story! That story reflects your process. Value that process. Don't rush it and don't let anyone else. Surely, there is a place for expediency, efficiency and effectiveness and life has a time limit attached. Indeed, time waits for no one, however purpose has a process, and for you to maximise the full life lessons from your process, you need to carefully and painstakingly, endure each phase and stage with the right attitude in order to, gain the corresponding altitude.

Advancing Through the Grades

I remember when I was in primary (then All Age School) in Jamaica in the early 1970s, as students we had to meticulously go through all the grades from one through to 9. I started my formal education about age 6 to prepare to pass the National Common Entrance, 11+ selection examinations for high for secondary school admission. We were not allowed to move on to a higher grade simply because it was the end of the school year and we had gained another year chronologically. No! In those days students would be kept back to repeat a whole year! Embarrassed or not they would remain behind in a class whilst their friends and classmates moved on to the next level. They would remain there and be kept back until sufficient process was made commensurate with the required progress for that stage of academic development and rigour. We had to go through due process.

On the contrary, a few students who had performed outstandingly over and beyond the requirement for that particular grade or year group, would be advanced to the next level even though they would be younger than the average age for that year group. I remember being thus advanced. I believe that similarly in life you may choose to underperform in your attitude to life's challenges and trials and be kept back to repeat a lesson or two if you refuse to value your processes. If you continue to react with anger, resentment, loss or lack of direction, blaming others, unforgiveness or other negative responses, you may have to keep repeating life's lessons until you learn the lesson, which that particular situation wants to teach you. No doubt, to develop character, purpose, passion and further to mould you into the image of Christ. Rick Warren (2002) notes that, 'God has a purpose behind every problem and often uses circumstances to develop our character' (p.193). Additionally, the late Dr Myles Munroe (2003) states that 'your purpose will become your passion' (p.32); 'every human being was created to accomplish something that no one else can accomplish' (p39).

You can choose to embrace the process, though painful and learn the lessons quickly. Thus, taking your exams in silence and matriculating to the next level or be out of season as age catches up with you and you are sitting in the same class with people so much younger than you are taking the same lessons or courses you should have taken years or decades ago! You are there looking a bit strange and out of place, why? Because you are too old for that stage of life. You should have taken those courses years ago. 'Make hay while the sun shines!' This is an interesting issue because, true, the Lord works differently in our lives as individuals. You may be called to a task and your period of preparation takes much longer, or is manifested much later in life.

I will hasten therefore to add this caveat, that chronological age is by no means necessarily a measure of the stage in life you are or should be at. Some young people have achieved more than someone in his or her nineties and the converse is true, where someone could be in a ripe old age before they embark on their purpose calling, if at all. I think Moses is a good case in point. He, after years of preparation was called to be the deliverer to the children of Israel from Pharoah's bondage in Egypt quite late in his life, aged 80. I believe that as individuals we should develop our personal relationship with God to a level where we are in communion sweet with Him, trust Him through His Word, and know His voice, as and when we embark on each stage of life and how we sojourn each process.

Value and Embrace the Process: Rehearsals And Recitals
The point I am making here is we should value and embrace our processes. Life challenges us in different ways. We can only be assured that 'the steps of a good man are ordered by the Lord and He delighteth in his ways (Psalm 37:23). I mentioned earlier I was a Music major in university and have sung in a few Classical, cultural and gospel choirs as well as play a little keyboard, rhythm and bass guitars in a few groups and worship bands over the last 40 years to present. I recall also as I use this example, in 1984 when I was rehearsing

diligently for my Grade 6 Pianoforte Royal Schools of Music Examination.

So please bear with me while I use this musical metaphor to illustrate my point. We tend to enjoy the recital but who enjoys the rehearsals? The recital then represents that time when after all the hard and laborious and seemingly uninspiring times of fervent rehearsals, we present to an audience that which was done in private over a period of time. That which was painstaking and sometimes isolating and tedious, now gets the pleasure of being presented to others for their listening pleasure.

The recital does present its own set of challenges, mind you. There are challenges of nervousness, technical issues, economic ramifications or just pressure to remember that which was practiced to recall and perform accurately. However, the rehearsal tends to present a process of repetition and drudgery leading to 'perfection' of sorts for the performance. Can you imagine having to repeat arpeggios, scales (major, minor or chromatic) or a phrase or several bars of music repeatedly, much to the irritation and annoyance of others? Rehearsals can be frustrating. Rehearsals can be discouraging. Rehearsals require resilience and an unimaginable degree of perseverance, stick-to-itiveness, resolve, determination, fortitude and grit. Whether your rehearsal is musical, academic (degree, vocational), you will have to endure your rehearsal process before you can enjoy the pleasure and satisfaction of the recital with all the glitter, glamour, the appreciation and applause.

If we look a bit deeper at an aspect of Moses' life on the backside of the desert tending Jethro's sheep, we see that it was not too glamourous a task with stubborn sheep and dung between his toes. Nevertheless, there he honed in on his craft, protecting the sheep and learning the skill of leadership, patience, empathy, resilience, courage, assertiveness, overcoming personal defects and private insecurities and setbacks. He had to learn to hear and recognise God's voice in the burning bush. He had to develop self-confidence and overcome his personal insecurities when he argued with God regarding his stutter and his stammer and inability to confront Pharaoh to release the Israelites form Egyptian bondage. He had to practice to throw down his rod to become a serpent, his hand in his bosom in and out to become leprous (Exodus 4) all in the privacy, loneliness and isolated environment of the backside of the dessert with dumb animals as his audience before he faced the power and might of Pharaoh and his magicians.

He 'rehearsed' in private before manifesting his 'recital' in pubic. This private rehearsal as part of his process gave him the confidence to perform publicly. Having to face the Red Sea, and so many other challenges, even with the very people he was sent to deliver, was no easy task for Moses to handle. Furthermore, his personal struggle with his own identity as a Hebrew and an Egyptian trained, educated and cultured man was even more challenging and conflicting to handle.

Moses thought he needed Aaron to help him speak because of his stammer and stutter however in the end, he really did not. In fact, it was Aaron who caused grave distress, problems and loss of life as he instructed the people to melt their jewellery into a golden calf for idol worship when Moses went to receive the tablets with the Commandments (Exodus 32:21-24).

Reflection: Who or what are you taking along your process that you think you need because of your insecurities and areas of deficiencies? Could it be that you really don't need who or what you think you cannot do without?

Maybe these 'crutches' could be liabilities and not assets to your God-given purpose and destiny. How do you differentiate between genuine support from liabilities in your life?

It Costs What it Costs
Sixthly, we learn the value of ourselves and that of our processes. Your process is not for sale, it costs what it costs. After that rigorous process to get the diamond and prepare it from earth to shelf, the truth is it costs what it costs! It is not a case like you haggle and negotiate the price of a lovely diamond ring in a top-end store. It costs what it costs; either you can afford it or not. It is for sale but it is not on sale.

After all you have been through, what is your value and worth? What have you learnt from your trials, hurts and disappointments? How much value do you actually place on the experiences you have had? What about your education, training and expertise? Often others want to undermine or devalue your worth and value whether financially or otherwise for the service or ministry you provide. However, your worth is not so much in monetary form in terms of your time, but rather what value you add to others and what problem do you solve by virtue of your education, training, expertise and process. There is a time and place for charity or a 'love gift' or 'travelling expenses' reimbursed, but there is also a time and place when your gifts, talents and abilities, capabilities must be valued, respected and appropriately remunerated, based on the value you bring. This is especially true when you are in Christian ministry.

It is my sincere belief that no experience is wasted and nothing happens by chance in the life of the believer. There is a cost to greatness and achieving your full potential. There is a price to be paid to realise your God-given purpose and this must be respected. You have to see the importance and significance of your personal contribution even if others do not. Understandably, you may have to process some traumatic experiences from your early formation. We all have to do that. It will be different for each one but we all have to face our fears, cares, tears and decide that regardless of what might have happened or failed to happen; that was then, this is now. You now have full responsibility for your life in terms of the decisions you will make from this day forward.

This is not easy. However, if you want to change your future you will have to face your past and develop a positive mindset that begins to see yourself as how Christ sees you. Cerullo (2014) in his book *'Take it Back – Reclaim Everything the Enemy Has Stolen'* writes:

> *When it comes to the battle of the mind, you aren't just a helpless victim or bystander. You have choices to make about what you allow to enter your mind,' (p.122).*

Part of that new perception and shift in paradigm and attitude means valuing your experiences and seeing them through new lens. Valuing the process means looking at what you have been through, or are going through as part of your character building experiences with opportunities to learn and grow. You totally resist any perception of anger, bitterness, resentment, frustration, loss or guilt, although they may be part of your process to closure.

I earlier mentioned, Sir James Dyson. He did 5127 prototypes of the hoover before the final product was agreed and mass produced! What determination and resilience. It takes all these characteristics, personal values and beliefs to keeping on keeping on; to be knocked back repeatedly and still believe that you will succeed and that 'after He tests me, I shall come forth as pure gold' (Job 23:10). All these 'failed' attempts were really 'rehearsals'. Now the Dyson brand of vacuum cleaners is one of the trusted cleaners in the world. So, whatever you are going through, you can succeed and come through using what you have left, not what you have lost.

Joyce Meyer (2015) puts it this way and writes,

> *'Don't spend your life mourning over what you have lost and what is already gone. Take an inventory of what you have left and keep going, one foot in front of the other, one step of faith at a time, remember, God is on your side!' (p. 12).*

Indeed, this is wonderfully said and beautifully expressed. Often the temptation is to moan over our losses. However, your destiny lies in your future. We learn from the past but we don't dwell on the past. We glance through the rear view and side mirrors intermittently but focus our attention through the windscreen on what lies ahead. 5,127 attempts, shows 5,126 ways that did not work!

So, you are not for sale! Value your process, Value your story. Believe in yourself and know all you have been through should be viewed through the correct lens; should make you a better person and shock your enemies and naysayers. You are one of a kind with no one else in the world having your unique voice stamp, iris or finger prints! You are a great original not a cheap copy of anything or anyone. Instead of letting others rejoice at your demise, turn your seemingly hopeless situations around. Thus, God will be glorified, the enemy will be horrified, you will be successful and others will be uplifted and edified.

You must demonstrate you have learnt from your process and can now use your experiences to benefit humanity. Some people have formed Charities, ministries and opportunities to be of help to others because of the brokenness they have suffered. No wonder the Bible say we should, 'comfort others with the same comfort wherewith we have been comforteth' (2 Corinthians 1:4); however, 'if you do not know peace and contentment you cannot bring comfort to the troubled heart' (Day, 2003, p.6).

Reflection: So, what is the value of your suffering? What was it for? What have you learnt from it and how do you now see your process?

The Decision Is Yours

Life affords you options in all of this. You have decisions and choices to make. You can throw it all away or pick up the broken pieces from life's shattered dreams and use them as catalysts for the next stage of your life. There has to be a reason for your pain. There has to be a purpose in your problems, stepping stones in your stumbling blocks, messages in your messes, opportunities in your obstacles and implements in your impediments. You cannot simply go through such ferocious storms and suffering for nothing – make a decision to turn it around for your good!

Regardless of your background, race or personal circumstances, start with how you see and value yourself. Speak the Words of God in your life. Mike Murdock states, 'The Word of God is a shield and enables you to see the attacks of others as opportunities rather than obstacles' (p. 10). Remember the sayings 'Life and death are in the power of the tongue', 'as a man thinketh so is he', and 'if there is no enemy within, the enemy without can do you no harm!'

6. So Near and Yet So Far!

'A man cannot discover new oceans unless he has the courage to lose sight of the shore'

(Dr Myles Munroe, 1991, p. 67)

'A smooth sea does not make a skilful sailor' (Proverb, Author Unknown)

Paul and the 275 others on the ship were two weeks into their perilous journey. Tossed back and forth on the boisterous waves and despairing for life, finally they drew close to an island called Malta, after days of sailing hopelessly with no sight of land. In the previous chapter, I mentioned the need to 'comfort others with the same comfort that we have been comforted with. Paul, who having been re-assured and illuminated by the Angel that there would be no loss of life, though the ship and its cargo would be lost; now comforted everyone on board and encouraged them to eat something.

It is quite interesting how the stresses and storms of life can remove our appetite and desire for food, leisure or pleasure. This sustenance however needs not only be physical, but also social, emotional, relational or spiritual nurturing. The loss of a sense of leisure, pleasure, meaning or direction can be an indicator of the measure of distress, discouragement, burnout or even depression. No wonder God told Elijah to 'arise and eat for the journey is too great for thee' (1 Kings 19:7). Interestingly, this was after his tremendous victory on Mount Carmel that he was subjected to a period of fear, burnout and discouragement in the cave. Sometimes the process costs so much that the celebration is nuanced, dampened, lost its significance or seems totally meaningless.

Battered by the gale force winds, the captain was determined to forge on against Paul's inspired intervention. He made a desperate effort to sail the ship toward the beach, however it crashed on some rocks. At this point Julius, the centurion was concerned about the prisoners escaping. The soldiers desired to kill them all to prevent them doing so; however, Paul had found favour with Julius. He demanded that they be not killed. Again, we see the power of association. The presence of Paul on the ship resulted in the saving of many lives. In like manner, your presence can and does make much difference in the lives of others in all spheres of your associations, mostly unbeknownst to you.

Instead of killing the prisoners, the order was given that anyone who could swim should. Others made it safely on planks and broken pieces of the ship to the nearby island. I must make an important observation here. It is the fact that calamity struck within sight of the destination but not their final destination. The final destination was Italy but they were shipwrecked in about 90 feet of water off the course of Malta. It is re-assuring to note that even in the midst of the storm, God provided a way of escape precisely at the right time and at a location that, although not ideal, still facilitated the survival of all. We are promised that God is faithful and will not suffer us to be tempted more than we are able to bear. He may not come when we want him to but He is always right on time. He may delay his coming as in the case of Lazarus but He showed up even after the situation seemed so hopeless.

For Paul, the buffeting and battering on the stormy sea were relentless. There was hopelessness, despair, and great fear for life. To make things worse, they hit the sand bank resulting in the breaking up of the ship. Yet, it was shallow enough for them to swim to shore. Life never removes everything from you all at once. As bad as things might seem, there is always a glimmer of hope in your situation. There is always a light at the end of your tunnel. When one door is closed, many more are opened. You may not think this is so but life always leaves something for you to work with. Yes, Paul and those on the ship struck disaster in deep waters, and that was bad; however, it was close enough to Malta where they had the opportunity to somehow get to shore. Let's be honest, disaster could have struck earlier when they were in much deeper waters, in the extreme dark, during the stormy blast with absolutely no proximity to land when it would have been absolute calamity.

A Ray of Hope in Each Situation
I strongly encourage you to always reflect on, search for and interrogate each situation in your life for that opening, that opportunity, that ray of hope. Yes, the door may be closed but a small opening in a window may be present as a way out. Search for and embrace it. Do not dwell on the negative. By so doing you miss opportunities, frustrate others with your negativity, stress yourself and abort your purpose. Be realistic and pragmatic yes, but do not burden, exasperate others, or contaminate an environment with abject pessimism repeatedly. Be balanced in your views when articulating your situations. Do not only dwell on and report the bad side. Instead, punctuate your report with good things. I am sure you can always find them if you are honest. For example, you may be having a tough time with your boss' attitude or the strict targets you have to meet at work, but you may have had a lovely card of gratitude from a satisfied customer that day or

better still, you have a job to complain about! How about giving thanks for that job you have?

Alternatively, you could look around for another source of employment if the stress level on that job is just about at or beyond your ability to cope. You could also find other support systems on the current position to cope; whether it is through the wellbeing intervention programmes or through a Welfare Officer or friends, families or other support systems. There is always a way, Find it! Scripture declares: 'Give thanks in all circumstances; for this is God's will for you in Christ Jesus (1 Thessalonians 5:18 NIV). Please note that we do not give thanks 'for' but we give thanks 'in' everything as we go through our trials. For over two decades, I have used as my footer on my email "In everything give thanks".

There is no temptation taking you but that, which is common to man, and God is faithful and will not allow you to be tempted above and beyond your ability to cope. You can take comfort therefore that regardless of what transpires in your life, God has graciously and faithfully made a way of escape for you. Your finances might be lacking but you have your health or the converse true. Your business or your marriage or your studies may suffer a bit but then your children may be doing extremely well in school.

NB: Life will always leave something for you to use, God uses what you have left not necessarily what you have lost.

Sure, what you have lost can be teaching moments, character building experiences and processes. God wants you to be filled with faith, hope, and gratitude and a positive attitude of gratitude as you move forward through your storms. Your attitude will determine your altitude! How high do you want to soar?

You may not see the outcome to your hopes, dreams, and destination but you will make it. You may encounter storms and despair in deep waters, but God will always make a way. Of this, I am confident! Sure, it is not good what has happened to you but develop a proper perspective on your situation: you were shipwrecked within close proximity to shore. Simply put, it could be worse. Indeed, it might not be your final destination but you are close enough to a place of safety. Notwithstanding it was still a life and death process to get there but you are within sight of shore. Even in the midst of your storms, you can see the faithfulness of God. Consider this one more time with me please: What might have happened if the ship had broken up in the middle of the dark ocean with no island in sight or even nearby? You can look at your circumstances and become bitter, resentful, angry, stressed out or purposeless, or you can evaluate them and see where God has been faithful even in your storm.

Reflection: As you consider your life, how has God been faithful to you in one specific situation? If you do not have a personal faith in Christ, what good can you see out of your 'storms' in life?

Perhaps you can appreciate the fact that you have a wonderful opportunity to make it to shore despite your 'shipwreck' whatever this may be a metaphor for. You can thank Him for his protection, guidance, faithfulness, provisions, job opportunities, family, health, and healing to name a few.

Within Sight of Shore
Disaster struck within sight of shore (v41); there is something very significant about circumstances happening within sight of

'shore.' For Paul, disaster struck within sight of Malta. So near and yet so far! How often you may have said those words? No doubt, you can think of times in your life when disaster, failure, lack, hurts, disappointment, and pains struck just within sight of victory. This can be painful. You may be wondering how inopportune a time it was for that situation to strike. What is your 'shore' or your 'almost there'?

I remember in 2011 when I was completing my Master's degree in Leadership and Management when my cousin in Gloucester, England sadly passed away. He was only in his mid-forties. It was an awkward time to drive 6 hours return on 3 separate occasions to comfort my aunt and family; view the body in the funeral home, then attend the funeral and gave a tribute. This was demanding, but the good in that situation was that I somehow weeks prior, felt the Lord prompting me to make a study schedule or timetable which led me to complete, bind my dissertation and submitted it a week in advance. This removed all the stresses and panic thereby allowing me to have the required time to support my family in that time of bereavement. Had I not done that it would certainly have been a different outcome, in that I probably would not be able to support my family in the way I was able to do.

Take the time to reflect on your situation today. Identify some good even in the midst of bad situations. Let this be a source of encouragement to you as to the goodness of God in your life; then seek for ways in which you can use your experiences to be a source of inspiration and comfort for others.

Remember also that sometimes you may have to take a detour or have to 'stop over' en route to destiny. Circumstances can and often force us to demonstrate our flexibility in life. True, Malta was not in their plans. It was not their final destination or even a port of call at all, but circumstances forced them there. That is life. You will find yourself having to deal with situations, which are not of your making. You did not plan for them, ask for them, budget for them or make allowance for them but here you are crashed and in great peril in deep waters.

It may be so difficult but think of your blessings. You may have suffered heavy losses: had to withdraw from completing your degree, had financial reversals, saw your investments failed, had health issues, suffered bereavement, been through a separation or divorce or had your children whom you poured all into turned out to be a source of ingratitude, embarrassment and shame. Like Paul, the Lord may give you favour with the 'powers that be'. He may have allowed the crash close enough to land and He may have equipped you with the wherewithal to make it safely through after giving you words of affirmation, comfort, and hope. You may not have reached your final destination as yet; but since you have reached a destination, howsoever caused, it is an opportunity to reflect, refresh and regroup in order to move on at the appropriate time.

Another crucial factor to consider when close to 'shore' or a destination is to guard against complacency and familiarity. This means that you are having a sense of self-satisfaction, contentment, coasting, 'taking your foot of the gas pedal' or simply being careless or too composed. Statistics show that a number of road crashes take place within a few miles or metres from home! In a study conducted by Progressive Insurance, they found that,

> *An estimated 52 percent of car accidents occur within 5 miles of a person's home, and 77 percent occur within*

15 miles or less, (Progressive Insurance, 6 November, 2016).

Sometimes after a long, dreary journey or process the thought of the comfort of home and getting a well-deserved rest or just the sigh of relief that you can soon take a break, can all lead to a measure of complacency. The challenge then is to be diligent and careful to the very end; it is not over until it is over. You have to fight on with deep resolve. It is no time to ease up or slow down until it is 'in the bag.' That was what my Professor told me. I had successfully defended my doctoral thesis. Nevertheless, I was a bit disappointed that I had to do some revision or corrections prior to final binding and submission. My professor said, 'It is in the bag!' In other words, since I had already passed, just to get on with the few, relatively minor corrections to seal the deal and get the graduation plans in motion!! Why moan and throw a pity party when you have succeeded? Yes, you might have a bit of disappointment, but don't let it get to an unhealthy stage before you crack on with the final tasks then start planning the celebrations!

Falling Short of The Mark
Crashed short of Malta meant they had fallen short from shore; 'For all have sinned and come short of the glory of God' (Romans 3:23). It is as simple as that, we have all fallen short and missed the mark in some way and at some point, in our lives, whether spiritually, relationally, professionally, mentally, physically, emotionally, financially, socially or otherwise. There are lessons to learn from missing our goals, especially within sight of achieving them.

From a spiritual point of view, missing the mark and falling short of God's glory requires us 'believing on the Lord Jesus

Christ and you shall be saved' (Acts 16:31). Yet, the process of sanctification and 'working out our salvation' remains a lifelong process and here we fall short repeatedly. However, we fall on the grace, mercy and favour of a loving God to sustain us. He remembers that we are dust. He does not treat us as our sins deserve (Psalm 103:14). In fact, He looks beyond our faults and sees our needs. We can take comfort in the fact that we 'have not a high Priest who cannot be touched by the feelings of our infirmities…' (Hebrews 4:15).

You may also fall short emotionally, financially, relationally, mentally, and importantly sometimes within reach of your goals. 'Fall short' implies that you have already begun and are in the process; but for some reason have failed to complete the process or achieve your desired goals or reach your set or intended destination. There will be different reasons for this, some justified, others mere excuses. Nevertheless, let us face the fact that at some point in our lives, regardless, we all will or have all fallen short of ours or others' expectations, goals, targets, purpose or destination.

A classic example I believe is of Jacob (the trickster, sur planter and con artist) in the Old Testament. He was married to Rachel after working 14 years to win her, being tricked several times by his uncle. Laban had originally and deceptively given her Rachel's older sister Leah in marriage. Jacob was sometimes referred to as 'Israel'. On this specific occasion, he was travelling with his heavily pregnant wife Rachel to Bethlehem. Along the way, but short of the destination, she went into labour and sadly died in childbirth.

> *Jacob and his group left Bethel. Before they came to Ephrath, Rachel began giving birth to her baby. She was having a lot of trouble with this birth. She was in*

great pain. When her nurse saw this, she said, "Don't be afraid, Rachel. You are giving birth to another son. "Rachel died while giving birth to the son. Before dying, she named the boy Benoni But Jacob called him Benjamin. (Genesis 35:16-18 NIV)

What a sad end to this love story. Jacob loved Rachel deeply. In fact, initially he worked seven years for her hand in marriage only to be tricked and given the older and not so attractive Leah! It Is quite interesting that after the first night of marriage only in the morning did Jacob realise that it was Leah and not Rachel he was given! Ouch, let's leave that as it may to your imagination!

Although Leah was producing many children to the sadness and disappointment of Rachel, she cried out to the Lord and did eventually produce her own. Leah had the children but not the physical beauty. On the other hand, Rachel was worth Jacob's fourteen years of hard labour for her hand in marriage. Sadly, she could not have children. In her desperation she had cried, 'Give me children lest I die!' It was sad indeed that the deepest desire of her heart also contributed and eventually led to her premature death. There is a saying, 'Be careful what you ask for, you might get it and not want it.' 'Life and death are in the power of the tongue' (Proverbs 18:21a).

The Power in a Name
Rachel in her grief and intense pain and suffering, uttered her parting words to the nurse to name her son 'Benoni' that means 'Son of my sorrow or suffering.'

Reflection: Have you ever named a permanent situation out of your temporary pain? Do you react impulsively to situations, or do you calmly reflect and then respond to circumstances strategically and purposefully?

Benoni - What a name to give an innocent infant! While we can understand the sadness and pain as the reality of death crept upon Rachel, yet this innocent child did not even have a minute to live before he was saddled with the prophetic utterance of sorrow and pain over his life! Names had tremendous significance in those days and still do, albeit less so for some. I mentioned earlier about- how we name our situations and ourselves. I spoke about the importance of correct self-perceptions, concept, image and worth. It is also important how you perceive your situations as well: as 'giants or grasshoppers' or as being well able to conquer 'the land' (Numbers 13:33); or as 'dead dogs' unworthy of the grace, favour of mercy extended to you by the King as in the case of Mephibosheth and King David (2 Samuel 9:8).

The point is, never allow a situation, temporary or otherwise, however painful, or howsoever caused, to make you stigmatise, label, pronounce or name yourself or that circumstance according to your current feelings, perceptions, or pain. Somehow, you have to find the strength to value yourself and see your worth and agree with Scripture on who and whose you are in Christ. Agree with the Word of God and what it says about you not what you think about you. There will be times when you do not feel very well or in reality your storms and situations may cause you to feel less valued than your potential or purpose stipulate. This is the time when you need to find that strength, resilience and deep resolve to urgently address that name or negative label.

I can also think of Jabez who was deemed 'more honourable than all his brethren' yet he was called 'Jabez' which meant 'sorrow or pain' (1 Chronicles 4:9-10). He came to a place where he recognised the negative label, stigma and prophetic utterance and their implications over his life. Like the Prodigal Son, he must have come to himself at some point and for some reasons, because he subsequently cried out to God. You too in like manner can arise and declare like Jabez who cried out to the God of Israel thus:

> "Oh, that you would bless me, and enlarge my territory! Let your hand be with me, and keep me from harm so that I will be free from pain." And God granted his request. (1 Chronicles 4:10)

What a powerful prayer! He recognised that his name meant 'pain' and made supplication to God that 'he would not cause pain.' He broke the curse and moved on to fulfil his potential and purpose because he realised the power of positive utterances and prophetic exclamations. You are not a 'Pain', but you are 'honourable.' You are blessed, with God's hands of protection on you and His everlasting arms undergird you. Furthermore, your borders are being enlarged.

Isaiah declares:

> "Enlarge the place of your tent, and let the curtains of your habitations be stretched out; do not hold back; lengthen your cords and strengthen your stakes (Isaiah 54:2, ESV).

Reflection: This begs the question, 'Who named you and have you been living out a negative prophesy over your life because of that name? In light of this revelation, what will be your new name?

Sometimes you could have been named quite innocently out of the distress, grief, pain, hurts, and disappointment of others. Perhaps you were called 'worthless, good for nothing, ugly, not going to amount to anything good' and the list goes on. However, you have the power to break that curse. You can break the curse or the cycle of pain, unproductivity, failure, procrastination, ineffectiveness, inefficiency, divorce, failing to complete tasks, fear, or low self-esteem.

You need not be angry with those who have named you wrongly; instead, you can address the problem, not the person. Undeniably, a part of healing may require you to confront and deal with issues as well as those who have wronged you. However, Jabez's example of praying about his name is a particularly good illustration of how you can reverse negative utterances over your life and future and thus chart a new path to blessing, capacity, favour, increase, purpose, health and wholeness.

As mentioned, Jabez lived with that name 'shame, sorrow, pain' for a long time. Imagine every time his mother called him she in fact was uttering 'Come here pain, come here sorrow, come here shame!' Thankfully Jabez like the Prodigal son 'came to himself' (Luke 15:17-20) in other words after going through his storms and through a process of deep reflection, simply said,

'Enough is enough!'

'I have enough pain, shame and sorrow in my life I will come through this!'

What is in the past is in the past, from this moment forward this is my life and what I do with it is now my responsibility. Yours therefore is the responsibility for your goals, targets, dreams, aspiration, accomplishments, purpose, and destiny. You may have been negatively named or labelled or failed by significant others close to achieving your goals, but you now have the power to make some serious changes in your life, just like Jabez. You will come through safely.

You may have to be assertive like Jacob who was alternating between driving the horses and being there for Rachel in the wagon; providing comfort and guiding the progress of the journey. This is a hard thing to do: to provide direction, guidance and dictate the progress and destination of your family, life or dreams while being there for those who need you most simultaneously, whilst processing your personal dilemmas. TD Jakes pointed out the challenge of these dichotomies. Excess mixing and mingling with the family could inhibit the pace of your progress towards your destination, but focusing primarily on your destination inhibits emotional support, fellowship, and the comfort you need to provide for those who rely on you.

Undoubtedly, it is a demanding task to be managing the pace of your mission, as you are within sight of, but far from your destination while being there for your loved ones. You cannot be too career, academic or purpose-driven that you ignore and forsake fellowship. Yet, you cannot be so fellowship oriented and socially inclined that your personal goals, purpose, and mission are sacrificed. These are the conflicts of life as you are near to shore. No wonder Jacob was torn being there in the wagon with Rachel and driving the horses to the desired destination. Despite this intense juggling, the time came when he was told of the death of his beloved wife, Rachel, the birth of his son and the name given in her parting words. The driving stopped. The journey halted. Jacob was needed urgently in the wagon. Despite your very best efforts, there will be times when you will lose some precious things, relationships or people along the path of life.

Change That Name!
Jacob crawled into the wagon and the Nurse told him Rachel's parting words. She told him that with her dying breath in her last moments, she had named her son 'Benoni – son of my sorrow.' Jacob knew exactly what was going on. He understood well, the implications of naming his son 'Benoni.' Consequently, without time to even grieve the sad passing of his dear wife, he uttered purposefully,

> 'My son shall not be called 'Benoni' (son of my sorrow or suffering); rather my son shall be called 'Benjamin' (Son of my strength, Son of my right hand!')

Isn't this powerful! This is the power of positive and prophetic utterances. You reflect the name you were given. Break that negative label today; but remember that as you do, part of your inner storms will be the conflict of your own duality and identity. By this I mean the conflict of living with the two sides to your person. In a sense both Benoni and Benjamin are true, so too are Israel and Jacob. In Romans, we find these words,

> 'For the good that I would I do not: but the evil, which I would not, that I do' (Romans 7:19).

Oh, the conflict of the human condition. The truth is, sorrow has strength and pain gives power, with passion and purpose delicately intertwined. Behind every *Benjamin* there is a *Benoni* and in every *Israel* there is a *Jacob*. Understanding your weaknesses, failures, and shortcoming along your path and in your processes will help you to balance your expectations of self and others in your storms. You will understand who named you and what were they probably going through at the time, under the circumstance why they did. This could lead to empathy and forgiveness. You will have to decide how you will retrieve and salvage the broken pieces and move forward to purpose and destiny. Murdock (2001) argues that:

> *'Destiny is in your real difference from others, your difference agitates others, your difference is in the greatness you want to birth in your future, that difference makes others uncomfortable, miserable and angry in your presence' (p.121).*

Jacob, short of his destination in Bethlehem now finds himself with another unforeseen problem. This was not in the original plan when he and his group with Rachel set out. It should be challenging and somewhat straightforward journey to Bethlehem, the 'place of bread.' He did not expect to fall short or having to face the death of his wife in childbirth. But then, that was what life, his path, his process threw at him. The issue was how he now deals with what he could not change.

> *'The things one worries about seldom happens, while objections and difficulties no one thought about, may suddenly turn out to be almost insurmountable obstacles' (Drucker, 1998, p.27).*

I like the prayer of serenity:

> *'Lord, grant me the serenity to accept the things I cannot change, courage to change the things I can and wisdom to know the difference.'*

Jacob chose to change the negative label Rachel in her moment of intense pain and hurt gave her son in her final moments. He could not change the fact that Rachel had died.

That he had to accept graciously. 'Trying to do what you can't only produces frustration and feelings of failure' (Meyer, 2015, p.127). Yet what we consider 'failure' could be used positively. For example, Scottish Author and Social Reformer, Samuel Smiles (1812-1904) writes, 'We learn wisdom from failure much more than success. We often discover what we will do by finding out what we will not do.'

Yes, this was the same Rachel, his first love for whom working 14 years at hard labour for her hand in marriage was just like an evening gone. She was dead!

Jacob after having renamed his son, *Benjamin* then grabbed his shovel and started digging her grave. This was not how the story was supposed to end.

Reflection: What sorrows are you carrying that broke your heart? What dream of yours died within plain sight of your destination? What have you buried in the place you fell short?

Like Jacob who buried Rachel short of Bethlehem, you no doubt buried your hopes, dreams, joy, fight, and resilience – part of you died in the place you fell short. Simply put, you were probably burnt out and lost your confidence; the process costs so much…. the confusion of the wagon and the horses – whether to make progress or to mingle in fellowship in the wagon; how can you balance the two and be present (TD Jakes, *'When Men Fall Short'*). Why must I too fall short? Why I cannot bring things to fruition and back on course? I was so near and yet so far – living with the losses of what you almost had: your dreams died: your degree, car, ministry, relationship, career, reputation, integrity, purpose, potential and destiny.

In his book, *'Wounded Soldier – A Greater Purpose'* Jason Mills (2017) offers a very helpful and insightful perception on loss, when he writes:

> *'We may perceive our losses to be a bad thing, but from a divine perspective it may be exactly what we need to reposition us for the purposes God has for our lives. Our duty is not to figure out God or what He allows to happen, not to play the blame game and beat ourselves up, not to wallow in self-pity and indulge in self-defeat, but to humbly submit to Him'* (p. 91).

You may have to deal with destructive criticisms for falling short by significant others. You tried to balance the inconsistencies along your path of life. Murdock (2001) has an interesting perspective on criticism. He encourages us to 'develop more wisdom regarding the purpose of attack. Criticism is an attack designed to distract you. Attack is an opposition designed to destroy you, criticism is designed to demoralise those around you, those desiring to help you, criticism is meant to make your future undesirable, adversaries fear your motives' (p. 131).

You may have done your best and now you simply need some encouragement. You may have sacrificed and given of your very best only to be told 'you were not there for me' or 'your best is not good enough.' You are hurting because like Jacob you were only trying to be there in the wagon while driving the horses, making progress to your destination while mingling with the family. One brings fellowship but not much progress and vice-versa. You are seeking hard to balance the two to satisfy all (TD Jakes).

Others may forget your sacrifices or not even recognise or remember that you contributed to their success. Instead, they might only recall where you fail to meet their unrealistic expectations. Yet, suffering and bleeding, you carry on. Nevertheless, you had to forge through your process to get to where you are through weakness and strength. You are not alone. You might have fallen short, but you are still special, 'the righteous man falleth seven times and rises up again (Proverbs 24:16), so get back on your feet. Take what is left and move on again. Do not give up at the place you fell short; achieve your full potential, God-given purpose and destiny. God wants to strengthen you and fortify and build you up, God knows where you are (Adam). When He asks a question, He is not seeking information. Instead, He wants to know, if you are aware of the place where you have fallen short and missed the mark.

Reflection: Are you aware of your location, position and condition in relation to your purpose and destination? God knows your needs and your destination. He knows how much you are hurting.

He declares:

> *For I know the plans I have for you saith the Lord, plans not to harm you but to give you a future and a hope' (Jeremiah 29:11).*

Despite this powerful Word of affirmation, we often resort to worry, anxiety and fear. We despair for life itself like Paul and those on board that ship when the winds and waves are contrary and danger to life and property are imminent. As mortals, we sometimes medicate our pains with unwholesome habits, activities, relationships and pursuits. At this point, you may be tired, burnt out and weary as you struggle with your 'Jacob and Israel, Benoni and Benjamin, Thomas and

Didymus, Peter and Simon' all struggling in the same place and in the same person.

Part of your maturity lies in your ability to control the negative voices, perceptions and labels: the Jacob (trickster, supplanter, con artist), Benoni (son of my sorrow), Jabez (shame or sorrow), Didymus (two or twin) and Simon (unstable); and bring forth your Israel, (Genesis 35:10), Benjamin (son of my right hand/strength), Thomas, and Peter (Rock). This will take more than positive thinking or self-effort. Only Divine intervention can make the difference.

What have you 'buried' short of your 'Bethlehem'? Like Jacob we bury what we cannot fix when the storms get tough. We bury our passion, sense of pleasure or leisure, our hopes, dreams, desires, aspiration, ambitions and abandon our God-inspired purpose. As you cast the last shovel full of earth over the hurriedly makeshift grave of your sad loss, Jesus said,

> 'Show me where you laid Lazarus?'
>
> 'By this time he stinketh...' The replied hopelessly.

Mary and Martha felt abandoned by their friend Jesus who could not even be bothered to attend the funeral of his dear friend Lazarus. Showing up four days after the funeral showed He had the power as the 'resurrection and the life' (John 11:17) to raise him from the dead. Yet, touched by the feeling of their infirmities and startled by their unbelief enough to cry with them, 'Jesus wept' (John 11:35).

Whatever you may consider to be 'stinking' in your life, what you have long buried short of your hopes and dreams, bring Jesus to the place whenever you fall short. Let him bring to life and reveal His purpose even in your problem and in your pain and give you power and passion in spite of your problematic process. Be specific: What fell short? What is the purpose?

For Jacob, his process though pain was a type and shadow of Jesus. As Joseph and Mary with Jesus on a donkey would later ride to Bethlehem, declaring the arrival of Jesus the Messiah! Where Jacob fell short, Joseph got to Bethlehem to fulfil prophesy of Jesus being the Messiah. The Kings of Israel later came through Benjamin. Change your name and your perspective. Benjamin was not meant to be born in Bethlehem for Jesus was predestined to be born there. Miracles come from messes…don't give up till you see the end! Don't die in your storms you will never know how your story would end if you stop short.

Your life can be the canvas on which others to come will paint the reality of their lives. Jesus compensates for your shortcomings. He endows upon you anointing, gifts, talents, abilities and capabilities to fulfil His purpose. Use what you have left, not what you have lost. Life will never leave with you nothing. For every failure, shortcoming, insufficiency. Remember this:

> *"So, I will restore to you the years that the swarming locust has eaten, the crawling locust, The consuming locust, and the chewing locust, My great army which I sent among you. You shall eat in plenty and be satisfied, (Joel 2:25-26, NKJV),*

Trusting Where You Cannot Trace
A major challenge is to find some good even in bad situations. In other words, making a desperate effort to change your paradigm and your perspective on whatever life hands you. Are you a 'grasshopper' or someone capable of victory and worthy of success; or are you a 'dead dog' or heir to the

throne, Mephibosheth? Only you can decide. It is really about your mind set. It is amazing the strength you have within you to change your circumstance! Take back control and decide how your story ends. Be proactive. Be determined. Possibly, you might have had words of affirmation, encouragement, faith and prophesy spoken over your life but you have to birth that which was planted in you. This might mean being in the right environment, socially, economically, morally, spiritually, physically, mentally, or academically to possess the right mind set in order to bring to fruition your goals, dreams and purpose. Like Paul, Jabez and Jacob you might have to take charge of your situation and be assertive to change what indeed you can change. You will pull through; even though you may have had a bad start in life or was disadvantaged in some way.

Inevitably, there will be storms you cannot calm; situations you cannot fix and brokenness that cannot be mended as well as dead dreams that cannot be resurrected. In these cases, you develop a correct mind set of faith and accepting God's sovereignty, 'trusting His heart where you cannot trace His hand.' You may be so close to realising your hopes and dreams and only feet away from achieving your goals when disaster strikes, and you are shattered and broken. Know that even in this process, just short of your destination God has a plan for your life, one that is for your good and not for your harm. Keep living. You have to see how your story ends! After all the pain, turmoil and suffering, there has to be something better on the other side of your pain. You have to see what your storms were all about. Do not suffer and sacrifice for nought, there is a reason for your pain. This will be the catalyst for your passion, purpose and power. Persevere and hold on to the very end. Take hold of and keep in mind a promise that cannot be repeated too much: Jeremiah 29:11 reminds us, 'For I know the plans I have for you said the Lord; plans not to harm you but to give you a future and an expected end.'

In this chapter, I focused on how to cope when you are so near and yet so far from your destination, when within striking distance of your goals. We looked at how you can draw some important life lessons when you are 'shipwrecked' within sight of your destination. Let us now focus in more detail on the key verse 44 of our discussion and hone in on the three categories that were identified to get all safely to shore.

7. The Swimmers, the Planks and the Broken Pieces

> *...But the centurion, wanting to spare Paul's life, thwarted their plan. He commanded those who could swim to jump overboard first and get to land.* **The rest were to follow on planks and on broken pieces of the ship**, *In this way everyone was brought safely to shore,* (Acts 27:43-44)

The journey had continued through the dark, dreary, dismal, and deadly process leading to the crash on the sand bank within sight of Malta, but yet a good distance from shore. The sailors had earlier checked the depth of the sea to be 120 feet but continued perilously on then sounded again at 90 feet. Crashing into the fierce waves where two seas met meant that there was little hope for all on board the ship. They had been, so far divinely protected through the revelation, inspiration, and Word through the Holy Spirit to Paul. While this divine intervention did not eliminate or avert trouble, consider what the journey would have been without Paul on board.

Consider also what the journey would have been had Paul not been 'at the place' in tune with God in such deep fellowship, to receive such divine revelation and angelic visitation. Furthermore, contemplate also how different things could have turned out had the centurion and the ship's owner listened to Paul's wise counsel initially. Never underestimate the power of one! You may feel insignificant, but your presence makes all the difference in the home, family, job, car, train, and airplane or wherever you go you carry the presence of God. Remember this verse:

> *For we have this treasure in earthen vessels that the excellency of the power may be of God. and not of us (2 Corinthians 4:7).*

What you consider to be alone could only mean that you forget that the Spirit resides within you, and He speaks to us words of comfort in our storms.

In the midst of the storm at this point, there was mass confusion. As the ship began to break apart, there was the fear that the prisoners would all escape. Even in this panic, Divine protection was affirmed: remain in the ship though some things will be lost. With authority, confidence and faith Paul declared, 'except ye abide in the ship ye cannot be saved (v31). All 2 hundred, 3 score and 16 souls (v37). This is an interesting scenario. Death was seemingly imminent. The waves were boisterous, the ship was falling apart, lives were in danger and the water was very deep. The temptation was to simply jump overboard. But alas, Paul admonished, 'stay calm and remain on the ship.'

These are powerful words. How often your storms are so bad that you are tempted to jump ship, give up, abandon your plans, and abort your vision. You may make a calculation where you thought it better to die trying to swim to shore rather than remain calm in the situation, while you evaluate your options. This might not make any sense sometimes because the situation may seem both important and urgent simultaneously and you feel pressured to make a decision at that moment! The proverbs 'Haste makes waste' and 'when emotions are high judgment is low' are very applicable here. Sometimes even when you fear disappointment and destruction, you may need to 'cast anchor and ride out the storm, wait for calm and *wish for 'day.'*

Consider Your Options and Choices

This might not seem like you are doing much but having done all just stand (Ephesians 6:13). Some storms require that you simply ride them out. Sometimes there is not much more you can do, except to contemplate, seriously reflect on and weigh up your options, before making any decision at all. It may be the only prudent and safe thing to do at that time. You may be one who reacts hastily to situations without thought of consequences. Perhaps you are more reactive than proactive, irritable than reflective. You may need to be more reflective and consider more carefully your options or choices prior to making life-changing decisions.

You may need to seek wise counsel from qualified people or seek Divine guidance on crucial decisions you have to make. These are difficult times especially if you are in leadership and the lives, livelihoods or health, safety and wellbeing of others are wholly dependent on your decisions and choices. This level of pressure and stress cannot be overstated or underestimated.

Through Paul and the favour, he found with the centurion all the prisoners were spared death. Again, it is worth noting the power of God's favour toward you. Favour or grace, God's unmerited goodness can come from strange places and through unexpected sources. This calls for openness, non-discrimination, flexibility and non-judgementalism. God can use anyone to bless you, even your enemy. He can grant you favour in that marriage, job, investment opportunity, studies, ministry, and family or personal life's goals. An important point to note is how the favour that God grants us affords us undeserved blessings, tremendously influence, impact, and even save the lives of significant others! Indeed, your attitude determines your altitude and 'your gift makes room for you and brings you before great men (Proverbs 18:16). It is interesting that Paul found favour in the first place. Notwithstanding, the time had come for a crucial decision to be made.

Reflection: How could your attitude to life, others and situations; (your mannerism, demeanour, deportment, personality, faith, and representation of Christ) daily propel you into a position of favour with significant others?

'Jump!'
The situation on the ship in the storm was a fluid one; one that called for wisdom, discernment, and faith. There was a time for remaining on the ship and riding out the storm. Then out of the noise of crashing waves and screams and confusion came the Centurion's orders, 'Jump!' When it is time to jump and not remain on the ship, you have to discern the moment and follow instructions. This was now time for action. The deliberation, panic, contemplation, and reflection had passed now it was time for decisive action. Jump! Stuck within sight of land but far out to sea, will take courage. Disaster struck within sight of shore (v41) so near, almost there but not the final destination. As earlier mentioned, there is always that pain of riding straight into a storm within sight of your hopes, dreams, and destination even though you are still in transition.

Have you ever been stuck betwixt and between? These are the conflict of the human condition. These are the vicissitudes of life; too far out to be in and too far in to be out. When to remain and when to jump, to speak or hold your peace; to resign or to remain, to leave a relationship or job or to stay, to invest or to wait, to terminate a contract or to sustain it. When you have weighed up your options and made a decision from your choices, it is reassuring; but you still need the courage and the faith now to Jump! In John 12:27, Jesus demonstrates this dichotomy: 'Now My soul is troubled, and what shall I say? "Father, save me from this hour"? No, it is for this purpose that I have come to this hour.' Let this cup pass, but not my will. The internal conflict and the intersection of your will and God's will formulate your cross!

Three Categories: Strategies to Safety
Although the order to jump was given, there was a systematic manner to do so. You would think that in the mass confusion, panic and fear it would have been a total free for all; an intensely clumsy and boisterous heaving, shoving, and panicking as each man for himself jumped into the sea to save 'number one.' But no, there was a strategy in the storm. Even when you are sure of your decision to cope with that stormy situation, you still need a strategy on how to progress. How will you approach your situation? Yes, all is pressing in and you have an important decision to make. No doubt the lives, livelihoods, health and wellbeing of others depend on your one decision. What is your strategy? The centurion identified three categories and allowed them off the broken vessel accordingly:

1. Swimming Unaided
Firstly, those who could swim were ordered to jump first and swim to shore. In every storm, you will find that you or others in your circle of association have the courage, power, anointing, gifts and talents and abilities to 'jump and swim to shore unaided.' That is, you may have the wherewithal to be proactive and to take the scary plunge to realise your goals, target, purpose, or destination. You may have had years of education, training, expertise, rehearsals, preparation, setbacks and sacrifices to qualify you to be in that first

category. Your success comes at a price and a great cost to you.

Some might look at you as you jump or prepare to jump and think 'oh, you are so gifted and talented' or you are so bright and clever or still, you were 'born with gold spoon in your mouth!' Alas, some of that might or might not be so. Yes, you might be gifted and talented or naturally endowed in some situations or areas of your life; however, there is a time when you have to earn your way to the top. The truth is, the glory has a story and people often tend to see the former and not contemplate the latter. People will see your successes, but you know your secrets. You know what it cost you to get there. You know the cares, the tears and the fears. They see your well-polished, successful, accomplished self, swimming to shore. However, do they consider your years of preparation, process, and problems? Do they consider your countless hours of rehearsals before your recital, or the number of failures, setbacks, mishaps, mistakes, and disappointments you have suffered en route? In fact, 'genius is nothing but labour and diligence' (Hogarth 1697-1764). Thomas Edison (1847-1931) also confirms that 'Genius is one per cent inspiration and ninety-nine per cent perspiration.' Indeed, the price must be paid, the course must be steered, and plans must be laid (Schuller).

You may fall in the category of the servant who was given 5 talents of his master's money (Matthew 25). As mentioned earlier, he wisely invested it and had 10 to return to his master by way of a return on his investments for which he was greatly praised and highly commended. However, investment is a risky business. He could have lost a part or the entirety thereof. Be careful how you judge those who can swim unaided to shore amidst the stormy blast from the stricken ship.

I will also refer to this category as the 'get on with it' people. There are people who whatever they face, they never get stressed, worked up and flustered; they simply get on with it. They are the ones who accomplished great things without complaining, whatever life threw at them. The problem is that they can be one of the most frequently misunderstood groups. This is so as others assume, quite wrongly, that they are always ok. Just because someone is quiet, pensive, or passive and simply carries on seemingly effortlessly without a fuss does not necessarily mean that they are all well.

They too have their cares, fears, and tears. They might be swimming unaided and could very well be doing so effortlessly. However, they could also be doing it afraid anyway. Being gifted, talented, or duly qualified does not necessarily remove fear, doubt, or stress. For courage, it is said, is not the absence of fear but the conquering of it. For Twain (1835-1910), 'Courage is resistance to fear, mastery of fear, not absence of fear.' Some people are just better at confronting, controlling and eventually conquering their complexities. This category of unaided swimmers was exposed to danger of death like everyone else but took a risk anyway. They may be numbered among those who suffer silently, scream inwardly and cry unseen in the still of night. Sadly, these are the screams of silent frustration. Unfortunately, few have the discernment to detect this. No wonder some ministers fall. I am not excusing the conduct or behaviours. However, without nurture, care, refreshing, replenishing the energies, as one ministers to others, this could be a recipe for burnout and ultimate disaster.

Never for once, believe that they are not in need of comfort, encouragement, and prayerful support. Never for once, confuse the person with the gift! Being able to swim unaided on the stormy seas out of a traumatic situation does not exempt you from stress, trauma, and personal issues. My mother would say, 'The higher you climb is the more you are exposed.' There is a different set of challenges that await, befall, and is encountered by the gifted, talented, anointed, and successful. There is a tendency for people to look at those who are deemed successful in whatever sphere of life and assume that their lives are perfect and that they have no challenges or problems. Being at the top in whatever sphere brings its own sets of challenges. It is not problem-free at all. The misconception is that once you get to a level of success, life will be smooth sailing and problem-free, how wrong.

Being at the top poses its own unique sets of challenges. Joseph and King David are two very good examples of managing ultimate power and success effectively. For Joseph, after being sold into slavery in Egypt and all the trials he underwent from the pit, the prison, the palace, to being Prime Minister, he still received and forgave his brothers who instigated such evil, forgivingly declaring,

> 'But as for you, you meant evil against me; but God meant it for good, in order to bring it about as it is this day, to save many people alive' (Genesis 50:20).

David similarly had suffered greatly at the hands of King Saul. Yet, in power as King he remembered the friendship he had with Saul's son, Jonathan. One day he asked the question:

> "Is there anyone still left of the house of Saul to whom I can show kindness for Jonathan's sake? 'And Mephibosheth lived in Jerusalem, because he always

ate at the king's table; he was lame in both feet, '(2 Samuels 9:1 & 13).

These are powerful examples of how King David and Joseph even at the epitome of success could still remember kindness and show forgiveness, grace and favour.

As some consider those who swam unaided, the sad comparison is often made at a very fundamental, elementary, and shallow level to their own area of deprivation and lack. Let's take for instance, someone with limited financial resources. Such a one might look with jealousy and resentment at another who is financially secure and incorrectly assumes that all is well with such one. According to Ashimolowo (2000),

'A twisted perception makes you want to be somebody else, therefore leading you to become envious and jealous' (p68).

The truth is that the wealth could be outward expressions and displays rather than genuine prosperity. They could be heavily in debt or living beyond their means. They could also be genuinely financially secure but have struggles in other areas. For example, they could be in poor health, having marital issues; children might be on drugs or on the brink of bankruptcy.

The same principle applies to any area of success. It could be that someone seems so confident and have it all together with all the trappings of success. Yet, it is possible they could be barely hanging on; outwardly confident but inwardly afraid. Nevertheless, if you are in the unaided category, do it afraid! Don't wait for perfection. Go ahead, take the plunge and swim for shore amidst the savage waves of your situation.

I would like to add another important point for this category: Never feel apologetic or ashamed of your accomplishments and successes. You may be made to feel insecure or even guilty for your success. Others may make you feel as if your achievement is just a coincidence. Possibly you were undermined, not recognised, rewarded, respectfully acknowledged, or celebrated for your accomplishments. Success costs, and at every stage thereof you will be required to show resilience and strength of character to stand not just the process, the storm, and the fear but also people's responses to your success.

I remember some years ago in my teaching. There was a student, let us call him 'Jake' He was a clever student who was about fifteen at the time. In fact, he had done so well in Mathematics that he was nationally recognised for his abilities in that area. Yet, the friends he had would disrupt lessons and produced very little work. For them it was not cool to be bright, clever or even respectful to teachers. Low aspiration, apathy, indifference, lack of attention and low-level disruption seem to be the mantra they live by. It was sad that Jake found this association to be desirable.

I will be remembered in my teaching career for one of my many 'wise-sayings' 'Birds of a feather flock together.' By flocking with those birds, Jake soon realised that his gifts, talents and successes, as a bright and clever student, were not recognised or celebrated in his circle. He wanted to be cool and to fit in but the price for him to fit in, was that he embraced their stupidity and adopted their poor attitudes to education and life. What a shame! Jake could be soaring with eagles and not scratching for worms like a chicken.

When you are created to soar. You must choose carefully other 'eagles' who will celebrate your successes and have the same mindset of high aspiration and achievement, without you feeling guilty for your success. True, you need to be humble, respectful, and caring, but that does not mean that you undermine, belittle or feel guilty or ashamed of the gifts, talents, abilities and successes that you have. 'Unto him whom much is given much is required (Luke 12:48).

If you are in the category of unaided swimmers, then take the plunge! Go for it and swim to shore because your life depends on it. Your purpose depends on it. Finding and fulfilling your destiny depend on it. The legacy you leave in the earth after you are long gone depends on it! 'It's not what you take when you leave the world behind you, it's what you leave behind you when you go' (Three Wooden Crosses, Randy Travis).

Be strong enough to resist and overcome the naysayers and swim to your 'shore.' Not everyone will appreciate you. Not everyone will celebrate your successes. Get used to it and move on to your goals.

I am not sure, of the 276 souls on the ship, the number of individuals who were in the category of unaided swimmers. What is clear is that even if you are surrounded by others of similar abilities, purpose or mindset, there comes a time when the storms of life crashes on you in such a way that you have to focus on your personal survival, a bit of 'proper selfishness.'

Nevertheless, being in a group with others of similar interests, abilities and purposes can provide some momentum for success. I am sure you are familiar with the metaphor of the geese flying in a 'V' formation. They build momentum from each other and take turns in leading the flock. Furthermore, it conserves their energy. Each bird flies slightly above the one in front. This results in a reduction of wind resistance. Another benefit to the 'V' formation is that the birds in the group can be accounted for. Flying in formation may also assist with the communication and coordination within the group.

That is very relevant, applicable and helpful as we sojourn the treacherous seas and navigate the hostile paths of life; nevertheless, there are times when you have to go it alone. These are times, when you will need to draw on God's power in a special way. You will need His strength and all the resilience and stick-to-itiveness He has so lavishly bestowed upon you.

2. Grab the Plank!

Secondly, the next category to be ordered off the stricken vessel were those who swam, holding on to planks, boards, timber or beams. These no doubt, had some swimming abilities but were not fully competent in that area, like those who could swim at that depth and for the boisterous duration to shore unaided. Those pieces of timber, beams or boards, all came from the ship, but somehow remained sufficiently intact to provide flotation, some security and support, to make it safely through within their ability range.

The important thing at the end of the day, is that you made it safely through. So often we are carried away with the saving vehicle of success, focusing on 'the what' of success rather than the fact that you are successful. God can use strange things to bless and rescue you! You might even be tempted to compare yourself with those who swam unaided. But use what you have. Use what life affords you. Grabbing and using a plank in this instance does not necessarily mean that you might not be an unaided swimmer in another situation or context! Life is far too complicated to be that linear. You could be strong in one situation and weak in another; you might be weak in one but strong in another. Perhaps, in more shallow waters or closer to shore, you would not need the plank to support you and would have been numbered among the unaided swimmers.

Your challenge, therefore, is to grab hold of your plank, from the raging sea that life affords you and pluck the courage to head for shore there on. Your long, flat piece of sawn timber or wood implies that it has been previously processed. Life sometimes hands you or provides on stormy seas, the raw materials for success through your trials and processes. You may also have been the recipient of the grace, mercy and favour of God. Others have gone before you to pave the way for you to follow to aspire, to achieve and to realise your God-given potential, purpose, and destiny. They provide resources, values, attitudes, and experiences to guide you.

In other words, others have suffered and sacrificed, laboured and languished, worked and worried, toiled and travelled in order to hand you or make available a plank to move on. It may be tossed all over on the raging seas and not necessarily handed to you; however, someone facilitated the opportunity whereby you could benefit from a plank.

I tell my students all the time that 'the students should be greater than the teacher.' All the storms I have been through, the incidents, accidents, traumas, and the harsh lessons I learnt from the school of hard knocks, I now package like a smoother plank that I endured, and use it to inspire, motivate, encourage, and challenge others. Therefore, if life hands you a smooth, shaven piece of wood, at least someone took the trouble to prepare it. This implies that you are the recipient of it and did not have to start from scratch to progress to your destination. Instead of comparisons or complaining therefore, you owe a debt of gratitude to those who prepared your plank so you have something to hold on to for dear life to get through your storms to safety!

Your teachers, parents, older siblings, friends, religious leaders, mentors, or any significant other may have poured into you and given you something to work with. Indeed, it might not be much. However, be thankful for and use 'not enough.' It could be that you were encouraged, supported, looked after, and equipped with the values, morals, beliefs, attitudes, skills, education, expertise, training, and the wherewithal to surmount the challenges of life. You may also have been the beneficiary of physical, emotionally, mental, psychological, spiritual, academic, or financial help to move forward in life. The point is that whatever you have gotten or not received to help you weather your storms in life, the truth is that life has given to all of us something to work with.

You may feel that you have been hard done by and that life has been unfair to you. No doubt when you look at your misfortunes and all the bad things that have befallen you, you may be justified in thinking that way. You have felt your pain, and no one can truly understands. However, I believe that there comes a time when we all have to face our worse fears and make a decision: either for growth and success or death of our dreams and stagnation and non-realisation of purpose. It is your choice.

Never forget that even though you were not in the category to swim unaided, you still have the ability to swim, albeit with the help of the plank. It is possible sometimes to disqualify yourself from the unaided category through fear. You may have remained on board 'the ship' when you should have gone unaided. Sometimes you may need to be more confident in yourself, knowing your strength, abilities, and capabilities. On other occasions, you might need someone to have the faith to believe for you until you can believe in and for yourself.

Reflection: Can you think of some opportunities you have missed in life through insecurities and fear?

You were just as good or even better than those or some of those who moved out unaided, but you were restrained by fear, doubt and insecurity. Maybe you were belittled, bullied, ridiculed, or told 'you would never amount to anything!' and you sadly, internalised that negativity.

Your early formation or even adult experiences could adversely affect your life chances. However, I want to help you to change your paradigm and adopt a new way of thinking; a new way of processing what happened to you, a new way of moving forward to achieve your full potential and be the best you can be. You have potential, talents, gifts, abilities, and capabilities. You may not be for whatever reason, in the unaided category but look at you…you have the wherewithal to swim!

For sure, life hands you a plank or better still, you had to jump from the stricken vessel and frantically ride the boisterous waves to grab one amidst the chaos and pandemonium, while so many others were reaching for the same plank. You are making progress to shore despite navigating your way through a storm, and undoubtedly, equipment that is more appropriate would have been so much better. Nevertheless, you have something to work with! Use what life affords you. Use the something that life gives you, even if it is the remnant of what used to be.

Never yield to the temptation of comparing yourself with others. I have a powerful statement for you:

You have all you need for your success!

You may say,

'I don't believe that!'

Well, others can believe in you until you believe in yourself, or they may even hand you a plank or otherwise facilitated the opportunity for you to obtain the plank yourself. Whatever it is, the fact is that you now have a plank. What are you going to do with it? You have decisions and choices to make in life. You can bemoan your situation and complain about who left, who were not there for you or who said you would fail. On the contrary, you can say 'That was then, this is now!' grab the plank, and head for shore!

What will you do? While some are fortunate enough to be handed a plank, you may have to swim and be tossed mercilessly about by the savage waves round and about the broken vessel to fetch your plank, then find a way to navigate the stormy blast to safety. Whatever is broken in your life, you may have to circumnavigate it, encompassing it about in desperate attempts with fervent resolve just to locate and lay hold on your piece of plank. The process can be daunting, draining, time-consuming and frustrating. As each time you identified and located a plank, the rough waves washed it a little way further from your reach, or another snatched it before you. This is part of the frustration that life's circumstances can pose. However, it provides an opportunity for your reach to surpass your immediate grasp.

The process of identifying what you need to help you fulfil your purpose and achieve your goals can be daunting. It takes courage to believe you can fit into this category, to swim to the shore of success from this distance out at sea. After you have identified and secured your plank, you now have the unenviable task of now making your way through your fears, through your doubts, through your limited resources to land. This requires self-confidence and faith in God, but also faith in yourself and your ability and capability. Paul said, 'I can do all things through Christ who strengths me' (Philippians 4:13). It is going to be through Christ, but you have to do it! He provides the people, the process and the plank but you make the journey, swallowing water, crashing into others, occasionally losing your plank and frantically grabbing it again, tossed violently by savage winds and boisterous waves, but making it safely through eventually.

Your 'plank' might be your faith, words of affirmation, prophesy and faith spoken over your life; it may be your skills, abilities, education, and training. Whatever or whoever life provides you with to help you make sense of your storm and assist you through its stormy blast, is your 'plank'. Whether your plank is temporal, spiritual or both, hold on with firm resolve and purpose in your heart to make it safely through whatever storms you are facing today. You need your source of strength for this test.

As God told Elijah as he sat hopelessly under the Juniper trees in deep depression, 'Arise and eat for the journey is too great for thee' (1 Kings 19:9). Sometimes you may have underestimated your process and not realised how much it costs you or how burnt out and drained you really are because of what you went through. Proverbs 17:22 (NLT) reminds us that 'A cheerful heart is good medicine, but a broken spirit saps a person's strength.' Life provides you with a plank; whether it was handed to you, or you had to survive some life-threatening storms to locate, secure it then then use it to your advantage to successfully navigate your way to safety and success.

3. The Broken Pieces

Thirdly, the final category is equally or even more intriguing. This category represents the ones who did not swim unaided, neither did they secure planks; instead, their only hope for safety was through identifying, locating, securing, and using the broken pieces of the ship to make it safely to shore. The crashing of the vessel into the sandbank where the two seas met was undeniably a terrifying experience for all on board the ship. So great was the devastation that the ship began to fall apart at the hind parts. The word of prophesy earlier given by Paul had now come to pass:

> 'There will be no loss of life, but there will be damage to the ship and property will be lost' (Acts 27:22).

This was not the time for fear but faith. The evidence did not support this position, but Paul knew the outcome based on his experiences and encounter with God. He held firmly to his faith even in the storm. Your personal faith and deep conviction could save not just your life, job, relationship, business, or health but also those around you whether in your family, job or sphere of influence and associations.

After those who plunged into the raging sea unaided and those on planks, the last category to head to shore was those who did so, on broken pieces. We do not know how many were in this category and how they felt about their lot. Was the choice made for them or did they believe that they could make it safely to shore on the broken pieces of the ship? It is possible that sometimes choices are made for us through the circumstances that life throws at us. Decisions and choices could also be made for us because of the selfishness, stubbornness, greed, and insensitivity of others; for example, the centurion and the ship's owner. The reality that you are now in that situation necessitates a critical response. Now is not the time for a post mortem. That can be done at another time, but now is the time for survival…it is now life or death.

I find it very interesting the stages of intervention police and rescue services employ especially when someone is missing. There is a stage for search and rescue; however, in some cases sadly it progresses to search and recover. Search and rescue implies that there is still hope for life; but this stage has a time limit. The rescuers feel immense pain, are drained, tired yet hopeful, until when they have to call off the search and rescue and declare it is now a search and recovery. This phase can be unbearable and traumatic for them as well as for the families of the missing loved ones.

When the ship was broken up, there was no longer any hope for the vessel. The once valuable cargo also was now useless, some of it already dumped to lighten the ship previously to prevent capsizing. The reality now is that property is lost, and the ship is broken, damaged beyond repair. All that can be done now is to move to the recovery stage. The command was given, to use broken pieces from the stricken vessel to head to shore. Interestingly, that was the strange provision made for this third category. It was their strategy and method to survival. No doubt, they paddled frantically in the deep and raging sea identifying and securing suitably safe broken pieces, upon which no doubt their lives depended.

I examine with keen interest those who swam unaided and those who made it safely through on planks; however, I am even more intrigued by this third and final category. The implication of brokenness is that the vessel was at one point whole and intact. The process of life on the stormy sea now rendered the once full, total, entire and unabridged vessel now broken. It was wrecked, fragmented, shattered, ruined, and destroyed.

Reflection: What in your life through the process you are going through has been shattered, broken, ruined, destroyed, and fragmented? Could it be your hopes and dreams, aspirations and plans, career, family, finances, marriage, business venture, reputation, or your faith?

The broken pieces of the ship where jagged, rough, and splinted with sharp and uncomfortable bits. I can understand those on planks with much smoother formations, but can you imagine the broken pieces that were not cut and carefully designed and shaped. Once they were, but now the broken pieces are mainly sharp, pointed, rough, serrated, and spiky. They were not carefully carved and shaped in the manufacturing process instead battered and broken by the deadly waves they were formed without due process and care for comfort, health, or safety. The truth is they started out beautifully carved and shaped in the same manufacturing process as the plank but now beaten down by life's storms, they were now a sharp, pointed and jagged broken piece.

Reflection: What do you do when life has beaten and broken you down into a pointy, fragmented, spiky piece of seemingly hopeless wood? Do you now hurt others or yourself in response to the traumatic experiences you may have had? Has the abused become an abuser?

You may have suffered greatly in your formative years, neglected, and abused, the dysfunction might have been too much for you, or later in life your decisions and choices or those made for you may land you in a sticky and prickly predicament. You feel hopeless and useless,

> *'My life is a wreck' you may say. 'I am no good or no use to anybody, I serve no useful purpose.'*

Nevertheless, just when you thought it was all hopeless and useless, in the midst of your wreck, your disaster and shattered dream, look! others have now gathered around in desperation to grab your broken pieces to use as catalysts to swim safely to shore.

Reflection: Can you for one minute imagine that your brokenness could be the implement of 'salvation' to someone's calamity? What you thought was useless junk now becomes the ultimate strategy and method of saving yours and others' lives, hopes and dreams in grave distress and danger of death. How do you feel about your shipwreck?

What is your attitude to your shattered dreams, fragmented future, destroyed destiny, smashed situations, cracked confidence, and ruined resolve? Could it be that your brokenness was intended to provide a safe passage to you or others to success along the stormy seas of life?

Although the vessel was shattered and broken with pieces scattered and drifting aimlessly in the boisterous seas, yet the broken pieces would be salvaged and turned into useful, life-saving flotation devices for the safe passage of desperate souls to ultimate safety. Indeed, do not cry over what you have lost, instead use what you have left!

All in This Together

Whether swimming unaided, on planks or on broken pieces, all souls were in the same situation; surrounded by deep, boisterous waves with the potential of death not far away. They encountered the danger of the distance and the darkness. There were different abilities, capabilities, gifts, talents and things to work with, but all had the chance for survival. The method, device or strategy might be different, however all had to use the same water to get to shore. They also had to use what they had left out of the situation. This is not the time to reminisce on how wonderful the 'ship' was in its whole state. It was time to grab what was left of the brokenness and use it to get to shore.

Firstly, the word of affirmation, assurance and prophesy was given that although there would be destruction of the ship and loss of the cargo, there would be no loss of life. Words may have been spoken over your life to the detriment of your dreams. I earlier spoke about reversing the negative utterances and speaking positively over your situation and life. You may have to take control of your life and start to move forward in confidence toward your dreams.

Paul says, '... One thing I do: Forgetting what is behind and straining toward what is ahead" (Philippians 3:13, NIV). So, whether you find the strength and resolve within you, or someone believes for you until you dare to believe and dream again, the responsibility rests solely on you to make your way to shore howsoever you will, using whatever life throws at you. You have to use what you have, as mentioned earlier not what you have lost. The past is gone, behind you; learn from it, and move on. Experiences are crucial. Your history can inform your present and future however, your future is not necessarily tied up in your past. Indeed, your past experiences on the seas do form part of your story which can now propel you into purpose and destiny and be a source of encouragement, comfort, and inspiration to countless others.

Characteristics of the Broken Pieces

A unique feature of this category lies with the composition of the floatation device. The jagged nature of the broken pieces is well established and documented. While those on the planks most certainly suffered grave discomfort of the wood being violently tossed back and forth, above and below on the treacherous waves, those on broken pieces had an additional source of pain and distress. As mentioned, the pointed, uneven, spiky, and sharp ends of the broken pieces as they were savagely ripped from the ship by the angry waves, now form the basis of all they had to hold on to in order to make it safely to shore.

Reflection: How do you respond when the thing you are holding on to for your change, hope, survival, livelihood, and life is hurting you?

You took the courage to plunge into the deep and mighty ocean of your situation, mustering the last ounce of faith and courage within you; desperately and frantically grabbing a broken piece of what used to be. You reached forth and held it not as if, but because life depended on it. Grabbing it in and of itself was no mean feat. There was a process and time lapse between making the plunge and identifying then grasping the shattered broken piece.

Only you know the fear you feel and the time that lapsed between these processes as you gasped your broken piece and while being tossed helplessly; propelled high then low then high again on the angry waves. You aimed and reached then grasped but it eluded you. Frantically you repeated this process so many times until you finally succeed. Then that was only part of the process, as now you have to lay hold on that which was shattered and broken and use the same for your only hope to safety and survival. You struggled desperately deep within, but you found the strength to start the process to shore…on broken pieces. Now the thing that should take you over is hurting you.

It is hard to conceptualise vaguely the fact, that your broken pieces are the remnants of what was previously whole, entire, unabridged, complete, full, and total in your life. All your hopes, dreams, plans, achievements and successes, now ruined and all that remain are broken pieces of the same. You may be tempted to throw it all away. You may think 'what a waste of my life, time, space, resources, emotional or financial investments. What if I had made different choices or how could things have turned out differently had I made the decisions and choices rather than having them made for me by others with their own motives and agenda; whether these were selfish or made out of love or care though misguided'. Maybe someone thought they were doing you a favour, but it backfired spectacularly now you have to pick up the broken pieces of your life and carry on.

For the Joy Ahead
As I reflect on the issue of keeping focus while on the broken pieces with the pain, humiliation, despair, disappointment, and destiny detour, I can only think of a powerful strategy that Jesus employed as He contemplated the cross. The Scripture declares that,

> *'But for the joy that was set before Him he endured the cross and despised the shame….' (Hebrews 12:2).*

This is indeed powerful. Having a goal and something to focus on through your pain and the storms of life is a helpful strategy to employ in order to help see you through. As dark as the path may be, there has to be a 'light at the end of the tunnel.'

It may seem so patronising and insensitive to believe that good can come out of all situations especially when we consider the death of our loved ones. No words can express the intense pain and emptiness that pierce your lonely heart in the stillness of night as alone you shed warm and bitter tears. As you grasp your broken piece of wood salvaged from the remnant of your former wholeness and what used to be. But 'everything has the same component as its source' (Munroe, 1991, p. 103). The broken pieces are remnants from the previously whole ship. So too, what you have left are remnants of what was previously whole in your life.

You feel and endure the pain of desperately holding on to the thing that should take you over, that is now hurting you. Is there something hurting you, that you are holding on to for your safety, security and survival? You need it but it hurts. You are spent emotionally, mentally, physically, spiritually and financially; yet you are holding on. Maybe it is your job that you have given so many years of your life to or your child into whom you have poured so much, your marriage, business or ministry. You need them to see you through to the next level, but the truth is that they are the broken pieces, which are hurting you. You love them but it hurts to love.

Hold on to your broken pieces and continue for shore. It is not your final destination, but it is your immediate destination along your path and process. Like the widow with the last of the flour and the oil, Moses with his stick and stammer, David with a rag and a rock, the disciples with twelve baskets of crumbs, all you have is what you have left. We are reminded that,

> *When they (the multitude) had all had enough to eat, he said to his disciples, "Gather the pieces that are left over. Let nothing be wasted." (Matthew 14:20).*

Your success does not lie in who left you or what you have lost along the way but in what you have left. In other words, your success, security, and safety lie in picking up the shattered dreams and broken pieces from what you had and using the broken pieces salvaged therefrom to now, chart a new course to success, purpose and destiny. Indeed, some through the water, some through the fire, some through the flood but all through the blood. So regardless of your path, problems, processes you have your own cross to bear. It is tailored and unique to you but will make it through even on broken pieces. Do not compare yourself with others, they too have their cross. If you have a personal relationship with Christ, then you would have come through His shed blood on Calvary's cross.

Don't Worry About What You Lost, Use What You Have Left

As we made it to shore, we look out for each other but understood every man must carry his load. There is a cross, a storm, a story, a process for each and every one of us. These will be different and initiated or instigated differently, but we will find ourselves in situations that require deep reflection, ingenuity, sacrifices, encouragement, prayer, resilience, coping strategies and faith.

Life, circumstances or others may have endowed differently but you use what life has given you. Whether swimming unaided, on planks or on the broken pieces of the ship, all were in the same depth of water, all faced death, all had the same distance to swim to shore and all faced the same fearful and angry waves, despite different abilities and categories.

The three categories indeed had different tools to work with, but each had something. Life will never leave you with nothing. Even if you have lost everything, you still have something, which you can be salvaged from your brokenness to resurrect and propel you into greatness. Businesses have failed and owners go into bankruptcy and later arise, rebrand, and start over to greater levels of success. Seemingly hopeless situations can be turned around and used for the benefit of self or others and God's glory.

I reiterate life is not a simple straightforward journey. There are mountains, valleys, highs, lows, sickness, health, riches, poverty, successes, failures, the bitter and the sweet, the good times and the bad. Whilst I have identified three categories that made it safely to shore, yet you may not be stuck in a particular category. It is possible to be in one category at a particular time in life when you are going through a particular storm and in another category or on another occasion. In one situation, you could be endowed bountifully to swim unaided. That is let us say for instance that you may be good at finances and investment planning, but a recession or Covid-19 caused your business to go under. You may have staff and expenses to pay while no income is coming in. You may have workers on the government's furlough scheme, but you have to subside it or the scheme ends.

You have difficult decisions to make about the future of your business and worse still, the livelihood of your loyal and dedicated staff. Can you retain them after furlough, or do you have to make them redundant or even close the business for good? These are stressful decisions to make. Yet some businesses, rebrand themselves, diversify and start doing something else from the shattered dreams of a family business going on for generations. They start to deliver meals instead of dining; some businesses even start producing hand sanitisers, face masks and ventilators as they grab hold of what they have left from the broken dreams and make it safely through on broken pieces.

So, you have strengths, talents and giftings in different places. In one storm you may also be the one on the plank and yet another, on broken pieces. Again, life is not straightforward, it requires flexibility and adaptability. You may start out unaided and later have to, later grab a plank or a broken piece. You have started out on broken pieces, but later grab hold of a plank or even develop the confidence to swim unaided. Maybe the pain from the broken piece was too great or you finally developed the confidence to go unaided!

Your well-planned out life can change in an instance, and how you move forward has a lot to do with your attitude, mindset and ability through faith to pick up the broken pieces of what used to be and make it safely through on your broken pieces. Whether you perceive yourself to be a 5, 2 or 1 talent servant (Matthew 25:14–30), use what life has given you and make a return on your Master's investment in you. Increase your profitability, and leave a legacy in the earth. If you are thus endowed to swim unaided then go for it, accomplish your goals, and seek new and more challenging ones. If on planks, then in like manner, achieve in proportion to your endowment of gifts and talents.

If all you have is the jagged remains of what used to be, then weep if you must, mourn as required but use the broken shattered, cracked, prickly, fragmented pieces to restart, continue, or progress with your life. It is your process on the stormy seas on broken pieces of board. Make something out of it.

Reflection: How do you process your journey, your circumstances and your storms? Do you buckle under fear, unbelief, hopelessness, numbness, lack or loss of direction, regret, guilt, or do you demonstrate faith hope, resilience, purpose and direction?

Accept the help that others may offer, it may be directing you to your plank or taking you to your broken pieces. Do not despise their help. Isn't it what Jesus asked of Martha, 'Show me where you lay him?' In other words, take me to the place of your brokenness, the place where your dreams were shattered and died; the lonely desolate place where it seems like nothing can ever be salvaged from your fragmented wreck. Help can come from strange places.

The prisoners on the ship did not even know Paul, yet they benefited from his favour. The favour shown to him by the centurion rubbed off on them. They were not killed for Paul's sake. In addition, the divine revelation he got paved the way for assurance that no lives would be lost despite destruction of the ship and loss of cargo. In fact, everyone on board including the centurion and the ship's owner benefited. Your help could be from strange places and persons.

Reflection: How open are you to receive such help and who could you be helping by your obedience and presence within your sphere of influence?

You will need to build on your perception, faith, personality, mindset, associations, attitudes, and actions. At whatever stage you are or category you are in, it is possible that your success will be a source of irritation to some; those who constantly focus on your successes and not your stories, your recitals and not your rehearsals, your glory and not the grinding process, your anointing but not your pressing. This can result in you feeling isolated and even apologetic for having made it through safely and successfully.

Doctoral Thesis Submission and Defence (Viva Voce) – The Process

As I reflect on this process and these categories, I once again contemplate my doctoral journey especially in the final year of my thesis writing and defence (Viva) preparation. Even with the help of supervisors and lecturers, it is not uncommon for students to feel isolated and under-supported and this was my experience at times. With one Methodology tutorial, I had to read extensively and worked independently and rigorously to grasp the concept of a methodology I had never heard of, let alone to use it in a doctoral thesis and be comfortable enough to successfully defend it. That was indeed a storm.

Furthermore, my final external examiner was different from the one mentioned at my final review (the last formal meeting with Chair and two supervisors) prior to final submission of thesis to external examiners. This meant working extremely hard independently and developing the correct mindset and attitude of success instead of murmuring and complaining or allowing myself to be stressed out or tempted to abandon the degree.

It dawned on me that whilst I might have felt this way, it could be that my supervisors saw that I was coping well and did not require as much intervention as I thought I needed. Thus, they gave their time to other students who perhaps needed the help more, possibly. However, I was not told this and if this were so, it would have been good to know that. On the one hand, it could have enhanced my confidence toward my final submission and defence; however, it could also engender a sense of complacency. There is always that difficult balance to strike. Despite all the struggles, academic reversals, the fears, cares and difficulties, I came through successfully even on those broken pieces.

Responses to Your Success: The Glory and the Story

I find it so interesting at times in like manner, as I suffer negatives attitudes and jealousies at my achievements; be it in some responses to achieving my doctorate, where I live or what I drive or my gifts and talents. These are the successes, the glory and the recitals. The process, secrets and the story tell a very different narrative. These were nasty, unflattering and even racist comments made to my face by a significantly small minority. They see the glory but they don't know my story: of hurts, pain, sacrifices, delayed gratification and fervent prayer.

In the late 1980s, due to the negligence of the housing officer at the university, I was briefly made homeless. With no room booked for me as requested in the Halls of residence, I briefly stayed with a friend for a while but also had to cope with many grave inconveniences and discomforts. I know what it is to teach full time in the Caribbean while painting houses, offering piano lessons and doing construction part time during my holidays and weekends.

In the UK, for a whole year after I moved out of London to the county of Kent for a better quality of life, the initial process of transition was challenging. Although we bought a new four-bedroom house, I had not gotten a job locally at the time. We had to consider the journey by train in the night and made a decision. Rhona then resigned her wonderful job. She was the Night Auditor at the prestigious Carlton Towers Hyatt Hotel in glamourous Knightsbridge in Westminster, close to world renowned Harrods. Initially she took on menial tasks in Kent.

I retained my teaching post in London at this time and continued my daily commute. I woke up 4am to travel 8 hours round trip to work to and from London, changing buses and trains 6 times daily. Of course, on those days when I had staff meetings or Parent consultation meetings, I would get home by or close to midnight. On the days when I got home late evenings, we would embark on our janitorial job and on Friday evenings and all-day Saturdays, stack supermarket shelves for £3.50 per hour. In addition to these, I would also serve as an Examiner, marking Citizenship General Certificate in Education (GCSE), Secondary School National Examination over 2 summer holidays at £3.00 per script.

To attend university and embark on 13 years of continuous study (3 degrees) with a full-time job teaching over 700 students every 10 days, simultaneously speaking and preaching in 7 churches, and managing our entrepreneurial venture, with little sleep and great sacrifices, deprivation and feeling of intense isolation. That is the reality. Yet by God's grace, I succeeded in all degrees (BA, First class Honours, and MA, Distinction), having never missed an assignment submission date or having to re-sit an exam. All tuition fees were fully paid. That is the part of the process and the story behind the glory, the rehearsal and the recital, the secret and the success! Indeed, as I learnt in primary school, the poet Henry Wadsworth Longfellow reminds us that,

> *'The heights by great men, reached and kept were not attained by sudden flight; But they while their companions slept, were toiling upward in the night.'*

So, whatever your rehearsal, storms and brokenness some very important questions are:

Reflection: 'Safely through for what, so what is next?' What was the purpose of your struggles? How can you use the process of your storm so that the experience is not wasted?

As you reflect on your storms and the process you just went through or are going through, you need to ascertain how you really feel about your process and how you are making sense of what you went through. It's not really about what happened to you but how you feel about what happened to you. You need to seriously reflect and ascertain whether it was worth it at all and how you can use the experiences, you have gleaned along the way, for the benefit of yours and others.

Success, Purpose and Thanksgiving

I would suggest that you develop a mindset of success, a mindset of purpose and one of thanksgiving. One that strives to be better, not bitter, to have a testimony out of your tests, and messages even out of your messes and triumphs out of your trials. I believe that you can reach forward and glance backwards. What do I mean by this? I mean that as you have come through your deadly storm, unaided, on planks or on broken pieces, or a combination; you do not dwell negatively on the process, instead you press ahead to greater purpose while glancing back to help someone else along the path of life. Possibly, someone might be struggling in the same or similar areas that you have just succeeded in. You are in a good position to offer help and support to them.

For me now, I am helping other doctoral candidates who are struggling with various issues at different stages of the doctoral programmes. I am able to do so because of my attitude through my storm and the fact that I was willing and able to grab a piece broken from my dreams and used it to successfully navigate the stormy blast. Among other things, I am currently lecturing and mentoring university and secondary school students; as well as providing academic references for postgraduate students and training teachers on the Postgraduate in Education Programme at Master's degree level.

Part of my academic storm included me not doing very well at my GCE in 1980 I was home for two weeks unwell during the middle of my GCE exams. I had to fight hard to process this issue and develop the confidence to believe that I had the potential and capability to successfully complete a doctoral degree. The reality hit me when my friend, a psychologist (as we were having an informal conversation), pointed out how well I had done to successfully process and survive so much to reach where I am today. Well, he's known me for nearly 30 years!

As you reach back to help others, you will be authentic, non-judgemental, caring and empathetic. I remember Ezekiel as he sat where the people sat (Ezekiel 3:15). He wanted to challenge them and straighten them out but as he shared their experiences and saw their plight, he was overwhelmed and moved with compassion as he sat where they sat for 7 days in silence. He developed the wherewithal to identify with them, to feel their pain, to care and to understand because he sat where they sat. "I sat among them for seven days--deeply distressed." (v15). Consider also the case with Job in his suffering when his friends came to see him. Then they sat on the ground with him for seven days and seven nights, but no one spoke a word to him because they saw how intense his suffering had become. (Job 2:13).

As you go through your rough times, purpose in your heart to make a difference. You will do so with care and empathy as you reach out to others because of what you have been through. It is possible to be hardened and judgemental because of what you went through; it is possible that you could say,

> *'I went through that and it did not bother me, why should you make it an issue'?*

The truth is you could be gifted and talented in an area that others are not. It could be that the particular challenge others struggle with, does not seem to bother you, because it may not be your 'cross.' However, you have a cross. I have a cross. A specific personally designed challenge that hurts to the core and breaks you in places, which will be different for each of us.

Now, let it go!
The plank and broken pieces: knowing when to let go, it is over! There is a time to hold on to the plank or broken pieces. They provide the hope and stability in the midst of the storm. They assist with flotation and buoyancy and help to allow the holder to keep the head above the water. Undoubtedly, the wood, be it smooth as the plank, or jagged as the broken piece, form a crucial part in the safe passage through the storm. It facilitates the survival of the bearer and provides a crucial solution in a life and death situation. Thus, the importance of the plank and the broken pieces cannot be overstated. However, they have one have common denominator:

they both have a shelf life. In other words, when it comes to their usefulness for this particular task, timing is a factor.

There is a time in life when we hold on dearly for life to that which is crucial for our health, safety, wellbeing or survival. Nonetheless, with experience, we also realise that there comes a time when the very thing that we held on to so desperately to take us over, must now be released as the mission is accomplished. It takes wisdom to discern and judge when that time is. In some situations, it might be more obvious than in others: when to speak or when to hold your peace, to invest or to wait. You may have difficult decisions regarding: whether to study the financial market or count the cost some more, to break off an association or friendship or to hold on; to divorce or remain married. Perhaps it is whether or not to voluntarily withdraw from that degree programme or to hold on, to remain in that job unfulfilled with low pay or hold on, to continue supporting a child who refuses to learn from his or her continued risk-taking behaviours and lifestyle or to bear with them some more. Life presents these difficult scenarios with no clear answers or manuals to guide your decisions and choices.

Notwithstanding, there comes a time when the plank and the broken pieces have served their useful purposes and must now be abandoned and discarded. Few times in life there are when these are kept on as reminders or souvenirs or as 'memorials' of thanksgiving. Some for instance, after extracting a tooth following a period of intense pain and discomfort ask the dentist for the tooth to be kept as a reminder of the process endured. I am not sure I want to keep it but then, to each his or her own.

Part of the success to deliverance after the storm is in knowing when to release what carried you over. This can sound a bit ungrateful however, it is not so. The reality is that the wood has served its purpose and now that you have reached safely to shore require that you release that which carried or supported you because its part in your story is physically over. Like the scaffolding on a building site to facilitate easy access during its construction or painting, it is useful during these processes but after the building is completed, the scaffolding is removed and rightly so. It would be strange and unsightly to retain the scaffolding after the completion of the building. One crucial essential in life is to know when to let go, that is to know, recognise and realise that something or someone's part in your story is over.

There is a time and place for gratitude and appreciation, I cannot emphasise this more. One of the things that greatly annoys me is ingratitude and lack of appreciation. I firmly believe that there is much room for these values and virtues to be promoted, preserved and protected in our relationships. We should remember those who have been there for us, who have helped us along the stormy seas and supported us along the narrow and winding path of life. How can we not show our appreciation and gratitude? We should be mindful of those who form part of our stories, who are there for us spiritually, emotionally, mentally, academically, socially and in every way. Yet, there is a time for wisdom, a time and place of separation like Ruth, Naomi and Orpah, like Abraham, Isaac and the servants, like Jesus who sent people outside the room before performing healing miracles.

This is not about discarding, using, or exploiting people or things but rather, it is about having the spirit of discernment to know when someone or something's part in your story is simply over. All 276 souls on the stricken ship had made it safely to shore; some swam unaided, others on planks and still others on broken pieces of the ship. There was no longer any need for the planks or the broken pieces. They could have been kept as souvenirs but that might not be very practical. Furthermore, the fire that was later kindled (in the next section), would not benefit from these pieces of wood, as they were soaked from the perilous journey and even then, too large for the purpose of firewood.

The simple fact was that their part and purpose in the story was over. Release it and let it go. It was necessary then but now it has served its role and is no longer needed.

Reflection: What or who do you need to 'release' that played a role in your life however, continued association may be toxic?

It does not have to be a person. It could be a thing or idea, attitude, value, mindset or perception. These could be counter-productive to health, wealth, well-being and success; although they have served their part in your story and are no longer required for the next season, chapter, or level in your life and story.

Take Up Your Bed and Walk
There is another important life lesson to reiterate from this. It has to do with times when the thing that once carried you is now the thing that you carry. This is an important and interesting concept. Let us think of the man who was lame and was carried to Jesus on the stretcher by his friends after making a mess of someone's roof in order to get this man to Jesus. Touched by their faith Jesus healed the man,

> *'Arise take up your bed and walk' Jesus said, 'your sins be forgiven thee' (Luke 7:48).*

Carrying the thing that once carried him was humbling but also served as a constant reminder of his story, process and the path through which he had come successfully. This process and humility kept him genuine and authentic, non-judgemental, caring and empathetic.

After the Storm
After your storm, you have a decision to make on your response. It is possible to have a sense of relief, gratitude, or numbness, shock, disbelief or even regret. It depends on how you pull through and your attitude, in through and after your storm. Sometimes the process might take too much. Nevertheless, it is important that you remain standing regardless of the challenge. Like Noah after the flood, you may build an altar of thanksgiving; or David after the baby born to Bathsheba died, he (after his period of intense grieving),

> *'Then David got up from the ground. After he had washed, put on lotions and changed his clothes, he went into the house of the LORD and worshiped. Then he went to his own house, and at his request they served him food, and he ate (2 Samuel 12:20 NIV).*

When you look back at your storm you have pulled through and the reality you actually made it that can be surreal. The truth is that after every storm you are building something. You can build an altar of worship, thanksgiving and praise; as you are amazed by the goodness of God and how he brought you safely through though so undeserving. On the contrary, you may build an altar of resentment, shock, anger, regret, bitterness and fear. However, you can choose to go to the house of the Lord to worship showing your appreciation, choosing rather the giver than the gift, the ways than the acts of God; or you can go to your 'own house' and relish in your own efforts, confiding in your own competence.

Deuteronomy 8 (NIV) reminds us to,

> *Be careful that you do not forget the Lord your God, failing to observe his commands, his laws and his decrees that I am giving you this day. Otherwise, when you eat and are satisfied, when you build fine houses and settle down, and when your herds and flocks grow large and your silver and gold increase and all you have is multiplied, then your heart will become proud and you will forget the Lord your God, who brought you out of Egypt, out of the land of slavery.'*

We are also reminded of the storms and trials He brought us through,

> *He led you through the vast and dreadful wilderness, that thirsty and waterless land, with its venomous snakes and scorpions. He brought you water out of hard rock. He gave you manna to eat in the wilderness, something your ancestors had never known, to humble and test you so that in the end it might go well with you.'*

Never for once think that you did it all by yourself and that your success is predicated on your status, wealth, training, expertise, education, gifts, talents or abilities.

> *'You may say to yourself, "My power and the strength of my hands have produced this wealth for me." But remember the Lord your God, for it is He who gives you the ability to produce wealth (NIV)*

The 'wealth' you have amassed may be in the form of prosperity, affluence, means, capital, treasure, fortune or riches; however, it may also be in the form of influence, spiritual growth, attitudes, values, renewed mind sets, changes in paradigm, extended Christian ministry and outreach to others. In fact,

> 'Beloved, I wish above all things that thou mayest prosper and be in health, even as thy soul prospereth' (3 John 2:2).

Reflection: What are your motives for building and are you traumatised by the experience or empowered thereby? How did you come through and what did you make of the experience and most importantly, what did the experience make of you?

If you build and remain in fear you would not have maximised the opportunities for progress and purpose. However, building in faith demonstrates gratitude and trust in God's sovereignty. Faith, because although you might have just had a traumatic experience and suffered loss, yet you rejoice that God brought you through safely and although you have lost some things along the way that are valuable to you, yet you trust Him to restore the lost and stolen years.

That measure of faith embraces the scripture that indeed, 'all things work together for the good of them who are called according to His purpose' (Romans 8:28); that faith knows that God will get the glory from your story, He will be magnified in the situation and others will benefit therefrom. Faith in thanksgiving realises that often God incubates greatness in tight places…places of affliction, of crushing and of trials. With this in mind, you can temper your perception and mindset to accept though painful, that God is in control and that it will in some seemingly strange and crazy way, work out eventually for your good. For Warren (2002),

> *'The events in your life work together in God's plan; they are not isolated acts, but interdependent parts of the process to make you Christ like' (p. 196).*

'Independent parts' like the planks or the broken pieces of the ships or like the left overs in a tasty meal, all form part of a previous whole.

Whenever I speak whether in England, Jamaica or the Cayman Islands and I sometimes refer to Romans 8:28. I refer to Rhona's baking. She will have the raisins being soaked in wine for months and can you imagine the flavour they add to the fruit cakes or bread pudding! When she is baking her Christmas fruit cakes, which she is very good at, I notice that she has all these ingredients which she adds: the egg, raisons, nutmeg, butter, vanilla, flour and so forth, the truth is I don't really know what else! The point though is that I would not partake of these or other ingredients of themselves singly; in fact, I could not relish the thought of eating any one of them separately.

However, when they are mixed together after that laborious process, they come together to make a most scrumptious cake. Admittedly, I do not participate in the act of preparation but do gladly help myself to the finished product! Sometimes, Rhona hides some of the finished product, but through divine revelation, I locate the finished product and gladly partake there-of. The point, life's experiences in and of themselves, though bitter and unpalatable, when viewed or perceived in isolation are not in and of themselves good. However, in the grand scheme of things or the overall picture, or at the end of all the troubles, will turn out well for you.

Greatness is borne out of affliction. 'The more they were afflicted the more they grew' (Genesis 1:12). This account depicts the story of the children of Israel in Egypt. I believe that this should be our response to life's adversity. Out of evil should come forth good and out of weakness, strength. I like the verse of Scripture that reminds us that, '...we have this treasure in earthen vessels that the excellency of the power may be of God and not of us' (2 Corinthians 4:7). We are flawed mortals, yet we can find strength in the power of our all-powerful and all-knowing God, the Omnipotent and Omniscient One. Munroe (2003) argues that:

> *'God often gives us dreams that initially confound us because He wants to make sure we don't attempt to fulfil them apart from Him...God will never give you a vision without the provision for it' (p. 166).*

Plan Your Celebrations

I personally believe in and strongly advocate the acknowledgement of success. I believe that successes should be recognised, acknowledged and celebrated. You have paid the price and been through your storm, now go give thanks and prayerfully celebrate.

As an Educator for over 38 years, I have seen and attended many Prize-giving and Award ceremonies. Here in England, I have attended three of my own graduations at the world-famous Canterbury Cathedral in Kent, UK. I have also sponsored an annual prize and monetary award, *'The Dr Phillip O'Connor's prize for Principles and Values'* at my own educational establishment, for the student who shows resilience and perseverance through grave setbacks and challenges yet overcame to achieve great things academically or personally. I believe in celebrating success. The late Doctor Myles Munroe (2003) states,

> *'Prayer sustains us in the demands of vision. God will bring you through your difficulties and give you the victory through prayer based on His Word' (p. 213).*

You know what it costs to get to where you are now. You know the storms, the problem and the process. The 'shipwreck' and the 'fierce storms' you have endured to get to where you are on life now. You have earned the right to celebrate your success. You took time for thanksgiving now celebrate!

In Genesis 1:31 it is interesting to note that at the end of each day of Creation:

'… God looked over all he had made, and he saw that it was very good!' I like that. Surely, the entire creation was not finished, yet God called what He had done that day, 'Good!' Paul and the others crashed off the shore of Malta. They were going to Italy. That was not their final destination.

Yet, build a fire, warm yourself, refresh yourself, be rejuvenated and receive the kind hospitality provided for the next leg of the journey. It is important that you take the time to recognise and celebrate the small steps (some call them 'marginal gains') en-route to your destiny.

Do not wait for success; get started without it. Do not wait for the final destination before celebrating, plan small acts of celebration along the path. You may plan the massive celebration when it is all over, that is what I did. However, for now you have made it through on broken pieces. Look at you,

you have survived and come through safely and successfully, you may still have a great distance to go but you have done well so far.

Be proud of yourself. Go and celebrate and do not allow the jealous naysayers to dampen, cramp your spirit or pollute the atmosphere of success with their toxic negativity. Go ahead and plan your thanksgiving celebration! Undoubtedly, you will have to deal with those who disagree with you and challenge you for doing so. However, you have paid the price and know exactly what it costs both to acquire what you have and to be you!

Do not allow others to belittle, negate, undermine or accuse you of simply 'showing off'. You need to be aware of the motives of those who challenge you. It could be based on jealousy and sheer failure to rejoice and celebrate others' success. It could be that they are fearful that your outstanding achievement will jeopardise their life chances. It could also be that they feel threatened or intimidated by your success. You might experience this in your family, circle of friends, community, your places of worship or places of work. Do not let it get to you.

Some people will never be happy for others. Wish them well, move on with your planning, and furthermore, choose people who value your experiences. This may mean casting over board those toxic unproductive and unhealthy associations that drains you of every ounce of positivity and aspiration. As the saying goes, 'Go where you are celebrated, not where you are tolerated.' Nothing is wrong with you! Just remain humble, respectful, approachable and thankful. Be sensitive also, and well measured in your celebrations.

Indeed, it would be wholly inappropriate to flaunt your celebrations and achievements around and constantly talk about yourself especially when others might be grieving or going through situations, which are not at the moment celebratory in nature. Ecclesiastes 3:1 is a good guide, 'To everything there is a time and season under the sun'. Know your times and seasons and act appropriately. Also, 'rejoice with those who rejoice and weep with those who weep' (Romans 12:15). This is a true reflection of empathy, care, thoughtfulness, maturity and sensitivity.

There is a time for celebrations. The story of the lost coin is a good case in point. *"Rejoice with me!"*

The widow exclaimed when she found he coin. The same is true for the lost sheep and the lost prodigal son. In all cases, there were great celebrations because 'my son who was lost is now found, was dead but is now alive!'

Reflection: What have you retrieved that was lost? What was 'dead' in your life that is now alive? Is it your dreams, degree, confidence, career, reputation, marriage, children, business venture, reputation, aspiration, drive, focus, Faith or spiritual life?

Whatever you have achieved, take your time to celebrate. We bear in mind also the greatest celebration ever as, 'there is rejoicing in heaven over one sinner that repents.' (Luke 15:7). What a celebration then and later at the Marriage supper of the Lamb, so get used to it!

8. Rescued on Malta

'All safely landed on Malta where it was cold and uncomfortable. The locals were very hospitable and began making a fire for the people from the ship. As Paul began to help by collecting fire woods, a poisonous snake jumped out and bit him. Paul just shook the snake off and threw it into the fire. The island people were amazed at this because anyone else who was bitten by a poisonous snake would certainly die. They had conflicting responses to this strange phenomenon. Paul received great hospitality from Publius the local leader' (Act 28).

The Hospitality of Strangers – Unexpected Favour
All made it safely through to shore, what a relief! Some swam unaided, others on planks and still others on broken pieces from the ship. The toil, struggles, fear, desperation, isolation and life-threatening situation is now behind. But successfully getting out of one situation does not necessarily mean that you are out of danger or that all is well. Sometimes, the end of one struggle only signals the start of another. This means that you have got to muster the strength, fortitude and resilience even after your storm to face even future or continued situations albeit, of different kinds.

This strength and resilience to stand even after a crisis can be had from within and as well from the support of others, without. In Matthew 4:11 after His temptation in the wilderness, help came from the Angels. However, Scriptures say that the devil left Jesus for a season. How long will your season of 'rest' be? I simply cannot tell. But, even after safely making it through a storm, there is no time for complacency. This does not mean that we do not deserve a break with sufficient time for recuperation. What it means is that sometimes in some situations, consecutive crises surface with little time for rest, relaxation or even celebration. These sometimes have to be postponed, thankfully not cancelled. Yet as I mentioned, a clear balance should be made between these times of transition and simply waiting for perfection.

For Paul and the others, a safe place, despite the storm and after the shipwreck was provided on the shores of Malta. All 276 souls made it safely to shore. The inhabitants greeted and graciously received them. God always make a way out and grant great favour. Even in your darkest and bleakest moments, God will provide a way out for you. I prophesy unexpected blessings from unexpected sources over your life today! If you are ready and prepared to be opened to receive, you will be the recipient of unmerited favour and unexpected blessings even out of the dark and desolate places of your life. You will now have a different mindset and see life's circumstances through the lens of faith, hope, thanksgiving and purpose.

Publius, the local leader was chief in leading the hospitality that was afforded this multitude of unexpected guests through this strange arrival. The challenge is not only for you to be prepared to receive such hospitality in your circumstances, but also to be ready to bless others with kindness as they cross your path. You too can offer to provide the warmth of fire and something for others to eat, metaphorically speaking. The warmth of fire could be comfort, comradery, security and a safe place to recover after a crisis. It could simply be lending a listening ear to someone who just wants to talk. This provision and intervention were most welcomed given the stress and trauma of the process. Be careful how you spell relief and where you lay your weary head for comfort and rest after a traumatic process. That is when you are most vulnerable.

> *Delilah lulled Samson to sleep with his head in her lap, and then she called in a man to shave off the seven locks of his hair. In this way she began to bring him down, and his strength left him (Judges 19:19 NLT).*

You may not know how far your provision of 'warmth' from the fire you built to others can go in helping them as they go through or have gone through their processes. It will cost you something as you receive them, hear their story, gather the wood and minister to them in their cold, wet, hungry and shivering state. Helping others costs. No wonder when Jesus healed the woman with the issue of blood, he asked the seemingly insignificant but profound question, 'Who touched me for virtue left me (Luke 8:46). You cannot genuinely and sincerely help and be there for someone without it costing you something. Ministry is sacrifice. That is the mistake that the recipients sometimes make; thinking that you are blessing and ministering to them out of your abundance, surplus and success when sometimes you are doing so out of great sacrifice.

It was amazing that Paul and the others got such warm reception. Sadly, receiving such hospitality is not the case for all. Some people would have been rejected, put back out to sea or attacked instead of being received and provided with a place of safety and refuge from the stormy blast and brokenness. As others crash onto the island and shore of your path, you may not physically build a fire for others to warm themselves around; however, you can kindle a fire of hope, faith, desire, aspiration, love, support, comfort, resolve and renewed zeal and purpose. Whether you are a key or essential worker in Health, Education, Social Care, Medicine, Business and Commerce, Religious or Charitable organisations, it really does not matter; you have a tremendous opportunity to make a significant difference in the lives of others by virtue of your strategic positioning, alignment and assignment.

The responses of others in your crises can make life a cold and desolate place. It may be so for you at this moment. Perhaps others are reaching out to you after your 'shipwreck' and you are resisting their offer of help. This is understandable. It could be that you have been let down so many times after your storms, that you find it difficult to love and trust again. It may be so hard for you to accept hospitality because of past experiences. Maybe you have faced rejection, judgementalism, ridicule, lack of appreciation or others misread your motives. This may be so but do not suffer in silence; find someone you trust to share with. I know this can be so difficult at times. You may find some folks very selfish; lacking empathy or being untrustworthy, not willing to make the sacrifice to put time into the relationship or simply lacking an understanding of confidentiality.

Notwithstanding, there must be even one person with whom you can share. You may have to share a little here and a little there and see how well they listen, care, share, empathise and reciprocate. Trust must be earned. Confidentiality and respect for privacy are earned. 'A problem shared is a problem halved.' It will benefit you greatly to graciously receive the kind, sincere and genuine provision from a trustworthy, non-judgemental, empathetic and caring source after or in the midst of your boisterous storm. However, remember, never 'cast your pearls to the swine' in desperation to 'get things off your chest!' Not everyone can handle sensitive, confidential or even controversial issues. Go carefully. In the absence of someone you really trust, develop your deep and personal relationship with God and like David, 'Encourage yourself in the Lord' (1 Samuel 30:6).

Reflection: Should you share everything (secrets, flaws, weaknesses) with another human being? Should you keep back some things as private, confidential, sensitive and personal between you and God? In other words, are some things better left unsaid? What impact might this have on your significant relationships? Are there legal, moral, spiritual, professional, relational implications? Should or can your spouse be your best friend with whom you share 'everything'? Are there exceptions?

The Venomous Snakebite
It is quite interesting that this section follows the issue of sharing problems, confidentiality and trust. You may find solace in such warm fellowship or your trust could be betrayed. You could 'share your heart' and be bitten, through scandal, gossip, lack of empathy, judgement, destructive criticism, undermining the gravity of your experiences, over spiritualising away your problems, minimising your pain or simply failing to make the sacrifice of time to listen to you.

The refuge from the storm on the shore in Malta was not the final destination, neither was it the anticipated end to the journey when embarked on initially. This is a significant life lesson. This highlights the flexibility and adjustments needed to be made to our plans even when they are derailed, howsoever caused. In the midst of provisions of hope and hospitality through the generosity of others, there were more challenges to overcome. While we are thankful for the kind hospitality, we are aware of the impending challenges.

Paul had gone through so much interrogation and stress in the defence of the Gospel in the trials with Felix, Festus and King Agrippa. He availed himself for Divine revelation and illumination, and displayed the courage to challenge the wisdom of the experienced centurion and ship's owner. This could be scary but with the sure Word from God and his previous experiences of God's faithfulness and goodness in his life, no doubt he was assured in challenging these experts in their respective fields. Paul had continued to be in tune with God along the way though destructive was the storm. Their lives were all in danger, even Paul's. Yet, he calmly assured them all and offered that earlier on the ship; they even 'break the fast and had something to eat!' What peace and assurance even in the midst of the storm?

Reflection: Have you ever had to stand up to experts in a particular field and respectfully challenge them? How do you navigate your treacherous seas? Are you in constant fear, panic, stress, worry or dread? Like the disciples who cried out to Jesus on the stormy sea, 'Carest thou not that we perish? (Mark 4:38).

Perhaps you are someone like Paul, who seeks God in and before each storm and can have a calm assurance that God is with you even in the fiercest of tempests: financially, martially, relationally, professionally, physically or emotionally. Paul even stood and again challenged the centurion when he was about to give the order for the prisoners to be killed as the ship struck the sand bank. 'Except these stay on board they will perish!' We are not sure how he made it to shore but all was saved in accordance with and in fulfilment of his prophesy, 'there will be no loss of life but of the ship and its cargo.'

Following this success and demanding leadership through the tempestuous journey, you may say and rightly so, that Paul deserved a time of refreshing, recuperation, rest and relaxation. Paul no doubt thought so too. He was human and no doubt was spiritually, mentally and physically spent, cold and hungry like everyone else. The process had cost him so much. He was warming himself by the fire and gathering woods to stoke the same when a venomous snake emerged and fastened itself on his hand!

> *'Oh no why him?' you asked. Why not someone else? It is not fair!*

Remember that firstly, the danger and perilous nature of your storm does not insulate or exempt you from future challenges. Sometimes you may feel that it is too much or why you. This might be a reasonable point for contemplation as long as you do not dwell on it and remain there with anger, resentment and bitterness indefinitely. To reiterate, our specifications are factored into our trials. We can therefore rest confidently in the knowledge that whatever transpires, however painful and howsoever caused, God's faithfulness will see us through. Remember, He will never allow any more than you are able to bear. This might mean accepting God's sovereignty and realise that in some cases we may never get an answer to our 'How, when or why me?' on this side of eternity.

The book of Job in the Bible is a good one to read to see how God's sovereignty and permissive will can lead, despite our frustrations, questionings and deep pain, to our ultimate understanding, acceptance and realisation of God's power and divine providence. Indeed, your latter days will be better than the former ones! Take some comfort in that knowledge.

It is important also to reiterate that even in the wilderness when Jesus was tempted forty days and forty nights as the angels came and ministered to Him, the Scripture says that the devil left him for a season (Luke 4:13). Regardless of how many storms you have been through or how successful you are, there will always be a battle to fight, a storm to navigate and obstacles to overcome. You may be successful in one area but life always throws something else at you; and these can be at the least opportune time. Brooker T, Washington (1856-1915) argues that,

> *'Success is to be measured not so much by the position one has reached in life, as by the obstacles which one has overcome while trying to succeed.'*

In Paul's case, it was just as he had survived a deadly storm, was gathering woods to prepare a fire to warm himself, get some well-deserved rest and relaxation at the hands of his hospitable hosts, that the serpent struck.

Secondly, you are not exempt from further challenges, reversals, setbacks, traumas, accidents and incidents just because you are anointed and in tune with God to the extent that you are the recipient of Divine revelations! 'In this life, those who live godly will suffer persecutions (2 Timothy 3:12); and Jesus asked, 'If these things be done in the dry tree what shall be done in the dry?' (Luke 23:31) We must take up our cross and follow him to be true and faithful disciples (Luke 9:23). I am not talking about suffering presumptuously or as busy-bodies' (1 Peter 4:15), I mean suffering while doing good deeds, suffering while serving the Lord, suffering while ministering to others, suffering as bad things happen to 'good' people.

I can understand that from a 'Word of Faith' Charismatic, Evangelical and Pentecostal perspective, there might be times to 'name it and claim it', 'declare and decree' 'bind and loose.' However, we all have our storms to endure and there are times in our lives when we simply have to go through some storms, process, situations and circumstances, and these wonderful Pentecostal, evangelical, Word of faith declarations will not necessarily prevent them! They may help if we sincerely and humbly pray according to God's will and be submissive to His higher good and ultimate purpose even if, as and when we do not understand or even accept them.

These are difficult concepts to grasp and I do not have the answers to them, philosophically or theologically. You may be struggling right now with the death of your dream: maybe of your only son or daughter in a senseless killing or drug over dose, drive-by shooting or road traffic collision. You may have lost your wealth or investment portfolio or your health through a terminal illness or had your life's work destroyed by the covid-19 pandemic, to name a few. There will be times when you will pray and receive Divine and spectacular miracles and other times you simply hear 'My grace is sufficient for thee' (2 Corinthians 12:9) as you bear your heavy cross and loss.

Not Another One! The Enemy Lurks
Safely through on broken pieces, yet another danger lurks. You are now safe from storm now the serpent lurks and lie in wait. The essence of life after the storm is to be aware of the danger of self-satisfaction. It is so easy for us to lay down arms and be comfortable and complacent presuming that all will be well. There are times when we have a period of rest after a

battle. In fact, in some cases after a particular storm and battle some people never had to endure that particular storm again, ever. However, there will always be other challenges awaiting us to conquer; another stumbling block to use as a stepping stone, another impediment to be seen as an implement, another trial to pave the path for overwhelming triumph and another test which will pave the way for a profound testimony.

I spoke earlier about the dichotomies of life. Things can be going well and wrong simultaneously. You may have just safely navigated the most dangerous and deadly storm in your life and are gathering woods figuratively to celebrate, rest and relax when here comes another storm, albeit of a different nature. Your finances maybe only just recover but here comes a health issue; your marriage may be as perfect as it can get but then the children are 'going off the rails'.

There always seems to be some challenges to overcome, storms to navigate, problems to solve, and processes to endure along the path to purpose. I guess it is called 'Life!' Nobody gets away without a storm. Regardless of wealth, health status, race, culture, religion, gender or age. You may look at others from the outside and desire their lifestyle but the truth is that you do not know what their true circumstances are. The grass may seem greener on the other side but the lawn has to be mowed. The lovely roses you see over the neighbour's fence also have thorns and prickles just like yours. They may or may not choose to divulge their secrets to you but trust me, even those who seem to have it all together, have areas of their lives that they wish they could change. We all have some areas of life that challenge us to the core and these are in spite of our successful passage through our storms.

Sara Henderson (1936-2005), Australian Outback Station Manager and Writer had her share of grave problems from financial reversals to terminal breast cancer. However, with great resilience she bounced back from her difficulties and wrote the book 'From strength to strength.' In a firm way, she states that,

> 'Problems are a major part of life. Don't whinge about why you always have problems...Get on with the solving. Take it from someone who has been there – the solving gets easier as you go along.'

With this inevitability of life in mind, it behoves us to save our strength for life's vicissitude. This means that we need to accept the permanency of change and make allowance in our plans for flexibility and fluidity. These natural change or mutations are to be expected in the affairs of humans. Therefore, we expect favourable or even unfavourable situations, circumstances or events that seem to happen by chance or unexpectedly. This means that we can also expect at some point in our lives, difficulties, hardships on our course of action, path or process beyond our control in any area of life. We will all have to endure alternating change in our lives. We take the bitter with the sweet.

My mother used to say to me as a child growing up 'save your tears and strength for the difficult times in life!' and she was so right. Do not major on minors and minor on majors. It is crucial that we not only save our strength for these trying times but that also during the good times, we stockpile and invest for the 'lean years'. Isn't that what Joseph in the Old Testament did? After the King had a dream, which no one could interpret, Joseph who was languishing in jail, forgotten by the baker, was suddenly remembered as an interpreter of dreams. It is interesting how people can forget you at their convenience and suddenly remember you when they need you or something from you! Nevertheless, thank God, there is a time, season and purpose to everything, so hold on.

Joseph was summoned before the Pharaoh to interpret his troubling dream of seven lean cows devouring the fat ones. The interpretation in part was that during the fat or prosperous times, the Pharaoh should save up, store and invest because surely, the lean or recessional years of seven would come (Genesis 41). Joseph's gift indeed opened doors for him and brought him before Potiphar, 'whose was blessed because Joseph was in charge' (Martin, 2000, p.15). Talking about the impact, influence and the difference your presence makes wherever you are and with whomever, like Paul on the ship. Joseph was selected, chosen and hand-picked as the most suitable candidate to lead and manage this project of storing and investing grains in the prosperous years of plenty in preparation for the inevitable lean and famine years ahead.

The Favour and the Famine
This is a powerful principle and life lesson! Whether in the realm of the physical, material, spiritual, financial, academic, mental or emotional, it really does not matter: the principle is the same, no investment no return! Balance your favour against your famine! Use your years of plenty: prosperity, strength, resilience or success to plan and prepare for the times of recession, famine and overall, life's vicissitudes; for undoubtedly, they will come, if not in one form, most certainly in another, keep living.

It is sad some people simply live from hand to mouth, month to month, pay cheque to pay cheque deliberately. I am not talking about hardworking, trying and diligent folks who are doing their very best against extremely exploitative employment, or health or other traumatic situations; working three jobs to make ends meet and giving the very best to the children out of great sacrifices. Rather, I am talking about people who can, but never save, invest or tuck away anything for a 'rainy day' because of their chosen careless lifestyles. They take expensive vacations and live beyond their means, partying and 'having fun' in the days of youth; and forget that the senior years of leanness are inevitable. These are they who later look with utter contempt, bitterness and jealousy at the prosperous among them who earlier made grave sacrifices and paid the price for their success through deferred gratification.

We are on the 'battlefield'; the 'enemy' does not fight to rules of engagement; as one storm is over another emerges. That is life. It may not seem fair and maybe it is not however; we accept the sovereignty of God and travel on through our storms with grace, faith, hope and dignity holding on to our integrity and remembering our years of leanness and sacrifices. As I write this, I remember a Pastor whose only son sadly died in a car collision. With deep sadness and grief yet, with resignation, a sense of closure and acceptance to the grace and sovereignty of God, he committed the body to the earth as the officiating minister at the funeral service. Wow, what grace, dignity and strength.

It seems unfair Paul was bitten while doing good and after all the ways in which he had helped others: encouraging, affirming, reassuring and providing strong and sustained leadership in the midst of adversity, and now instead of sitting down and waiting to be served, was actually still serving others, gathering firewood. These all contributed to the saving of so many lives from death. You too will have to navigate these discouraging, difficult, devastating or even deadly processes. You may be too young to have experienced them or you may be going through some currently. I wish you well in your processes; this too came to pass and for what does not pass, His grace will sustain you. There is a wise saying I heard from my father that I must share with you: 'What you cannot cure, you endure.' This will be so although you are bitten while anointed, doing good, serving the Lord, loving, serving others and they 'bite' you.

Managing Expectations

I think an important aspect of life is managing our expectations. At some point in our lives, we will be 'bitten.' For Paul it was a venomous snake literally, but for most of us, the snake will be metaphorical. Your snake could be any aspect of life already mentioned, including people. Yes, people do bite! It could be through ingratitude, jealousy, vindictiveness, maliciousness, insensitivity, uncaring, unreasonable or simply wicked. You may experience the warmth and kind hospitality of so many, the goodness, grace and mercy of God to safely and successfully guide you through a deadly storm, benefited from the warmth and comfort of the fire to warm you when cold and destitute, yet that old 'Serpent' lurks in hiding to 'kill, steal and destroy' (John 10:10).

The enemy seeks to kill your attitude of gratitude, aspirations, hopes, faith and dreams you have developed from the process you just went through and miraculously survived. Yes, it is still painful, particularly because you were bitten whilst doing good. It is a hard thing to be bitten while helping others. You know the sacrifices you have and continue to make on their behalf and yet you receive nothing but ingratitude and backstabbing. You may feel like giving up and never help anyone ever again, but the truth is that your blessing may come from another source. For Jesus, of ten lepers, the return rate was 10%! He asked with disappointment,

> *Were not all ten cleansed? Where are the other nine? (Luke 17:17 NIV).*

Very few people remember kindness, sad but true.

However, do not stop doing good deeds. The one you help may not necessarily be the exact same one who will reciprocate and return to bless you. Furthermore, the one person that you did not help could just be the one who turned out to be most successful and you failed to help such a one. That has certainly been my experience when others did not help me when needed, so I can just imagine how you would feel, the hurt, the regret the disappointment. However, never lose hope, continue to use wisdom and discretion when to walk away, when to 'knock the dust off your shoes' and move on (Matthew 10:14) and when to bear and forebear, like the loving father in the story of the Prodigal son who never gave up (Luke 15:20) but knew how and when to simply 'shake it off!' Some things you simply shake off and do not personalise or internalise. This word can save you a lot of stress.

Although a venous snake bit Paul, God protected him from the effects of the venom. Whilst some circumstances might hurt you, they will not kill you! Benjamin Franklin sates that 'Those things that hurt, instruct' (*The Complete Pocket Positives*). A crucial thing to remember is your attitude to the bite. Whilst there are so many things that happen to us outside of our control, we can still manage things through our attitude towards what happened to us. You cannot change people. You may not be able to change the situation you are in but for sure, you can change your attitude and perception;

remember? 'What you cannot cure, you endure.' Of course, there is a time to walk away and not endure toxic circumstances or people. Use wisdom and discretion.

The Venom and the Serum

The snake venom is the poisonous, usually yellow fluid, which is stored in the adapted salivary glands of venomous snakes. They rely on the venom, which they produce to debilitate and immobilize their prey. The venom has an effect when it enters the bloodstream or is injected into the tissues. The effects can be varied but devastating, affecting the nervous system, muscles causing paralysis, respiratory failure or worse. The National Health Service (NHS) in the UK advises the patients should among others: stay calm, keep the part of their body that was bitten as still as you can and lie in the recovery position. It further advises that people do not:

- Go near the snake, or try to catch or kill it.
- Try to suck or cut the venom out of the bite.
- Tie anything tightly around the part of the body where the bite is.

These are very useful preliminary precautionary measures. Nevertheless, the ultimate treatment for a snake bite is administering anti-venom as quickly as possible after the bite. Even so, knowing the size, colour and shape of the snake can assist medical staff to determine which anti-venom is best suited for that particular situation. It is interesting to note that anti-venom is made by actually collecting venom from the relevant snake and injecting small amounts of it into a domestic animal. The antibodies that form, are then collected from the domestic animal's blood and purified.

According to the World Health Organisation (WHO), anti-venoms work by boosting our immune response after snakebites. The anti-venom is actually produced by immunising donor animals with robust immune systems, for example, sheep and horses with the snake venom! Anti-venoms are obtained by harvesting and then purifying the antibodies from plasma produced by the donor animal. This produces powerful antibodies that 'can bind to snake venom components, enabling the victim's immune defences to eliminate these toxins.'

Shake it Off Into the Fire!
Paul's response to the bite of the venomous snake was almost instinctive…to shake it off! He certainly did not have access to these modern medical procedures. However, he was exposed to the same danger as any and the locals knew it well. Such venomous bite was intended to immobilise (stop, halt and restrain), neutralise (nullify, deactivate and reduce the effect of) and debilitate (incapacitate, weaken and hinder) and ultimately kill.

We behave differently in our pain and grave distress, whether fight, flight, freeze or in faith depends on a whole range of factors. For some it could be based on past experiences with similar situations and having developed the courage to stand and fight, or to take flight. Others might, for whatever reason freeze in fear, disbelief, panic and pain. However, having the presence of mind to not only shake it off, but to be purposeful in where he shook it, raises Paul's reaction to another level of faith I believe.

Paul shook off the serpent into the fire. This shows a quick, calculated and deliberate response to an urgent imminent danger. It also shows his presence of mind not simply to act in panic of disposing the venomous creature, but to aim specifically for the fire! This deliberate act ensures that the snake was not allowed to run wild or be dropped in a position to return to do further harm to him or others. This quick thinking undoubtedly saved lives. Paul was expected to literally drop dead on the spot! (Acts 28:6).

Reflection: How do you deal with situations that are urgent and/or important and demand quick judgement? Are you prone to panic, fear, freeze or run away from situations or issues? Do you respond in faith? What does responding in faith mean and look like?

Sometimes we may even go through these stages (fight, flight, freeze), so quickly that we might not even be aware. As human beings, these are natural responses; however, as individuals, we might respond differently for a number of reasons. A crucial point may be to manage carefully how long we spend in each stage especially those that could be destructive in so many areas of life. There is a time and place to stand, hold your ground and fight for your rights, entitlements, truth, justice and privileges. However, there is also a time and place to walk out strategically and tactically walk away for a greater good or purpose. It could be that your health, safety or life of yourself or others may be at stake. Perhaps it may seem urgent but not really important. Some issues are there to distract from the real ones, in other words, they may be merely symptomatic of something more serious.

Taking flight therefore has its place and time. In fact, the Bible admonished us to 'Flee fornication' (1 Corinthians 6:18). There are times and circumstances when negotiating and arguing or even fighting maybe be ill-advised, unhelpful, counterproductive or even dangerous. Joseph and his experience with Potiphar's wife in the Old Testament is a good case in point (Genesis 39:7).

In life we should have core and non-negotiable values. Core beliefs, morals, values and mindsets that are simple not up for discussion. Deep-seated principles that sit at the core of our character that are not for sale, negotiation or settling. Maintaining these may require a firm stance of fighting to hold your ground or it could mean fleeing from situations that could result in the compromise of these core values and principles. Having these can instil 'greater respect for others' values and beliefs while embracing my core commitments, non-negotiable position...' (O'Connor, 2017, p84). Our responses then may take us through these processes and stages. Our goal should be not to remain stuck or frozen in fear, disbelief, anger, numbness, helplessness, resentment, rebellion but to strive for a place a faith, hope and purpose.

The Fickleness of Human Responses
Having a deep sense of conviction and core values, which are non-negotiable, is crucial to realising your potential, goals and purpose in life. Indeed, there is a place for flexibility and compromise. Notwithstanding, without this sense of knowing who and whose you are, can result in you being swayed by circumstances as well as the opinions of people. It is quite interesting to me that after Paul was bitten by the venomous snake, the locals gathered around in eager anticipation that he would simply fall over and died (Acts 28:6). They knew exactly what to expect, that he 'should have swollen, or fallen down dead suddenly.' No doubt, they have seen it happened before. Why should Paul be any different? Nevertheless, he was different.

It is important to note that Paul was not exempt from trouble, yet from the start of this trip, we have seen the power of God being manifested in his life. This manifestation whether through his word of knowledge, admonition, rebuke, encouragement or instruction through Angelic visitation, undoubtedly had a tremendous impact on the lives of all onboard the ship and later those on the island of Malta and beyond.

Even after Paul shook the venomous snake into the fire and the locals watched the demise of this deadly creature, their next anticipated spectacle was the demise of Paul himself. In fact, the minute the 'venomous beast' fastened itself to Paul's hand, the locals formed their own judgement! They said among themselves,

> *'No doubt this man is a murderer whom though he hath escaped the sea; yet vengeance suffereth him not to live' (v4).*

It is quite extraordinary the conclusion they arrived at without even having the facts; and yet no doubt this was part of their tradition and belief system or even their lived experiences. Making hasty judgements, generalising, jumping to conclusion, stereotyping, labelling or projecting our experiences on others can be unhelpful and ill advised. There is a place for sharing our stories and using them as inspirational and motivational tools in the lives of others, however, each person has his or her own process to pursue.

Nevertheless, the natives' anticipation of imminent death soon transforms into absolute shock and amazement and even worship! Paul shook off the viper into the fire and 'felt no harm!' As mentioned by the WHO, the venom is dangerous if, as and when it enters the bloodstream or tissues. Neither of which seems to happen to Paul, miraculously! This is testament to the amazing and protective power of God to defy the laws of nature and to show Himself far superior to them. The crucial lesson here is that if we can so isolate ourselves from the venomous influences of life, we can be protected. We are harmed when the thing on the outside gets on the inside whether of our bodies, minds or spirits.

It is one thing for a ship to sail on water, it is quite another for the same water to get inside the ship. Many people can sail on what others sink in. Whether it is infections or influences, you can be kept safe if only you guard your heart, body, mind, soul and spirit from such contamination that can neutralise, immobilise or debilitate. You go under when that which is on the outside gains entry to the inside.

When the locals saw that Paul was alive after the viper had fastened itself onto his hand and he was unarmed they quickly changed their story! From being a 'Murderer fleeing justice who was now facing retribution', he was now elevated to the status and position of 'a god!' People will always formulate their own opinions of you whatever your situation or progress. You have got to know who you are and whose you are, having those core and non-negotiable values, principles and beliefs I earlier mentioned so that in the face of the judgements, criticisms, labelling, stereotyping or malicious rumours of others you can stand firm in the knowledge of your own identity, position and condition in Christ.

Try not to be intoxicated from the praise, compliments or criticisms of people because people will always be fickle and change their minds about you as the situations change. It is okay for people to change their minds of course. Sometimes, we judge people harshly and prematurely. It is quite in order to apologise and move on to accept people and adjust our expectations and assumptions in the face of or in light of new evidence, circumstance or illuminations.

The Last Laugh
I remember as a teenage in University in Jamaica doing my teacher training, a gentleman came to address an assembly of all the final year student-teachers on travel and tourist opportunities in the United States. As he entered the auditorium, there were bouts of giggling all over the room. It was sad because the laughter as we understood it started because the conclusion drawn from a number of students was that the gentleman was not particularly handsome to behold. Sadly, he was judged by his physical appearance even before he had a chance to take his seat. He humbly sat there through all the preliminaries of the assembly and finally the introduction for him to speak. I am not sure if he was aware of the hostile environment into which he had entered. Nevertheless, he sat there composed and waited patiently until the floor was his.

Confidently, he rose and walked to the podium. In a calm but confident tone he introduced himself and stated his mission and purpose for his visit. Such was the decorum, confidence and presentation that soon there was a hush over the entire auditorium. No one was snickering any more about his physical appearance. He had grabbed the attention of his audience with his confidence, eloquence and flawless presentation. When he was finished, he simply invited questions at the end of the assembly and took his seat.

Surprisingly, he moved from someone who was perceived by some to be a person who was not very fair to look upon, to one who was desired to know and associate with! Extremely beautiful ladies flocked to register for the exchange programme in the USA! What changed? Like Paul, he moved from one end of the continuum from negativity to the other of positivity, and in such a short time! Maybe you too have your own story of how you were initially judged negatively and how you dramatically turned things around, using the gifts, talents and abilities, you have. You need not worry about what you lack because life always gives you something to work with for your ultimate success – even the broken pieces. You have what you need for your success; use what you have!

Zig Ziglar, American Motivational speaker and writer reminds us,

> *'Our problem is that we make the mistake of comparing ourselves with other people. You are not inferior or superior to any other human being…You do not determine success by comparing yourself to others; rather you determine success by comparing your accomplishments to your capabilities. You are "number One" when you do the best you can with what you have.'*

Additionally, we seek the will, mind and purpose of God for our lives and walk therein to fulfil His agenda for our lives. Of course, in the end, we are accountable to Him as to whether we accomplished our life's work,

> *'I have fought the good fight, I have finished the race, I have kept the faith. Finally, there is laid up for me the crown of righteousness, which the Lord, the righteous Judge, will give to me on that Day, and not to me only but also to all who have loved His appearing (2 Timothy 4:7-8 NKJV);*

And leave a legacy in the earth.

> *And I heard a voice from heaven saying unto me, Write, Blessed are the dead which die in the Lord from henceforth: Yea, saith the Spirit, that they may rest from their labours; and their works do follow them (Revelation 14:13).*

'If it's Going to be, it's up to you!'

I believe that no one can stunt your growth, purpose and destiny but yourself. You can either allow the compliments or the criticisms of others to get into you and influence negatively your self-perception, abilities, capabilities and purpose or you can 'shake it off into the fire' and move on to prove the naysayers wrong. But, wait! Don't do it for them, instead, you go on to achieve the best that God has in store for you simply because you were created for greatness and no one can stop you from achieving it! What a shame to live your life for people or to have not achieved your purpose and full potential.

People's perception will most likely and often change about you, therefore you must have a firm sense of your own identity and hold fast that the 'profession of your faith, (Hebrews 10:23) pursue your plans, hopes, dreams, potential and God-given purpose. You too can turn it around for good and use what others consider deficiency and liability to become sufficiency and assets.

Your response to the bite is as crucial and your response to the naysayers. I earlier mentioned how Jesus skilfully dealt with the situation when he asked his disciples 'who do men say that I, the Son of Man am?' (Matthew 16:13). The many and various responses of 'some say you are (this)' and 'some say you are (the other),' demonstrate the fact that you cannot necessarily change the opinions of 'some say' People will believe whatever they want to believe but; who do you say that I am? And who do you say that you are! Reflection is crucial and indeed the opinions of 'some say' can be useful in planning your directions or gauging how to improve your future strategy.

However, the problem is when there is an imbalance in how you receive or reject the opinions of 'some say' and if you allow their toxic influences to get inside of you. Someone said, 'you cannot stop the birds from flying over your head but you can most certainly prevent them building a nest in your head!' Additionally, 'If there is no enemy within the enemy without can do you no harm.' These place a lot of responsibility on you. Fan away those birds and guard your heart.

So, shake it off: negativity, anger, bitterness, unforgiveness, toxic comments, influences and relationships that come your way simply to debilitate, neutralise and immobilise. Guard your mind, body and spirit. This means also watching your physical diet, what you watch, see or hear. That is, guard the eye, mouth, ear and mind gates against anything that could be destructive or toxic if only they enter within. You have the power to determine your response to the 'bite' you can choose to be bitter or better though bitten. It is useful to remember that the bite could actually make you better. It is not good that you were bitten. It was not good that you were shipwrecked and had such a devastating process however, you are safely on shore! You make it thus far, whether unaided, on planks or on broken pieces of your shattered dreams, look at you! You may not be at your final destination, but you are safe and you weathered the storm safely. Furthermore, the bite did not harm you…Celebrate that!

As you reflect on your bite, remember that there is a cut to hurt and a cut to cure. If you have an operation, the surgeon will most likely have to cut you or laparoscopically make an incision. Whichever, you may be under local or general anaesthesia but the intention is to cure and not to hurt or kill you. This principle of understanding that life can throw things your way which may seem like a cut to kill however, that deep wound of rejection, denial, betrayal, loss or broken dreams could be an opportunity for healing and restoration and possibilities for changing the trajectory of yours or others' lives in the achievement of goals, purpose and destiny. Remember, that ultimately, the venom in the snakebite is used to cure the snakebite; the serum is in the venom.

Bitten but Blessed
It is necessary then to have the right response to people's opinions of you as well as to the fact that you were bitten. It is painful to be bitten while doing good or serving the Lord. It is also painful to be bitten in public; handling life's storms and the bite under the microscope of the public glare and scrutiny. It is one thing to be hurt, embarrassed or 'bitten' in private. There you can grieve without the glare, stare, and opinions of others to judge. However, alas, what gives additional pain when dealing with the bite is having to do so without the dignity of private pain, grieving, closure but simply opened to unsavoury comments and reactions, especially in these days of social media.

David found himself in a similar situation. There he had to encourage himself in the Lord at Ziglag. His men wanted to stone him after the Amalekites burnt their city and captured their goods, women and children! Interestingly, you can be a trusted leader and hero on one instance and worthy of being stoned the next when people's expectations of what they had in mind are not met. Oh, the fickle nature of mortals: 'Hosanna!' one day then 'Crucify Him!' the next couple of days!

Like David, never mind you are in the same position as your soldiers at Ziglag…you too have suffered loss. You too are hurting, grieving and trying to make sense of your storms. As a leader you could argue that he had to assume full responsibility. Nevertheless, in the absence of compassion, empathy and understanding from his soldiers, David 'encouraged himself in the Lord' (1 Samuel 30:6). Likewise, you are called upon to 'Build up yourself on your most holy faith praying in the Holy Ghost' (Jude 1: 20). You may not cause the situation you are in, yet you are suffering the consequences of others' poor choices, decisions and actions.

Reflection: What could the Lord have in store for you, and what great victories might await you? Could this storm be merely a pre-requisite for success? Could it be that others stand to be blessed, influenced, motivated, challenged and inspired from your life and it is necessary for you to go through this storm successfully?

Dining in the Storm

You are blessed, though bitten. Your blessings have burdens. You have come through safely. In some situations, you cannot go over them, you cannot go under or around them, but you have to go through them. I took note of the fact that Paul led 275 folks on the ship in a service of thanksgiving in the midst of the storm! They were not even believers and certainly, they were all panicking frantically and had refused to eat for two solid weeks. However, Paul encouraged them thus:

> *'Wherefore I pray you to take some meat: for this is for your health, and for there shall not a hair fall from the head of any of you' (Acts 27:34).*

That is confidence. Paul was in the same situation and yet he exuded such confidence and faith in God to the extent that he demonstrated such amazing leadership and faith in the midst of a life and death situation. Dr Floyd Antonio (2016), states that, 'Spiritual leadership involves the ability to lead others towards greater faith even in challenging circumstances' (p.94).

They had not yet agreed to eat, yet Paul took and broke the bread and publicly gave thanks. Giving thanks in the storm (Verse 35) Paul took bread and gave thanks in the presence of sinners; they ate and were of good cheer. They then gained strength to lighten the ship.

That could be very difficult; to maintain a Christian witness in the face of such adversity. Yet, this act of ministry and faith led to the strengthening of all on board; hope arose in them and the strength to lighten the ship and cast over board the excess weight that could jeopardize their safety (v35). Whatever your situation, you too may need to, like Elijah who was broken and burnt out after ministry and sitting in abject despair and discouragement, 'arise and eat, for the journey is too great for thee' (1 Kings 19:7). This instruction holds the secret to your progress through the process of your despair. Indeed, God can and does furnish a table in the wilderness (Psalm 78:19) and in the 'presence of your enemies' (Psalm 23:5). Eating physically as well as emotionally and spiritually can and will nourish you to embark on the next phase of your process and challenge. For Elijah, it was to arise and appoint a successor and for Paul and the others on board, to lighten the ship to make progress and avoid sinking. 'If you have achieved any level of success, pour it into someone else! Success is not success without a successor!' (Jakes1996 p.59).

Reflection: Are there things in your life that need to be lightened or could it be that you are at a stage in your life and ministry where you need to start seriously considering appointing a successor. You must accept that you are blessed though bitten. This can be a difficult concept to grasp: How can I be blessed when so many bad things have happened to me? How can I be blessed when the bad things happened to me in the full glare of the public?

Maybe you were made redundant or laid off after being furloughed because your employer could not afford to maintain your services in the company. Maybe you have lost loved ones to the Covid-19 pandemic and you were not there physically with them as they passed away. Maybe you had a very public and acrimonious divorce, a financial reversal, reputational damage or had your house or car repossessed. These are deeply hurtful, embarrassing and devastating circumstances and no one can even begin to conceptualise vaguely the pain they inflict. As you reflect, pray, and look at your situation, you will have to admit that you made it safely through now only to be bitten so publicly.

Reflection: Can any good come out of your pain though it seems so unfair and undeserving? Can you be blessed even though bitten? What would being 'blessed' mean and look like for you?

PART 3

Impact, Relevance and Application: Bitten, Better, Not Bitter but Believing

9. Bitten, Better, Not Bitter but Believing

In the same quarters were possessions of the chief man of the island, whose name was Publius; who received us, and lodged us three days courteously.

And it came to pass, that the father of Publius lay sick of a fever and of a bloody flux: to whom Paul entered in, and prayed, and laid his hands on him, and healed him.

So, when this was done, others also, which had diseases in the island, came, and were healed:

Who also honoured us with many honours; and when we departed, they laded us with such things as were necessary (Act 28:7-10)

Decide How Your Story Ends
After the horrendous journey at sea with imminent danger to life and property, Paul safely reached the shore. Despite all that, he went through in the process to that point, good that came out of that situation despite the challenges. For example, Paul had a warm reception and hospitable treatment of the locals on arrival. They rushed to gather sticks to build a fire to warm him and the others as they were soaking wet and very cold from the rain and the passage by sea. Despite their initial misjudgement and fickleness in their social interaction; from referring to him as a 'murderer' when bitten by the viper to hailing him as a 'god' when he survived, yet they somehow redeemed themselves by being kind and hospitable.

Paul, therefore, was the recipient of their kind generosity, gracious welcome and warmth. Can you find it in your heart to forgive those who hurt you?

> *"But I say unto you, Love your enemies, bless them that curse you, do good to them that hate you, and pray for them which despitefully use you, and persecute you"* (Matthew 5:44).

It could have gone completely differently; to compound an already nearly disastrous situation he and others could have stumbled on a totally different situation where their health, safety and lives were in danger. The locals were described as 'barbarians' yet somehow received them warmly. Paul's blessings indeed came from unexpected places and sources.

It is also worth noting that Publius, the chief man of the island received them and provided accommodation for three days and treated them courteously. This is significant as the one with the power, position and influence reached out to Paul in his moment of need. We can see a pattern of blessings, grace, mercy and favour even in the midst of a terrible situation. Things were bad but delicately interspersed with good things and blessings along the way. I like to examine situations and analyse them for some good.

Paul through his ability to defend his faith was brought before King Agrippa, Governor Festus, Felix, the Centurion, the ship's owners and now Publius and all this en route to his appointment for his ultimate defence in Rome before Caesar. Some of these encounters did not seem all positive ones; however, in the grand scheme of things, they all play an important role in contributing to an overall good. Of course, we know and have established that not all things are good but they indeed contribute to the ultimate good. Through these divinely orchestrated connections and interventions, a path would be paved for the Gospel to be preached and the lives of countless others would be blessed, enriched and influenced even to this day through the Pauline epistles. That is a demonstration of purpose in problems and purpose through the process.

As you look back over your life, whether in a general way or at specific situations, I am sure that you can connect the dots and see how God has divinely orchestrated your path. It might be through, then unwelcomed processes at the time. However, later you may have had to admit that 'the steps of a good man are ordered by the Lord and he delighteth in his ways' (Psalm 37:23). It may be in that business venture, a career or academic choice, a relationship or life-changing decision and choice you had to make. You now look back and see a pattern of people, places, occasions, incidents, accidents, even setbacks, disappointments and even traumas that now lead you safely through to the success you now enjoy. The process was painful but now you rejoice. As you went through that storm like Jesus, you use the joy that was awaiting you to enable, encourage and sustain you to endure your trials and challenges.

The Bitten Hand Becomes the Healing Hand
The process and principle of Divine connections is a powerful aspect of life's journey. God orders your steps and brings you before the right people at the right time to fulfil His will, purpose and way. Jesus must needs be go through Samaria (John 4:4). He had a mission and purpose there for the woman of Samaria. Despite the situation prior, He fulfilled that purpose and ultimately many were saved through the ministry and testimony of that woman who was an outcast as the Jews and the Samaritans had no dealings then. Crossing the cultural

and racial divide led to a tremendous evangelical thrust, which resulted in many coming to the saving knowledge of Jesus Christ, isn't that wonderful?

So let us continue to look at Paul's situation. As he enjoyed the kind hospitality of Publius, his father sadly became gravely ill. By virtue of this illness, Paul was able to pray for him and he was healed! What a setup, what a divinely orchestrated situation! Nothing happens by chance in the life of the Believer. You may feel despondent and discouraged at the things that are happening in your life but take courage that God is able to use them for His glory, your blessing and for the benefit of others. Therein you can take some comfort despite the gruesome process because, 'no suffering at the moment is joyous but grievous, and nevertheless, afterwards it yields the peaceable fruits of righteousness (Hebrews 12:11).

Not only was Publius' father healed but as word spread of this miracle, others came and they too were healed. This tremendous ministry was birthed out of absolute devastation and trauma. **The hand that was bitten became the instrument of healing for others!** A ministry that could have been aborted at any stage of the process, from the beatings Paul had prior, the trial process, the nearly fatal journey on the perilous and tempestuous sea, casting away the cargo, the shipwreck to the bite of the venomous snake! Yet all these individually and combined situations that were unwelcomed and not good in and of themselves, all paved the way for this wonderful healing ministry and outpouring of love, provision, hospitality. Furthermore, Paul was the recipient of much respect, honour, hospitality and blessing of provision for the onward journey when the time came for his onward journey. No doubt there was a bond that was forged that made departure meaningful and even difficult.

You maybe have asked a poignant question, 'What if Paul did not have to appear before Festus and Felix, and be shipwrecked with all the imminent danger of death that he faced? What if he had not demanded a hearing with Caesar in Rome, would all the sequence of events transpired where others were healed, blessed and delivered? Well, who could be blessed by your pain and storms?

Reflection: How do you apply this question to your own situation? After all that you have gone through, can you now look back over your life and ask what if I have not gone through my storms, would I be here today and would others have been blessed and healed? Can you actually say, 'If was good that I was afflicted' (Psalm 119:71)?

As you apply this lesson to your life, it is important to remember that the process of life will open many avenues for hurt, pain and disappointments through which ministry opportunities can arise. These include opportunities to share, testify, inspire, motivate, pray for and reflect the power of God in the lives and circumstances of people. You may have been bitten; well, we all have been bitten in some ways or areas of our lives.

Reflection: How do you deal with your bite, or shipwreck or the fickleness of people or when life throws you a curve ball? How do you respond to the incidents, accidents, traumas and vicissitudes of life in light of this analysis?

A crucial take away point to remember is that:

> **The bitten hand became the healing hand. The hand on which the venomous snake fixed itself became the hand that was later used as an instrument of healing not only for Publius' father but all those on the island who had diseases and came forward to be healed.**

Your bite could be for the healing of others and their healing depends on your ability to shake 'it' off and have the correct attitude in your painful processes; whatever your 'it' might, be. It is possible that all the traumatic things you have or are going through will have little to do with you. It could be that whilst you will benefit from the lessons from your processes but the greater good might be for the blessing, healing and restoration of others.

This thought could make you filled with joy, explanation and purpose. It could add meaning, illumination and closure to your suffering. It could also make you sad or even uncomfortable and angry as you may ask 'why me'? and declare how unfair it is that you have to suffer for the benefit of others. To be honest, I do not know; neither can I explain it. I know however, that God is sovereign and will certainly 'work it for your good'. That is not to over simplify, trivialise or spiritualise your trauma. Good could be realised relatively soon (over days, weeks months or even years), like Paul in this situation or it might be good in the very long term in or not in your lifetime. It could like other areas of Paul's life, be a part of your legacy in the earth. I am not sure if Paul realised then the impact his Pauline New Testament writings would have on the Church today! The Scriptures declare, 'Blessed are the dead who died in the Lord, they rest from their labour and their work follow them.' Your bite could be about others not you!

Your Life and Story as a 'Type and Shadow'

I reflect on the story of the Prophet Hosea in the Bible (Hosea 1:2). As he preached and warned Israel of their sin in falling away from God, his life was used as a model, a type and shadow or example of how the relationship between God and Israel had broken down and the extent to which God would go to redeem them. Hosea married a prostitute called Goma to reflect the sad, backslidden state of Israel. To think that Hosea the righteous prophet was declaring the Word of God with powerful and anointed prophetic utterances, while his wife was 'cruising the red-light district' was unthinkable, but true.

On so many occasions, he would go after her and woo her back but she would simply return to her abominable lifestyle, her familiar path. Under pressure, we tend to return to our familiar paths, our unconverted characteristics. Amidst the glares, the stares, the whispers and the scandals, Hosea reached out to reflect the unconditional love of God for his people. You may also consider the love of God as He sent His only Son Jesus to dwell among us and take on flesh; lived among us and be a part of the sinful human experiences to redeem man back to himself (John 3:16). As you reflect on these cases, you may ask, 'was it fair?' 'Was the lesson, type, shadow or the reality of the cross worth the outcome and effects on the holy man of God?

Reflection: How about you? Is your suffering worth the outcome of the life lessons learnt or the countless others who could be uplifted, blessed, challenged and changed for now and eternity through your suffering?

The anointing comes through broken places. I repeat my saying that no scars, no stars and no cross, no crown. Through God's grace, your impediments can be implements to success, your messes can be used as messages and miracles, your tests can be used as testimonies, your trials as triumphs, life's stumbling blocks can be used as stepping stones and the obstacles you face can be tremendous opportunities for ministry, healing, personal attainment, purpose, destiny and legacy in the earth.

Shake It Off and Stomp on It!
You will not only survive but also thrive in what could have killed others. The power of the anointing on your life as well as your positive attitude of gratitude will lead you to shake off some things that were designed to take you out. As I write this, I recall the story of an old mule. Now this story might be a bit upsetting to some, however for the purposes of illustration, I will relay it as best as I can. As the mule was so old and was no longer useful to its master, the most humane way at the time in history (without the animal rights we have today), to put it down was to pile dirt or soil on top of it in a hole.

As the farmer shovelled dirt onto the poor animal, it just stood there almost helplessly as the volume of soil piled up. However, as the reality of its imminent demise hit the old mule, it came up with the brilliant idea of shaking off the dirt and stomping on it. The mule continued this process. As the dirt was thrown on it, it simply shook it off and stomped on it. This process continued until, it's head was above the hole and was it was able to crawl out and bolted of for dear life!

This old mule realised that it had more life than its owner believed. Even when others pour 'dirt' on you metaphorically speaking, you have the power to shake it off and stomp on it. You also have the option and choice to simply stand there and be buried alive to a point of being neutralised, immobilised and suffocated. You can be proactive and take decisive action to fight back in order to be free to fulfil your dreams and purpose. Benjamin Disraeli (1804-1881) British Prime Minister and Writer argue that 'Actions may not always bring happiness, but there is no happiness without action.'

This is not glorifying individualism and legalism, rather it is stating a fact that in order to achieve success, and you must actually do something with your life; not just think, talk or wish. You too have much life left in you. Do not let others decide your times and seasons. 'Be not weary in well-doing for you will reap if you faint not' (Galatians 6:9). Use the bad things that happen to you in life as a catalyst for change and success. In response to those who were not there for you, who said you would not amount to anything or those who rejected or betrayed your trust, do not get bitter, simply get better! Frank Sinatra said, 'The sweetest revenge is massive success.' Be successful and do all you can to achieve your purpose and God-given potential not merely as a tool of revenge or to prove anything to others. They will see and hear of your success.

In fact, what your naysayers might not realise is that the very thing they pour on you to keep you down or to harm you will only propel you into your destiny. Put another way, Steve Harvey points out that the nutrients are in the dirt and that which was intended to suffocate and immobilise can provide nourishment to facilitate germination, growth, development and fruitfulness. It all depends on your attitude and perspective. 'None of the rulers of this age knew this wisdom, because if they had known it, they would not have crucified the Lord of glory.' (1 Corinthians 2:8) No wonder the Scripture confirmed that 'unless a grain of wheat falls in the ground and dies it abides alone...' (John 12:24). Your trials, crosses, pain and storms can be dirt that provides nutrients to facilitate your development. While no suffering is joyous, we can appreciate its part in our ultimate victory.

Pain, Power and Purpose

Your power is in your pain. This leads to your passion and ultimately guides and informs your purpose. Unaided, on planks or even on broken pieces you will safely make it to shore regardless of the problem. You have a firm promise of success in the challenging process. You can be confident of ultimate purpose. To reiterate, your anointing comes through broken places. Through your promise, process and pain will come your power and in the process, you will be propelled to your purpose through your problems. When you have paid the price and have been through the fire, the water, the flood and the blood you know what it takes for success. That is after you have 'suffered awhile' (1 Peter 5:10). You know the sacrifices it cost you. True, it is by grace and not that of ourselves lest any man should boast (Ephesians 2:9).

Consequently, you will not let it go so easily. You will hold steadfast to what you have achieved with undiluted fervour because you know pain you endured and the price you paid for your success. You know the depth of your pain and the passion from your process. Do not be silenced, neither allow the toxic utterances of jealous naysayers to distract and detour you from your purpose. Like blind Bartimaeus who cried,

> 'Jesus Thou Son of David, have mercy on me!'
> (Luke 18:38).

Likewise, the woman with the alabaster box of precious anointment lavishly poured it on Jesus' feet (John 12:3) despite the criticisms. Indeed, she knew the cost of her oil in her alabaster box. She knew the life she lived before and how Jesus saved her.

> 'Therefore, I say unto thee, her sins, which are many, are forgiven, for she loved much. But to whom little is forgiven, the same loveth little." (Luke 7:47).

Herein lies the passion and power. When others wonder whence lie your strength or why are you so passionate? It's the pain of the process that facilitates your powerful anointing. You minister in your pain and therein lies your genuine, authentic, and credible ministry. This ministry is not simply based on 'book knowledge'; which has its place, but experiential knowledge of your lived and often painful narrative.

10. Personal Brokenness

A cheerful heart is good medicine, but a broken spirit saps a person's strength (Proverbs 17:22, NLT).

Then saith he unto them, 'My soul is exceeding sorrowful, even unto death: tarry ye here, and watch with me' (Matthew 26:38).

Safely Through but at What Personal Cost

As the ship hit the sandbank where the two seas met, it broke at the end. Aside from those who were capable of swimming unaided to shore, it was the planks and the broken pieces from the ship that provided the only means of transport to help guide all souls safely to shore. I earlier discussed the powerful opportunities these played in making a difference in the lives of those who dared to know their abilities, capabilities and had the confidence to launch out using these methods to navigate the boisterous waves. The process through the stormy sea lies partially between the place of your 'shipwreck' and the destination. Never mind the fact that it is an unplanned destination, your challenge is to secure your broken piece from your shattered wreck and purposefully navigate your tempestuous path to an inadvertent place of safety.

There was no time to wait for perfection. There was no lifeboat. This meant, using what you had or potentially lose your life. That is how brutal life can be sometimes. We find ourselves in situations where we have to use what we have to overcome obstacles, triumph over trials, advance or adversities and to navigate our storms. We cannot wait for the ideal set of circumstances to launch out; rather we move out with what we have. We set out to face our fears and conquer them by using the shattered, wrecked, fragmented and damaged pieces of our broken dreams, circumstances and even life.

My main concern in this chapter, however, is to focus on the broken person, not the broken pieces. Your blessings may be predicated on the extent to which you have been broken.

Previously my focus was on the broken pieces of the ship that provided a lifeline amidst the angry waves. The broken pieces provided a safe but boisterous and life-threatening passage to the shore.

Reflection: How do you minister to others in your brokenness?

This is not about your 'ship', the owner, sailors, soldiers, centurion, prisoners or the possessions you have lost along the process, but the broken *you*. The 'you' that is in the process of your storms or have survived and now living and dealing with the ramifications of its aftermath. The 'you' that everyone thinks is okay because of the powerful ministry and anointing on your life, but who suffers in silent frustration; the 'you' who quietly shed a tear in the stillness the night in the absence of sweet repose. Be encouraged. Your blessing comes through your breaking in your process. Warren (2002) sums it up thus:

> 'Your most profound and intimate experiences of worship will likely be in your darkest days – when your heart is broken, when you feel abandoned, when you're out of options, when the pain is great – and you turn to God alone' (p.194).

Sometimes, coming out of a terrible accident and looking back on the shattered wreck can be just as or even more traumatic for some than actually being in the accident. The post-traumatic stress can take years or even a lifetime to overcome for some. It is very important therefore to pay special attention not only to the process and the storms but also the person who made it safely through on broken pieces. Just because you made it safely through does not mean that, you are necessarily okay.

Reflection: Yes, safely through, but at what cost to you as a person? Yes, safely through but what state are you currently in after the storm?

You have made it safely to shore, you may have had a warm, hospitable reception, a warm place and environment to recuperate or even a celebration ceremony. You may have had a powerful time of success in ministry with many being healed and blessed by your compelling testimony and story of how you made safely through on broken pieces. However, permit me to ask you one profound question, which maybe you have not been asked to this point or even if you were asked, it was casually as a polite greeting or as pleasantry:

'How are you?'
I do not know where you are in your life, experiences and processes and ministry but I am sure like me, you wish and silently long for someone to ask you that simple yet profound question! I heard the story of someone who was asked this question. Unexpectedly but almost immediately he burst in tears.

'Does anyone really care?' He hastily pondered.

If you are someone who is always there for others, encouraging, supporting, ministering to and helping; if you are the one that others frequently call on for a range of support; then chances are, you have more withdrawals than deposits in your life. In other words, you have more going out than coming in and this is recipe for frustration, burnout, silent frustration, depression, isolation and even worse. You may be the one in your family who knows the birthdays of everyone, who faithfully keeps in contact out of love, commitment, care and loyalty, expecting nothing in return. Nevertheless, would it not be wonderful to enjoy a bit of reciprocity? You have to carefully manage yourself. As you give and minister to others, you must ensure that spiritually, emotionally, physically, intellectually, socially and mentally you are being replenished.

Nurture Self: *'Sharpen the Saw'*

I remember well after I completed my Doctorate in Education. I simply wanted to just rest and replenish my energy. Besides much relaxation and later planning a thanksgiving celebration, I did a medical check-up: eyesight, blood pressure, cholesterol, prostate and full blood works. I simply wanted to. I had been carrying a heavy load having done three degrees back-to-back over a 12-year period. Probably I overlooked the gravity and the magnitude of such accomplishment. Honestly, I tend to simply get on with life; full-time teaching, preaching, youth seminars in a few churches, counselling and mentoring others, playing bass guitar in the church worship band, managing our investments, part-time work, domestic chores among other engagements, whilst I did my Bachelors (First-class Honours), Masters (Distinction) and Doctoral degrees non-stop.

Dr Stephen Covey in *'The Seven Habits of Highly Effective People'* encourages us to nurture self. In one of his seven habits, he challenges us to 'sharpen the saw.' This is very important. By this he means, that time should be taken for self-renewal. In the Ecclesiastics 10:10 we learn that 'Using a dull axe requires great strength', so sharpen the blade. That is the value of wisdom; it helps you succeed. Far too often we minister to everyone but neglect ourselves. Whether or not we feel we have the support of others, it is incumbent on us to look after ourselves in all aspects.

Having made it safely through your storm on broken pieces, you have the power and passion to fulfil your purpose. You will thrive where others faltered because of the powerful anointing on your life, gained through the pain you have suffered. However, this can bring with it a down side of sorts. It is possible that others not only come to you for 'healing' like Publius' father, but also lead others to you for ministry as well. How wonderful and powerful an experience that can and should be as you minister to others out of your painful experiences. However, this is so as long as you are being personally 'refilled'. You minister at great personal costs.

I preached on and often ask the question: 'Who ministers to the minister?' Those who having been through the fire and the floods of life, now ministering to and serving others diligently, are sadly sometimes seen for their anointing and not as persons. I have preached on the number of ministers who are sad, isolated, depressed or even suicidal. People can sometimes be unreasonable in their demand on your time and resources emotionally, physically, spiritually or generally. Sometimes the demand is so great that left unchecked, you can burn out as your resources are depleted. Often others might forget that you are ministering out of your personal brokenness. You are praying for and 'healing' others through Christ but out of your own sacrifice and broken places; thus, the need to draw from the 'fountain' as you minister. You must be replenished in the process. You must take the time to sharpen the saw!

I wonder if during the process of encouraging those on the ship, receiving divine and angelic visitation, of gathering firewood, admonishing and giving thanks, serving others food in their fasting and famine, laying on of hands-on Publius' father and all the others who came for healing, if Paul felt tired. I wonder if he even thought about his own pain, exhaustion and the upcoming trial he had in Rome before Caesar, plus savage beatings, imprisonment, isolations, unanswered prayers and death that awaited him.

A Cry for Help: Power to Discern

I remember about twenty years ago I was watching Christian television in the Cayman Islands and I heard a well-known American footballer shared his testimony. As I remember it, he spoke of a time in his life when he had all going for him: wealth and fame, fortune, status, success and great recognition. Yet, he spoke of the emptiness and the deep sense of isolation he was feeling. The trappings and external displays of wealth and success did not seem to satisfy his longings, cravings and the yearnings of his heart, mind, spirit and soul.

He had tried so many things in his quest to find meaning and purpose but sadly to no avail. In his deep distress, he contemplated ending it all. One night as he walked and wandered along a lonely path, hoping against hope that somehow even one person would see him for who he really was…not merely as a successful and wealthy sports personality, but as a person. As he stood by a bridge and contemplated the end, a police patrol car turned up.

Filled with hope, he glanced up as the police patrol car pulled up and the Officer approached him. The Officer recognised him, went back to the car, got his note pad and asked for his autograph! I have heard world famous personalities, some well-known televangelists too, lament the fact that so often people will request 'selfies' to post on social media without even recognising that it is a person behind the image. One asked 'why so enamoured with the image when you could get to know the person?' We do have a responsibility to remember the persons behind the personalities and the flawed mortals behind the faith-filled and anointed preachers; the humans behind the titles, degrees, wealth, power, status and positions of influence.

The good news is that the young sportsman above, went home that night still sad, wounded and broken, confounded by the insensitivity of others, but later found faith in the Lord Jesus Christ that now forms the basis of his meaning and purpose to life, and thankfully part of his testimony and story. That is what I am talking about; being able to make it safely through your trials and troubles successfully, regardless of the hurt from the splinters from the jagged, uneven and sharp ends of the broken pieces, then use your story as a testimony to help others. Indeed,

> *He (God) healeth the broken in heart, and bindeth up their wounds (Psalm 147:3).*

May we be caring, thoughtful and sensitive enough to discern when others are crying for help even when they may not directly ask for it. Sometimes they may drop subtle hints or test your sensitivity in other ways. You may respond in a manner that confirms their perception that you are an encourager worthy of their trust and confidence in their moment of grave distress. On the contrary, your response may confirm to them that you are insensitive, judgemental and uncaring. The truth is that you may never really know what someone is going through. When help, support, encouragement are required of you, be never found wanting – Indeed you may save a life!

Come Apart or Fall Apart
Jesus ministered to the multitude and was very tired. He healed their diseases fed them and ministered to the diverse needs; now he withdrew himself to a quiet place to replenish and renew His strength and fellowshipped with His heavenly Father. In addition, he had just gotten the sad and disturbing news that his cousin John the Baptist had been savagely killed by Herod. Despite His ministry, He was tired and drained.

As he rested alas, the multitude came to Him. Even in this state Jesus ministered to the multitude and met their needs (Luke 6:12). This is a powerful image of His grace, selflessness, power and compassion. Yet, I cannot neglect to illuminate and highlight the need for our 'multitude' to be sensitive to the needs and brokenness of those who minister. In reality, we not only do so out of our personal brokenness, we are simply flawed mortals with limited resources.

As ministers, we have to draw our strength from God as others reach out to us. We must never become so anointed that we forget to minister to our own needs while meeting those of others. Furthermore, we must never attempt to fix people or to minister in our own strength. 'The excellency of the power is of God and not of us, the treasure is in earthen vessel (2 Corinthians 4:7). Be careful not to preach out yourself as you preach in others. Paul warns us,

'I buffet my body lest I win others and be a cast away'
(1 Corinthians 9:27)

This is not selfish it is being prudent. It is being sensible and looking after your personal health and wellbeing. Your family needs you and furthermore, if you are sick, you cannot do any or as much in ministry anyway as you could accomplish healthily. This may mean being able to understand the nature of your associations and how they fit into your process and purpose.

Let us look at the example of Jesus for instance in the Garden of Gethsemane. He had the multitude that he fed (Mark 6:30), the over seventy that he sent forth (Luke 10), the twelve that were his disciples (John 21:15), Peter, James and John that he further mentored and exposed to experiences that all the previous groups were not privy to, for example at the Mount of Transfiguration (Matthew 17). Furthermore, Jesus had a special relationship with John, the one who Jesus loved (John 19:26). Despite the dynamics of these diverse relationships yet, in Gethsemane, the place of pressing, He prayed alone. He was broken, crushed and shattered as he agonised at the heavy cross and the bitter cup ahead of him, as on Him the sins of the world would be laid.

Jesus departed just a stone's throw from them and prayed. Three times he sought their support, 'Watch with me' (Matthew 26:40) yet, 'Worn out by their sorrow they slept away'. Checking on them repeatedly, Jesus finally had to find closure as he said, 'Sleep on. The spirit is willing but the flesh is weak' (Matthew 26:41). He most importantly found closure as He prayed, 'Not my will but thine be done' (Luke 22:42). 'The sorrow in my heart is so great that it almost crushes me. Stay here and keep watch with me." (Matt 26:38). As you go through your storms and come safely through, it is important to understand the categories of associations you have to contend with; from the multitude, the seventy, the twelve, the three, the one and times when you have to face life and life's circumstances alone. Come apart or you will fall apart.

Discerning Associations

You may and will have people around but you can take them so far and no further, for different reasons. Some may not understand the magnitude of the call or mission on your life or relate to you in your situation. Others might simply do not care, still others are selfish and lack the sensitivity to empathise and minister to you. Some people may have good intentions but lack the wherewithal to remain focused throughout the duration of your storm. Some lack the faith to believe at the level of your expectation, while others may be following you to exploit, dilute or pollute your anointing, reputation, qualification or title, seeking to use you as a 'launching pad' for their own selfish agendas. Remember on some occasions, Jesus had to ask some folks to leave or he simply shut the door before performing some miracles (Matthew 9:1-8).

The truth is, not everyone sees what you see, or has a mindset of faith, hope or positivity. Some people will encourage and support you while others are liabilities. Les Brown speaks of 'toxic and nurturing relationships.' Some relationships drain you and contribute very little or nothing positive to your life. Les Brown jokes 'that some people are so negative they can go in a dark room and start to develop!' This does not mean that all associations should be all encouraging. There is a place for critical friendships and we should be humble and gracious enough to receive constructive criticisms; but that is the point, they should be constructive not destructive.

Surrounding yourself with only people who agree with you all the time could be a sign of personal inadequacies. Maybe you are insecure, territorial or easily intimidated. A well-rounded, confident, humble and secure person welcomes others who can challenge them appropriately, respectfully and speak powerfully into their lives even if that might be in the form of a rebuke. The proverb states, 'Better are the wounds of a friend than the kisses of an enemy' (Proverbs 27:6). You need people who can add value to your life. They recognise, celebrate and promote your worth, and significance. They respect your time, expertise, training, experiences and values. They can challenge you without being toxic, unkind, confrontational, argumentative, defensive, critical, judgemental or jealous.

They recognise that your success is not at their expense; henceforth they are in no wise jealous of your achievements or accomplishments. Neither are they in competition with you because they know their own worth, values, purpose, potential and identity. In his book, *'Understanding Your Potential'* the late Doctor Myles Munroe (1991) concluded 'If you feel good about yourself, you will feel good about other people' (p. 55). In other words, something is going on for them in their lives. People who are busy pursuing their own goals and purpose generally do not have time for jealousy, comparison or competition. Adding value can mean sharing at a deep, insightful and helpful level where you can relate to each other.

The Value of Distant Support - Childhood Memories
I believe all of us need to appreciate the help from each category as you identify your 'multitude', 'seventy', 'twelve', 'three', 'one' plus your individual resilience and personal resolve in your storms. It is also important as well, that we recognise the help of distant support that others provide even

if they cannot physically or even emotionally be available to us in our most intense moments of brokenness. So many people have contributed to your success from your early formation to present realisation.

Some of your support bases maybe in distant lands and can only connect through social media, phone or prayerful support. Those who were there for you in your formative years and help to lay a foundation, on which you now build, form a crucial part in your current achievement. Some of your distant support may be physically present but are emotionally, spiritually or academically unavailable. This unavailability may not be out of malice or prejudice but out of inadequacies or ignorance. By this I mean, like the disciples 'the spirit may be willing but the flesh is weak.' Some folks may desperately desire to help minister, nurture and support but their level of training, understanding and depth may not allow them to do so at the level commensurate with your requirements, expectations and need.

Reflection: How can you help and support someone who is at a higher level than yourself spiritually, financially or academically but nonetheless need help but you feel inadequate or intimidated by their success and achievement? How can you see them as real persons?

I remember when I was a teenager studying for my General Certificate of Education Ordinary Level (GCE) Examinations. I was about sixteen years old. Our parents, Lamech and Thelma O'Connor had worked so hard to provide for us and instilled in us the values and attitudes to become successful, worthwhile persons with high aspirations. They had migrated to the United Kingdom in the later 1950s and had worked extremely hard to provide for the family. Lonnie, Ronnie and I were born here in England and later in Jamaica, Sharon, Brenda, Collin, Barrington and Sylvia were born.

It was a challenging time establishing life in Jamaica, working relentlessly on the farm producing crops for sale in the market. As we progressed in our academic career and moved into High or Secondary school, I remember Mom saying that she will support us in every way she can despite the fact that she did not understand the subjects at the level we were at. This humble admission was so moving. 'I pray that God provide the friends and support you all need, who can help you at the level you are at' Mom would say.

As I studied for my exams, I remember Mom would sit in the sofa close by with her head bowed and she would remain there silently for the entire duration of my studies; night after night, even if that meant to midnight and beyond! That was support! She was always within close proximity. However; the moral support and prayers were near and yet distant in the sense that they were not direct tutoring or help literally in completely the assignments. Nevertheless, the support was real, tangible, and very effective. She desperately wanted to do more practically. However, she was constrained by her own educational limitations of her formative years. She had done all she could to educate herself and what an awesome job she did!

I knew she was praying and what an answer to prayer: with only primary school education, my parents raised 8 children: all teachers and nurses (Brenda is a mental Health Nurses with a Master's degree and Sharon a Midwife) with education ranging from Teacher Diploma to Doctorate. This is testament to the value of support at a distance or in close proximity. There is no distance in prayer, furthermore in this age of social media, there is no excuse for not supporting your loved ones and friends through their storms.

Be thankful for the help and support you have from all quarters. However, be resilient and resolute as overall, your most stable, sure and firm support is alone on bended knees when to your Heavenly Father you cry your hurts, fears, tears, cares and open to Him the bitterness of the cup from which you must drink; of the cup that will not pass. Oh, how you wish things were different; nevertheless 'not my will but thine be done.' Therein lies the very essence of closure, as you face your personal brokenness. Your life, hopes and plans may be wrecked, fragmented, smashed, ruined and damaged but you will come through safely even on the broken pieces of your shattered dreams.

Delegate and Regulate
In addition to all the help and support you may receive as you come through your challenges and storms, sometimes you have to understand and appreciate the place of delegation. Especially if you are in leadership, a powerful lesson to remember is that you are a limited resource and you were not meant to carry the burden alone. We all have a part to play, however it is important to be realistic in what you take on. Sometimes you may feel that others will not do as good a job as you can so you embark on more than your fair share.

You may also be territorial, seizing, and holding on to power because of your own insecurities. You may want the glory for yourselves when a task is done. You may even be intimidated by having successful and highly 'intelligent' people on your team lest they 'overshadow' or outshine you.

However, as a leader, you definitely will need to address your personal insecurities and train others, develop leaders, delegate responsibilities, distribute leadership and encourage transformational leadership styles. You are as good as your staff. Avoid being intimidated by the success of your staff. Celebrate their success, locate, and deploy as according to their training, education, gifting, abilities, calling, anointing and passion. Delegate and regulate, but also give space for individuality and creativity. Know when to pass the baton for without a successor there is no success. Bishop TD Jakes, puts it this way, 'Good leadership works itself out of a job!'

A positive quality in leadership is the ability to appreciate the quality of your staff; whether it is in a family, professional setting, church, charitable or organisational setting. A good leader will celebrate the achievement, excellent skills and qualities their staff bring to the table rather than be jealous of or be intimidated thereby. (See John Maxwell or Myles Munroe, TD Jakes on leadership). This is all very relevant to the issues as without a proper and balanced attitude to delegation of responsibilities, the path for isolation, burnout and brokenness is already secure.

A Lesson from Moses
In Number 11: 16 and 17 we read,

> *The LORD therefore said to Moses, "Gather for Me seventy men from the elders of Israel, whom you know to be the elders of the people and their officers and bring them to the tent of meeting, and let them take their stand there with you. Then I will come down and speak with you there, and **I will take of the Spirit who is upon you, and will put Him upon them; and they shall bear the burden of the people with you, so that you will not bear it all alone.***

As outstanding and powerful a leader as Moses was, he was strongly encouraged to share the load. In another case his Father-in-law and Priest, Jethro had to firmly advise him to delegate. In Exodus 18: 13-24 we read the interesting and insightful account:

> *The next day Moses took his seat to serve as judge for the people, and they stood around him from morning till evening. When his father-in-law saw all that Moses was doing for the people, he said, "What is this you are doing for the people? Why do you alone sit as judge, while all these people stand around you from morning till evening?"*
>
> *Moses answered him, "Because the people come to me to seek God's will. Whenever they have a dispute, it is brought to me, and I decide between the parties and inform them of God's decrees and instructions."*
>
> *Moses' father-in-law replied, "What you are doing is not good. You and these people who come to you will only wear yourselves out. The work is too heavy for you; you cannot handle it alone. Listen now to me and I will give you some advice, and may God be with you. You must be the people's representative before God and bring their disputes to him.*
>
> *Teach them his decrees and instructions, and show them the way they are to live and how they are to behave. But select capable men from all the people—men who fear God, trustworthy men who hate dishonest gain—and appoint them as officials over thousands, hundreds, fifties and tens. Have them serve as judges for the people at all times, but have them bring every difficult case to you; the simple cases they*

> *can decide themselves. That will make your load lighter, because they will share it with you. If you do this and God so commands, you will be able to stand the strain, and all these people will go home satisfied."*
>
> *Moses listened to his father-in-law and did everything he said. He chose capable men from all Israel and made them leaders of the people, officials over thousands, hundreds, fifties and tens. They served as judges for the people at all times. The difficult cases they brought to Moses, but the simple ones they decided themselves."*

This is a very lengthy but a perfect example of delegation, but also of one, which clearly demonstrates how easy it is to be burnt out without it. Your approach may be wrong simply because you want to do a good job, but all by yourself. Your intentions are good but your methods and strategies may need adjusting. The observation and advice of Jethro is sound and well founded. Sometimes when you are going through your storms, challenges and hardships you cannot see or even feel the toll it is having on you. Sometimes, it takes a 'Jethro' to reach out to you with helpful suggestions, observations and advice to make the load lighter. Crucially though, will you listen and take heed? To put your spirit in 70 men or to have men set up over thousands, hundred, fifties and tens, exemplifies the epitome of stress, magnitude of the mission and fervent workload Moses was carrying single-handedly before the well-needed intervention.

Social and Emotional Intelligence in Leadership

Goleman (1998) in his research targeting nearly 200 large international companies, found that traditionally held perceptions of successful leadership qualities like intelligence, toughness, determination and vision were simply insufficient. He suggests that a high degree of emotional intelligence through self-awareness, regulation, motivation, empathy and social skill distinguished highly effective leaders. Alongside increased self-awareness, Rogers (1986a) in Tew (2007) identifies three core conditions necessary for personal growth and learning to take place:

(1) Congruence (genuineness), authenticity, 'It enhances the quality of …relationships leading to trust, leading to open and honest discussion on social, emotional and behavioural issues' (p13).

(2) Empathy (non-judgemental attitude), seeing from another person's perspective. This gives freedom and respect to the perceptions of another while still holding on to your personal view

(3) Unconditional acceptance. This enhances self-confidence and engenders authentic responses as the need to camouflage one's true self is diminished.

Ministering to the Ministers – Leaders Nurturing Themselves

The nurturing of yourself as a leader therefore remains a critical part of this self-giving and modelling process. As a leader you need to encourage yourself in order to be able to care for and minister to others. Care must be taken to be faithful to your roles but also yourself. You must remain in tune with your emotions and be true to yourself. Tomlinson (2004) argues that leaders should actually reveal their weaknesses 'showing their humanity, confirming that they are 'people' not simply their roles (p119). However, it is of crucial importance that you carefully choose those to whom you share at this deep, personal and intimate level. Clear categories of associations must therefore be established and adhered to for reasons already mentioned. Not everyone can handle this level of access and remain respectful and committed to their purpose and vision.

Nevertheless, leadership must also remain connected to those being served. Here, as Ackerman and Maslin-Ostrowski argue, the conflict between leadership role and your identity must be managed as it can 'diminish your chances of being genuine.' Day (2004) citing Farber and Miller (1981) speaking from an educational perspective, notes effectiveness is greatly reduced and being sympathetic will be adversely affected if one is 'emotionally exhausted.'

Encouraging Scriptures in Your Brokenness

'The LORD [is] nigh unto them that are of a broken heart; and saveth such as be of a contrite spirit' (Psalm 34:18).

'The sacrifices of God [are] a broken spirit: a broken and a contrite heart, O God, thou wilt not despise' (Psalm 51:17).

'He healeth the broken in heart, and bindeth up their wounds' (Psalm 147:3).

'Verily, verily, I say unto you, Except a corn of wheat falls into the ground and die, it abideth alone: but if it die, it bringeth forth much fruit' (John 12:24).

'Trust in the LORD with all thine heart; and lean not unto thine own understanding' (Proverbs 3:5).

'For thus saith the high and lofty One that inhabiteth eternity, whose name [is] Holy; I dwell in the high and holy [place], with him also [that is] of a contrite and humble spirit, to revive the spirit of the humble, and to revive the heart of the contrite ones' (Isaiah 57:15).

'I am forgotten as a dead man out of mind: I am like a broken vessel' (Psalm 31:12 ESV).

'We do not want you to be uninformed, brothers and sisters, about the troubles we experienced in the province of Asia. We were under great pressure, far beyond our ability to endure, so that we despaired of life itself. Indeed, we felt we had received the sentence of death. But this happened that we might not rely on ourselves but on God, who raises the dead. He has delivered us from such a deadly peril, and he will deliver us again' (2 Corinthians 1:8-10).

'But he giveth more grace. Wherefore he saith, God resisteth the proud, but giveth grace unto the humble' (James 4:6).

'I am crucified with Christ: nevertheless, I live; yet not I, but Christ liveth in me: and the life which I now live in the flesh I live by the faith of the Son of God, who loved me, and gave himself for me' (Galatians 2:20).

'Confess [your] faults one to another, and pray one for another, that ye may be healed. The effectual fervent prayer of a righteous man availeth much' (James 5:16).

'The Spirit of the Lord is upon me, because he hath anointed me to preach the gospel to the poor; he hath sent me to heal the broken-hearted, to preach deliverance to the captives, and recovering of sight to the blind, to set at liberty them that are bruised' (Luke 4:18).

'When they had all had enough to eat, he said to his disciples, "Gather the pieces that are left over. Let nothing be wasted."' (John 6:12, NIV).

'O Lord my God, I cried out to you, and you healed me' (Psalm 30:2, NKJV).

'Heal me, O Lord, and I shall be healed; save me, and I shall be saved: for thou art my praise' (Jeremiah 17:14).

'Why are you downcast, O my soul? Why the unease within me? Put your hope in God, for I shall yet praise Him for the salvation of His presence' (Psalm 42:5).

'A cheerful heart is good medicine, but a broken spirit saps a person's strength' (Proverbs 17:22, NLT).

11. Recapping Some Important Life Lessons

When goals go, meaning goes. When meaning goes, purpose goes. When purpose goes, life goes dead on our hands'

(Carl Jung, 1875-1961, Swiss Psychiatrist)

Further Applications

As you face the storms or challenges in your life, it is necessary that you develop relevant strategies to handle them, whether they are of your own making or of others. In this chapter, I want to recap some of the life lessons and strategies you can glean in order to deal effectively with circumstances as you face them. To begin, it is of crucial importance to have a clear sense of your own identity, whether personally, culturally, spiritually or otherwise.

From a spiritual point of view, you can make a clear distinction between your position (Ephesians 2:6, NKJV) and raised us up together, and made us sit together in the heavenly places in Christ Jesus; and your condition, that is to say, who you are and what you do. A good place to start is in 2 Corinthians 5:21:

> "For he hath made him to be sin for us, who knew no sin; that we might be made the righteousness of God in him. [that is, we would be made acceptable to God and placed in a right relationship with Him by His gracious lovingkindness]."

This clear sense of identity will guide you in determining your core, beliefs and non-negotiable values. Life and situations will always demand that you defend your faith, values, morals and beliefs. There will be times when you will have to find the courage to change some circumstances in your life and accept others; yet be discerning enough to know how and when to decipher between the two. You need to understand your modus operandi in handling your daily routine as well as how you manage the more serious issues of life, whether analytically, systematically or in a flexible manner. There has to be a degree of flexibility to change course as and when needed. Life's detours are not necessarily denials and your disappointments could be God's appointments.

As you travel the path of life, you will gather and accumulate so many things: experiences, attitudes, beliefs and patterns. Some of these may reflect your understanding and a particular truth, which might be useful, relevant and helpful at a set time, age and stage in your life. However, as situations, relationships and paradigms change, you may need to 'lay aside the weigh which beset you and lighten the ship' metaphorically speaking. This is not about being fickle, uncertain or unstable. These are not helpful traits. I am talking about having the wisdom to discern when a mindset, value, attitude, person, relationship or situation might no longer be an asset in your life but a devastating liability. When holding on to them is only toxic and not in any way, nurturing your body, soul, mind or spirit.

Lightening the ship or casting cargo overboard is a deliberate and delicate act where occasionally, even essentials have to go. Life depends on it. In Philippians 3:3-7, Paul recounts his pedigree and acknowledged their total worthlessness in light of all he gained in Christ, 'Whatever things were gained to me I counted as loss for Christ' he writes.

Note that on the ship, the cargo was first to go. All the excess baggage you collect along the path of life, the things that happened in the past that add to the weight must go: toxic associations, experiences, your negative attitude or utterances. You have to deliberately dispose of them. Weight can be fear, regrets, guilt, pride, arrogance, selfishness, pride, conceit, self-righteousness, jealousy, shame, loss, unforgiveness. 'Cargo' or 'weight' can also be important aspects of our lives, which were of great value at one stage or phase in life or in a particular situation. However, in a different situation or time; and under different set of circumstances, now move from being assets to liabilities. It could also be things we put our faith in, like education, training, expertise, backgrounds, culture or ethnicity. But it could be 'filthiness of the flesh and of the spirit (2 Corinthians 7:1). For instance, the elder brother in the story of the Prodigal Son might not have gone out and wasted his substance in riotous living but was as much filthy in attitude and spirit (Luke 15:28).

Casting and Keeping
Another important life lesson and application I want to point out is that even though the cargo was cast overboard, as the journey progressed and the storms grew fiercer, more possessions that were valuable had to be disposed of or cast away. The captain/owner took about three days after commanding that the ship be lightened before they had to make a crucial decision: to unfasten and unhook the ship's tackle and cast it overboard too! Letting go of what you consider valuable and of real importance whether of values, associations, mindsets, attitudes or things can be painful. The process can indeed take time. Only you can decide when you

have gotten to the place when and where you are ready to let go of anything that potentially could take you under. Sometimes significant others may advise, counsel, beg, admonish or suggest; however, you have to 'come to yourself' like the Prodigal son. Hopefully, it will not require a 'Damascus Road or hog pen experience' to get there.

Unlike the cargo, the tackle is part of the structure of the ship. "It is an assemblage of ropes and pulleys arranged to gain mechanical advantage for hoisting and pulling, or any system of leverage using pulleys, as a combination of ropes and blocks as for hoisting or lowering objects. It is the gear and running rigging of a ship (google). It's easy to cast away something you are not connected to but when there is a connection, a bond and relationship, then it is quite another story. It is easy to judge someone and demand that they simply get over what is bothering them! But the truth is they may be 'connected' in some unhealthy way like the tackle to that thing, be it a habit, stronghold, addiction, attitude, association, mindset or even a person.

Like in the case of Abraham,

> *Wherefore she (Sarah) said unto Abraham, Cast out this bondwoman and her son: for the son of this bondwoman shall not be heir with my son, even with Isaac (Genesis 21:10).*

Arguably, it was easier for Sarah to demand that her husband cast out Haggai the bondwoman and her unborn son, Ishmael. She was not that emotionally or sexually invested. Never mind the fact that she suggested in the first place that her husband produce an offspring through the maid in light of her then inability to do so, despite the promise of God that she would.

The deeper the bond, connection and the investment, the more difficult the 'casting'. The stronger the bond, then the weaker the determination and proclivity will be to dispose of it.

Your core and non-negotiable values may be wholesome and wholly desirable pursuits yet can be hindrances if wrongly prioritised or even idolised. Interestingly, traumas, accidents, hurts and pains are deeply personal and form part of your story, experiences and life. Extricating yourself from them can be painfully difficult. But removing your 'tackle' to eventually save your life, can be painful but has to be deliberate and done by you. Retaining it eventually jeopardises your very survival with potential impact on significant others. Thus, divine help and faith are needed to navigate these choppy seas and deadly storms without your safety crutch, especially if in place and had been part of your life's journey for years.

A Complete Sacrifice
The story is told of the chicken and the pig, who on a farm one day had a heated discussion. They were not really quarrelling, just having what I will call, an intense moment of fellowship about who made their master a more scrumptious breakfast. The chicken boasted of the different ways in which the eggs can be used: fried, boiled, poached, scrambled, omelettes while the pig listened intently. When it was his time to speak, the pig agreed with all the chicken had said, but poignantly added, 'for me to make my master a breakfast, I have to make the ultimate sacrifice! I must die to provide the ham, bacon or sausage!' Some things are valuable and maybe difficult to cast aside because they cost a part of you or your very life in its entirety.

Reflection: What are you carrying that may be of worth and value but is impeding or hindering your destiny?

There will be times in your storms when you are not gaining ground or making progress, sometimes you may be making some progress, but do not feel that way. These are the times when you simply 'stand ye therefore'. You differentiate between the negative mindset of condemnation that you are not doing enough or making sufficient progress for your age and stage, from those really crushing moments when you have done all you can do in all areas to successfully manage that situation and yet you come to a crashing halt. What do you do? You still hold on to your faith and maintain your integrity and resolve; determine to hold your ground and simply ride out the storm, and wait for calm *for 'day'*...Weeping may endure for the night but joy comes in the morning (Psalm 30:5); Never forget that,

> *'He that goeth forth weeping will doubtless come again bearing precious sheaves (Psalm 126:6).*

As you stand, you guard your heart, mind and spirit. According to Jakes (1996)

> *'The turbulence of change can be overpowering...So if you are going to have peace in your process, you must guard your heart and mind with prayer.' (p29).*

Personal Protective Equipment (PPE)

You protect your inner person from the toxicity of that which is without; remembering that you are safe once that which is on the outside does not enter and contaminate you. Each profession from medicine, science, technology, construction, security or engineering has its own personal protective equipment (PPE). This point has become known even more so in the coronavirus pandemic when we came to value the crucial importance of PPE especially for front line essential key medical staff as well as face masks or shields for the general public. If the virus from without does not infiltrate within, one will not be infected.

Noah in Genesis 6:14, (NASB) was given this strict instruction: 'Make for yourself an ark of gopher wood; you shall make the ark with rooms, and shall cover it inside and out with pitch.' Another translation puts it this way, 'Build a large boat from cypress wood and waterproof it with tar, inside and out. Then construct decks and stalls throughout its interior." (Genesis 6:14, NLT). *"Pitch was traditionally used to help seal or waterproof the seams of wooden sailing vessels (see shipbuilding). Pitch may also be used to waterproof wooden containers and in the making of torches."*

As long as the water was kept out of the ark, it was in absolutely no danger of sinking. However, any breach in the ship howsoever small, if left unchecked, will undoubtedly lead to disaster. Provided the water remains without, the buoyancy of the ship is assured and the water remains a method of transportation but not destruction. As the saying goes, 'if there is no enemy within, the enemy without can do you no harm.' This means guarding your eye-gate, ear gate and your mind gate; relationships, social and mainstream media as well as prevailing attitudes, trends, values, beliefs and values imposed upon you from without.

Narrow Your Circle of Association Closer to Your Destination

The closer you get to your destination it is crucial that you not only avoid complacency but that you also narrow your circle. Not everyone is called to go to the pinnacle of success with you; not everyone who started out with you, is necessarily called or destined to finish with you. This does not mean that you are discriminating or are selfish and forget your roots.

Rather, it means that you have to be discerning enough to know when someone's part in your story is simply over; when their continued impact and influence in your life is no longer helpful or fruitful, rather is toxic, a distraction and a liability.

The truth is that the higher you get to your goals, the narrower your circle becomes. The higher you get to the top, the more isolated is gets. True, it is lonely at the top because few there be that aspire thus. Sadly, some will try to hold you back as you progress, with their negative words, attitudes and actions. But if you associate with people who will, as my mantra says, 'Motivate, inspire, challenge and encourage' you then you will sail and navigate the choppy and stormy seas with the wind of their support beneath your sails. With or without the help and support of significant others, you press on towards your destiny, towards your hopes, dreams, goals and God-given, God-ordained purpose.

Self-Renewal and Refreshing
As you press on however, you remember the need for self-renewal and refreshing, as earlier discussed. It is possible to feed everyone and you become malnourished physically, emotionally, spiritually, mentally or relationally. Permit me to reiterate that it is possible to become so entrenched and enamoured in your vision or purpose that you forget to as Dr Stephen Covey in *'The Seven Habits of Highly Effective People'* identifies the value of 'Sharpen the saw.' Don't over work yourself, instead do strive for a sustainable lifestyle that affords you time to recuperate, recharge and be effective in the long-term. Learn from Moses, delegate and regulate.

Remember that God's divine presence is there with you even in contrary winds and that all things will work for your good ultimately (Romans 8:28). The circumstances of your life may set in motion a progression from 'contrary winds' (Acts 27:4), winds not suffering us (v6), sailing through winds that are dangerous (v9) and then posing imminent danger to life and property (v10). Even in such a tumultuous and dire situation with all seemingly lost, God uses what you have left. The temptation is to bemoan your situation and lament the grave injustices life handed down to you. But be encouraged and reminded that God uses not what you have lost necessarily but what you have left. So as tempting as it might be and as justified as it might seem and perhaps reasonably so, shun with great haste the temptation to join the club of complainers and negative proclaimers of how unfair life is to you and instead, frantically cling to the remnants of your broken hopes, dreams, relationships and life and head for shore.

Salvage and Use What You Have Left
Hasten to salvage any usable part, whether a smooth plank or the broken pieces with the jagged ends and despite its painful infliction of grave discomfort, hold on and relentlessly navigate your way through this stormy blast, setting your face like flint and fervent resolve to achieve your purpose and destiny! "Because the Sovereign LORD helps me, I will not be disgraced. Therefore, have I set my face like flint, and I know I will not be put to shame" (Isaiah 50:7). Now when the time was approaching for Him to be taken up [to heaven], He was determined to go to Jerusalem [to fulfil His purpose, steadfastly and with determination] (Luke 9:51, AMP).

With this kind of resolve you do not have time to cry or be stressed out over who does not like you or who is talking about you and all the 'light afflictions.' Strive not to major on minor and minor on majors rather, choose your battles in life. I am sure; there are more serious things of concern to you; concerns that require every ounce of your mental, emotional, spiritual fortitude and stamina. Remember the words of my mother as a child to me, 'save your strength for the difficult issues of life, don't waste your tears!' This is not meant to be unsupportive or unkind but in the spirit in which they were given, are sound words of advice that will and are useful for life. It is all about priorities. As you develop this sense of determination and resolve, you will be confident in yourself and in the knowledge of who, and whose you are.

You can rejoice with, and celebrate the achievements of others and not compare yourself with others. Indeed, a wise person learns from the life experiences of others; however, you carve a path for yourself that appreciates and values the uniqueness of your calling, purpose and destiny. Consequently, your experiences can and will be different from others. You will not be jealous of or intimidated by others' success. You will survive what could hurt others.

Find Your Purpose for Your Suffering
From the snake bite the local inhabitants genuinely expected Paul to fall over, swell up and die. That was what happened to others, but that was certainly not Paul's experience or portion. Without being arrogant or conceited you too can accept and appreciate the life experiences of others and the consequences of actions but with a sense of discernment and resolve. You can press forward with steadfast determination to fulfil your unique calling and purpose God designed for you and no one else. Thus, you survived your storm for a reason; do not let your suffering be in vain. Such survival indicates your special anointing, purpose and mission. Others have theirs that they must find and pursue for themselves. Murdock (2001) states:

> 'Somebody needs you! your words will motivate someone incapable of seeing what you see…God has qualified you to be a perfect solution to someone' (p. 83-84).

You may be a blessing or the catalyst in the lives of others to point them to their purpose! How can this be, you may ask? Well, by virtue of the things you suffered, I will hastily add. You can now share your experiences through various media, platforms. You can comfort others with the same comfort wherewith you have been comforted. Christ comforts us in all our troubles so that we can comfort others. The Scriptures put it this way: 'When they are troubled, we will be able to give them the same comfort God has given us' (2 Corinthians 1:4, NLT).

Alvin Day (2003) puts it this way:

> 'Your obligation is to be strong, grow, and educate yourself. Achieve your goals and become a significant force in the lives of others…expand your ability to touch the lives of more people by first touching your own' (p.6).

So, while you go through your trials, troubles and tribulations it is not all about you. You have a responsibility to learn life's lessons so that you can be a blessing; blessed to be a blessing. This is part of the whole reason for this book; to share some of my personal stories and how I have learnt from them to use life's lessons to motivate, inspire, challenge and encourage! That is what it is all about.

Do not be discouraged for 'God is a very present help in times of trouble (Psalm 46:1). The darkest part of the night is just before dawn and a smooth sea does not make a skilful sailor.

It is not the ease of life that shows your resilience but how you surmount your highest mountains and weather the fiercest storms. You achieve the best version of yourself in the stormiest of gale because 'the one who regards the weather never sows' (Ecclesiastes 11:4).

Some Things are Beyond Explanation

You learn from life's distress howsoever caused. Not all your suffering and troubles will be of your own making; sometimes you will suffer as result of the actions of others, deliberate or unintentional. Sometimes you will have to pick up the broken pieces of your and others' mistakes. Pickford (1893-1979) re-assures us that,

> *'If you make mistakes…there is always another chance for you. You may have a fresh start at any moment you choose, for this thing we call "failure" is not the falling down but the staying down.'*

The things that happened to you may not be fair, sadly, that is life. Nevertheless, you can maintain a right attitude in the storms of life. It is said, 'your attitude, determines your altitude.' Henry Ford argues that, 'Even a mistake may turn out to be the one thing necessary to be a worthwhile achievement.'

Like Paul, seek the Lord in the storm and be prepared to give a prophetic Word if you are thus inspired. Even if this is ignored, persist by faith with your reassurance and encouragement. There will be times when it may be appropriate to give words of challenge, admonition and firm rebuke. However, this should be done respectfully and in love. Be confident in yourself and in your relationship with God and do nothing outside of the peace of God (Philippians 4:7,

Romans 15:3) which acts as your umpire. Hold fast the profession of your faith even in the midst of rejection, ridicule or refutation, for great will be your reward.

Be reminded that getting divine revelation and illumination does not necessarily exempt you from being 'bitten'; you can still get hurt or 'bitten' when you are doing what's right. According to Martin (2000),

> *'Having favour doesn't mean you won't have problems. It just means problems won't have you because you will rise above them (p,15).*

The Scripture makes it quite plain that suffering persecution is inevitable for those who choose to live Godly (2 Timothy 3:12). Jesus asked, 'If these things be done in the green tree what will be done in the dry?' (Luke 23:31). Furthermore, Jesus told his disciples, "If anyone would come after me, let him deny himself and take up his cross and follow me (Matthew 16:24). Therefore, remember that in those situations and at those times when you cannot 'trace his hand, you trust his heart' holding on to the fact that His grace is sufficient and that God is a present help in times of trouble.

Even if you are bitten when doing well, have the presence of mind to 'shake it off in the fire.' This is significant, you shake it off where it will not return to do you harm.

Advance to the Next Level
There are some tests and trials that you confront once. Provided you successfully navigate them, there is no need for a re-sit. My days in school in Jamaica were quite different from my current experience of education in the United Kingdom. During my primary and secondary school experiences, for instance, simply remained in one class until they 'passed' or

successfully met the requirements to matriculate or move on to the next level, year or grade. It meant these students remained in a particular class well beyond the dictates of chronological age; if that was what it took for them to reach the required standard to be admitted to the next level!

Certainly, that could and most definitely would be embarrassing, but the converse was also true whereby students could skip a grade if their progress and academic performance indicated that they were working at a level commensurate with the standard of the next level or grade. I must add that here in England, I have seen few cases where students had to repeat a whole year especially at Advanced level or in sixth form, however, this seems extremely rare.

I believe that this experience can present a powerful teaching moment. If you fail to learn the lesson of life in a particular trial, trouble or storm, but emerge with a negative attitude or mindset that could mean you having to re-sit that test! It is therefore incumbent on you to internalise and display the right attitude; one of resilience, gratitude, humility and teachability to ensure a reasonably smooth transition to the next level of your character development. Thus, you will be ready for the celebration as well as the next trial appropriate for that level of success and victory.

I mentioned earlier, that there are some trials (troubles, storms, persecutions and crosses); that you face once in your life at a particular time and stage. Undoubtedly, you will face many more, but not those exact ones again because you have passed that stage of testing successfully. For example, you have done your entrance examination to get into Secondary school. You will never do that again. Similarly, your end of secondary school exam, Bachelor, Master's, Doctoral or PhD degree depending on the stage you are at on the academic ladder. If you have successfully completed any of these levels, there would be no need for you to repeat them. You may go higher but these stages are now in the past. Appreciate, celebrate and learn from them. Use the learning to improve self, society and others.

All in the Past – You Will See These No More!
Let us reflect briefly on Job and Joseph in Scripture as examples. After all that Job went through when he lost all and suffered greatly in his health, reputation, finances, business, relationships and family, he emerged successfully after the difficulties of his process. He was blessed doubled and nowhere have we read of Job going through those same trials again. The Scripture declares:

> *'So, the LORD blessed the second part of Job's life more than the first. He had 14,000 sheep, 6,000 camels, 1,000 yoke of oxen, and 1,000 female donkeys (Job 42:12, Net Bible).*

The same is true for Joseph. After all the trials, tribulation and sufferings; the lies, humiliation, jealousies, abuse, rejections, exploitation, isolation, punishments from the pit to prison to the palace, he maintained a positive attitude and mind set and successfully completed all his tests at each age, phase and stage. His ultimate success and reward are summed up thus with this proclamation:

> *"You shall be in charge of my house, and all my people are to obey your commands. Only with regard to the throne will I be greater than you. Pharaoh also told Joseph; I hereby place you over all the land of Egypt. Then Pharaoh removed the signet ring from his finger,*

put it on Joseph's finger, clothed him in garments of fine linen, and placed a gold chain around his neck.(Genesis 440-41, Berean Study Bible)

After all that Joseph endured, he reached the pinnacle of success, the epitome of high attainment, and nowhere in Scripture have we seen that he ever went through those same tests again. He no doubt had more challenges personally, relationally and perhaps professionally as he oversaw the management of resources during the famine. However, he came through safely on broken pieces using what he had left after all he went through! Never again did he go through those exact trials again, not enslavement, a pit, prison, lies or betrayal.

'Each level brings new devils' the saying goes. Commensurate with each stage and phase of your development and achievement will be challenges appropriate thereto. Sadly, there is no stage in life when you will be totally trouble free. Each age, stage or phase brings its own unique set of challenges whether during infancy, childhood, adolescence, young adulthood, adulthood or old age; whether married or single, educated or uneducated, prosperous or in need in any area of life. Regardless of how badly you have been bitten and how embarrassing it might have been to bear your cross and shame publicly, never let such a venomous bite abort your destiny. Indeed, that was the intention but never allow it to immobilise (stop, halt and restrain), neutralise (nullify, deactivate and reduce the effect of) and debilitate (incapacitate, weaken and hinder) and ultimately kill your hopes, dreams, purpose, plans, vision and legacy in the earth. Most importantly, never let it miss your eternal destiny.

Reflection: This is the time for legacy contemplation. What do you want your legacy to be? What will you leave in the earth that will outlast and outlive you? How do you want to be remembered? What specifically will you leave behind that will benefit countless others across the nations of the earth in a tangible way?

Post Storm Perceptions

After you have come safely through your storm, there should be a period of reflection, restoration and refreshing. Sometimes there may be successive storms but when it is all over The LORD says, 'I will give you back what you lost to the swarming locusts, the hopping locusts, the stripping locusts, and the cutting locusts. It was I who sent this great destroying army against you' (Joel 2:25, NLT). Never mind the host that encamp about you to destroy you. God is with you (Psalm 27:3). Greater is he that is in you than he that is in the world (1 John 4:4). Never mind how slow your progress might seem, 'the steps of a good man are ordered by the Lord' (Psalm 37:23). You might have envisaged or hoped you would have been much further on in life by now. Nevertheless, continue on from where you are with what you have left. Never give up.

Even if you are 'cut', remember there is a cut to kill and a cut to cure, medically speaking. Let the savage cutting from the challenges of life serve to enhance your healing and not destroy you. You may be stripped of your hope, faith, identity, confidence, and zest for life, aspiration or even the will to live. Be reminded, that if God allows the test, it is all in the plan. The fight is fixed. Your victory is guaranteed. I will restate this verse again and again for emphasis: 'For I know the plans I have for you,' declares the Lord, 'plans to prosper you and not to harm you, plans to give you hope and a future' (Jeremiah

29:11, NIV). This is a good verse to remember especially in those moments when you might feel that life is unfair to you.

Find the strength to minister in, through and after the storm. Comfort, inspire, encourage, motivate, admonish and pray for others. You may even need to do these before, in, through or after your storm. Publius' father and others need your help. Countless others need to hear your story. You may think that it is too insignificant but do not think that way, change that negative mindset now. Believe in the power of your story. Believe that you definitely have something constructive, insightful and helpful to contribute that will make a real difference in the lives of many.

Ministering to others may sometimes mean that you are hesitant to accept help from others. This is understandable but it is something to guard against. There could be a feeling, whatever the reason, that you do not need support, encouragement, hospitality or intervention. This feeling could be borne out of pride, conceit, fear or insecurities. Furthermore, it could be as a result of frustrations at the selfishness of others, after always being the one ministering to others and not getting reciprocity. You may be distrustful of others' motives as well. By this, I mean that you may question the reasons why the help is being offered and in whose interest, it is offered. This level of suspicion and scepticism could be unfounded or based on real life experiences. Despite this, it is necessary at some point, to accept help, support, care, hospitality and constructive intervention as you deal with the issues of life.

As we come to the end of the penultimate chapter, I would like to recap two more issues; firstly, the need for flexibility. Being open and not too rigid can be a positive way to deal with the challenges of life. Besides allowing you to be adaptable, pliable and accommodating to challenges as and when they appear. Flexibility can undoubtedly contribute positively to your health and wellbeing by reducing stress, anxieties and care.

However, you should not be too flexible at the expense of structure, order, organisation, boundary and being systematic to some degree. For Paul, this meant remaining in Malta another three years before moving on to Italy. That was long and certainly not in the original plan. You would think that it would have been a simple straightforward journey from Jerusalem. Even with the storm and the tragedy at sea, no one could have predicted or envisaged such changes in circumstances and outcome. There is a saying that 'things turn out the best for those who make the best of how things turn out.' This is flexibility; facing whatever life throws at you and dealing with it to the best of your ability by God's grace and having a positive attitude and mind set in the process.

The second point I will mention is your attitude to self, others, life and even to God after your storm. So often you may be tempted to think that once the storm is over or you are safely through whether unaided, on planks or on broken pieces that the issues are over. In some cases, this might be so. However, at other times, this can be so far from reality. It is possible to pull through safely and not survive the healing process. No wonder the words of admonition continue to reverberate: 'Having done all, stand ye therefore.' This is powerful. It is not enough to simply come through safely. It is also possible to come through safely with an attitude of superiority, judgementalism, pride and conceit. This is to say, your heart is hardened to the needs of those going through their processes, lacking understanding, care and empathy.

I am sure you have heard people say 'I have made it, so can you' or 'I paid the price to be here so go do likewise', 'you will not get anything from me'; or 'how could you let that bother you'? There might be a time and place when challenge, rebuke, admonition or constructive feedback will be appropriate. However, the attitude and spirit in which they are uttered should be in love and with understanding and non-judgementalism. Your cross will be different from others. It is so easy to compare yourself with others and judge them harshly. I pray that as you have come through safely you will remain humble, thankful, approachable and empathetic. Do not be hardened or embittered by your experiences. Rather, prayerfully reflect and seek how you can use the life lessons from your dire process to benefit humanity.

Reflection:

What do you do when the process seems to cost too much? What do you have left after all you have expended to survive? How do you now feel about your storms with these fresh insights? What can you offer to others because of what you have been through? How will you use the lessons learnt from your trials to benefit others, who, how, why and when? What specifically will you do? How do you feel after the storm?

12. Parting Words – You will Make it Safely Through, Even on Broken Pieces!

'Don't be afraid to take a big step if one is indicated. You can't cross a chasm in two small jumps'

(David Lloyd George, 1863-1945, British Prime Minister and Statesman)

These are my prophetic and parting words to you today:

"You will make it safely through even on broken pieces!" Will you receive this 'Word' today? I know that you might not feel that this applies to you because of the gravity and the magnitude of your situation. Your heart may be broken in many pieces. Perhaps, you feel isolated, dejected, sad, overlooked, ostracised, used or even exploited. Possibly, you have trained someone for a position on the job only for you to be made redundant and your trainee got your post with promotion. It could be that you have poured your all into a marriage or relationship or your children and they rise to say 'you were not there for me!' It is possible that you were frugal, diligent and extremely careful with your financial planning and management only for recession and Covid-19 to set you back by years. Maybe your investments instruments, stocks, shares, equity, business or pension all dwindle away or were drastically reduced or even disappeared before your very eyes.

Could it be that you had to downsize, relocate, or change your lifestyle drastically through no fault of your own? In other words, you had to 'step down' in your standard of living and you are embarrassed, hurt, disappointed, bitter, ridiculed or in despair. Are you struggling with an incurable health issue? No doubt, the treatment is frightening with painful side effects. These 'storms' and others, no doubt push you to desperation and the limit of your endurance and ability to cope.

Did you have to put your studies on hold after years of academic rigour and costly tuition fees or even had to voluntarily withdraw from your degree because of ill health, stress, unexpected or unforeseen circumstances? Maybe you feel unsupported by your teachers, lecturers, supervisors and professors. It could be that you are not coping well with the online teaching arrangements, as you would benefit much more from regular face-to-face interactions, lectures and tutorials. Perhaps you have lost a loved one and you could not be there for such a one in the final moments of life. These and other situations are all fervently painful, and vaguely can anyone even begin to conceptualise your trauma.

You may have started out well and like Paul, storms developed along the way, unexpected storms. Paul had a personal encounter and relationship with the living Christ and this meant that he trusted Him even in that situation. He did not become bitter and blame God for, in or after the situation. He did not remind God of his ministry and service to Him. He did not become angry, abandon his faith and stop serving God. His deep fellowship and divine revelation and illumination from God did not prevent his storms; instead, they supported, comforted and inspired him and others through the storms. How do you feel about your incidences, accidents, traumas and life's vicissitudes? You may argue that 'serve him right', he is having is just desserts for all the evil he did in his lifetime. God is the Sovereign God of purpose and destiny. He uses even our mistakes, accidents, incidents, traumas and flaws for His glory! No experience is ever wasted. Nothing happens by chance in the life of the believer.

Like Job (in the Bible), you may have tough questions for God, for example,

> 'Why wasn't I born dead? Why didn't I die as I came from the womb' (Job 3:11 NLT).

That is part of being human. Elijah was depressed after his experiences on Mount Carmel. 'But he went on a day's journey into the wilderness. He sat down under a broom tree and prayed that he might die. He cried out to God is desperation,

> 'I have had enough! LORD, take my life, for I'm no better than my fathers' (1 Kings 19:4, Christian Standard Bible).

Jesus asked,

> 'My God, my God, why hath thou forsaken me'?

And declared in distress,

> 'My soul is exceedingly sorrowful even unto death'

God Can Handle the Cry of Your Broken Heart
So regardless of how you feel, God can handle the cry of your broken heart. Like Paul, God can give you divine revelation on how to handle your storms. We walk by faith and not by sight. 'The steps of a good man are ordered by the Lord...' (Psalm 37:23); so, whilst in some situations we get divine revelation and illumination, there are other times when God says nothing. This calls for trust.

Do you remember the story of my SatNav? Set your destination before your start your journey. Preview your journey before you set out and after you have done all these precautionary interventions, be flexible and remember that even if you are prompted to take a detour or you have missed your turn or failed to follow a given instruction, you will be recalibrated back on course. Furthermore, if you have not received any instruction from your SatNav; that is, you have driven for quite a while in silence, you can rest assured that you are still on the right track; just keep going straight ahead.

Similar to when you are taking your driving examination, in the absence of any instructions from your examiner, simply keep straight ahead. For a number of these devices (SatNav) and in life you receive instructions mainly for major life-changing events. This does not mean that God has no interest in the seemingly minute and mundane issues of life. Be reminded that even the hairs on your head are numbered (Luke 12:7), not counted. 'Counted' implies how many are present, however 'numbered' means that each strand can be identified and accounted for.

According to TD Jakes (2017) assures us that,

> *'This process of growing in experience strengthens your ability to see where you are going and to adjust course as necessary based on variable conditions to ensure that your destinations remains in sight' (p. 154).*

The truth is that you may not even be able to see the path or the destination but you remain steadfast in your faith. A detour is not a denial and man's disappointment could be God's appointment. Your journey may, and certainly will have many detours, delays and disappointments but your destination of ultimate success is assured. Your process may be long and lonesome, dire and dreary but you will make it, even on broken pieces.

For Paul, the word of comfort, assurance and affirmation was 'there will be no loss of life!', so whilst others were in panic mode, he was calm and trusting God. How about you? Can you trust God where you may or may not have a direct word from Him in your storm? If you have no personal Faith and have not yet come into a personal encounter and relationship with the risen living Christ, you may want to consider your position in relation to faith in Christ. He gives peace in the midst of your storm and fulfilment, meaning and purpose in life's conflicting circumstances. You may not necessarily have all the answers but you will certainly grow in your faith to trust God's heart even when you cannot trace his hand or understand His works and ways. God can and will handle the cry of your broken heart.

His Acts and His Ways
I like the Psalm that says, 'Moses knew God's ways and the children of Israel sought His acts' (Psalm 103:7). Do you always have to see your way through at all times, or can you live by faith where you trust God even when you cannot see your way clearly? Are you concerned about the provisions as well as the principles of God? Jesus said, 'Blessed are those who believe yet they have not seen' (John 20:29). Furthermore, you trust God because of His character and principles, attributes and qualities. He is faithful, trustworthy and dependable.

Even without His acts, these ways or character traits are enough to rely on. My word to you, therefore, is that you will make it, firstly, "Safely" – You will make it safely over the other side of your pain, disappointment hurts, and reversals regardless of your process. Regardless of the 'cuts, bruises and trauma, the important thing is that you have made it and you are now safe. The process took a lot out of you but look at you now! You are safe and well. Sure, you may need support, counselling, healing and nurture but you are safe.

Secondly, you will make it "through": You will go through and not get stuck, over and not under. Jesus told the disciples 'Let us go over to the other side'. From end to end, it is a process. It might be as if you are stuck now but you will make it 'through.' Your process has an expected end, this too came 'to pass' and not to remain. Your troubles will terminate somewhere; they have a destination.

Sail through what was designed to sink or drown you; managing the water on the outside and preventing it from getting on the inside. Like Noah, pitch your 'ark' within and without. Seal your heart, mind, soul, spirit, relationships and vision. Managing people, News, social media, perceptions, influences, associations, thoughts, responses and reactions, what is on the outside that could jeopardise your stability and equilibrium. Reject negativity, poor attitudes and toxicity. Embrace challenging, critical but nurturing relationships. Seal your mouth too if, like Zachariah, you are tempted to negate your own blessing with destructive and toxic utterances (2 Kings 20:13).

Thirdly, you will make it 'On' - you will ride out the storms.... you will carry what was carrying you! Jesus told the lame man, 'Arise take up your bed and walk! (John 5:8). It may be embarrassing to face those who know you while you carry your bed, but it can be a celebration and testimony that the thing that once conquered and had you bound is now subject to you; that is to say, you are now well and healed enough to be carrying the thing that once carried you. Hang on therefore to the broken, shattered pieces of the wreck of what used to be in your life. Seize the positive influences. Salvage as much as you can and embrace the life lessons learnt from each situation but release the junk and useless remains of your past.

Fourthly, you will make it on 'Broken' – you do not need to have it all together to make it safely over! Stop waiting for perfection to start. You may be broken and spilled out, which is required for effective ministry. Use 'not enough', 'do it afraid' because 'courage is conquering fear not the absence of it.' Everyone is broken in some areas of life. You can have it all together in finances but have health issues that money cannot fix, perfect health but broke, finances healthy but no children, perfect family but poor, prosperous but lonely and lack peace, have it all together but miserable inside. Any area of our lives can be fragmented, shattered, cracked, smashed, damaged, flawed, destroyed, splintered or ruined. The challenge is to take the fragments of these and use them for your success.

Fifthly, you will make it safely through on broken "Pieces": waiting for perfection or 'wholeness' in all areas of life could delay your destiny, purpose and effectiveness. He who regards the weather never sows! Start where you are with what you have. This does not mean that you have not counted the cost and planned sensibly. Start where you are with the information and experience you have and move forward. You may be broken but you are blessed.

'Pieces' imply part of the whole though broken and shattered…in this case the planks or broken pieces were from the ship. Sometimes all we have is remnants of what used to be. What has shattered your 'whole', status quo, heart, normal or expected end? For Paul, it was the storms and contrary winds based on the poor decisions and choices of others. What caused your whole to be shattered into pieces? Remnant of a marriage, job, relationship, finances, health, goals, ambitions, aspiration or business venture; but these pieces reflect segments, albeit, small and broken pieces of the previous whole! These pieces or fragments can be used, salvaged and embraced to go over and through your storms. For instance, think of the 5 barley loaves and 2 fish of a boy's lunch that Jesus used to feed a multitude of over five thousand (Mark 14:13-21) or of the widow with the cruise of oil and a little flour that was greatly multiplied as she responded in faith and obedience to the Prophet, Elijah (1 Kings 17:7-16).

Relevance

As we sojourn, we will encounter a range of relationships that have to be managed appropriately. For Paul, he had to navigate his way from the ship's owners, centurion, soldiers, sailors and fellow prisoners through to the inhabitants of the Island. In all of his interactions, he respectfully, yet on occasions forcefully, manage each social interaction appropriately. For example, respecting the rights of the Captain's authority to command and recognising the power the soldiers hold as well as the duty of care the Captain and sailors hold for the safety of the souls on board.

Mention must also be made of the prisoners who rose to the occasion as and when so directed by Paul to ensure the safety of all concerned. Whether it was to remain on the ship, to lighten the load, to eventually eat and refresh themselves or to jump and swim to shores, unaided, on planks or on broken pieces of the ship. I am sure that Paul also had distant support in the form of those who prayed for him and supported his ministry and trials whether in Jerusalem or beyond.

Regardless of what you are going through today, you do have the respect and admiration of others. It may not seem so as this may not be frequently articulated. However, you have a lot to offer and others do value the contribution that you make. Additionally, you have distant support in the form of those who supported you in your formative years; those who prayed for you and encouraged you in tangible and intangible ways from far or near.

Application
You too will recognise and hopefully appreciate the many stakeholders in your life's journey. The many and varied people in your life along your journey will similarly necessitate appropriate responses, recognition and respect. They will most certainly play a different role as you navigate life's tumultuous waves. There will be times of fellowship, challenge, rebuke, affirmation, encouragement, disappointments, regrets, fear, panic, dread, warmth, hospitality, criticism, acceptance and ministry.

As you reflect on these possible experiences along your voyage, it is worth asking again, 'What is it in your hands that has been shattered and broken?' These could include your goals, dreams, finances, relationships, or health, and how can they be salvaged? I have already established that in some cases in life, there could be a total restoration of all things or even a doubling of what you have lost, for instance in Job's case. Also, there may be challenging times to pull through as you cast aside some weight, even of things precious and valuable, but which are now liabilities in your life.

As we navigate this largely unexpected Covid-19 pandemic, it is unimaginable to fathom the untold death rate around the world; so sad and what a senseless loss of precious lives, gone far too soon. Whether death through this terrible coronavirus or otherwise caused, our hope is in the scriptures that 'to be absent from the body is to be present with the Lord' (II Corinthians 5:8) and that 'to live is Christ and to die is gain' (Philippians 1:21). These might seem like empty words in your time of grief. However, my encouragement to you is to hold fast to the profession of your faith without wavering (Hebrews 10:23) and be not weary in well-doing for you will reap if you faint not (Galatians 6:9-10).

Reflection: As you reflect on the impact of the story of Paul's life, defence, shipwreck and journey, rescue, landing and hospitality and ministry opportunities, what will do now do? What action points, goals, aspirations, purposes or potential you will now realise? What is your God-given purpose in your storm? How have you been motivated, inspired, challenged and or encouraged?

Like Paul, you may have to pray for some folks who have landed you in your predicament. Yes, Paul had done some terrible things in his past life, but his immediate danger was not of his making. He interceded for the centurion, the ship's owner, the soldiers, and fellow prisoners. In your dark moments, you may need to release some things and people who might have hurt you. The darkness of the storm may obscure the sun and the blackness of your night conceals the moon and stars. Your heart is covered with the blanket of despair and hopelessness. You are wet, cold, hungry and seasick spiritually, mentally and emotionally and seem to have lost all hope. Nevertheless, the words of J.C. Penney (1875-1971) American retailing Magnate can add some hope,

> *'I'm grateful for all my problems. As each of them was overcome, I became stronger and was more able to meet those yet to come. I grew on my difficulties.'*

God reaches out to you in your storm howsoever caused. Through personal disobedience or that of others, when in desperation, you cry, 'If only!' These are teachable moments; can you embrace the moment as such? Life will afford you close escapes where you come through 'smelling of smoke'... escaping with just your life because you have had to cast aside so much overboard just to make it through! Not all storms result from disobedience; it could be an attack on your faith, to teach life lessons, develop character and spiritual development among others.

In your storm, it is useful to ascertain your location. God asked 'Adam where are you?' not for information; but to see if Adam knew the state, position or condition he was in (Genesis 3:9). As it is said, 'step one in problem solving, is recognition of the problem,' Having the right perspective on your location, identity, purpose, goals and vision even in the midst of shattered dreams and brokenness, will help to provide direction and resilience to make it safely through.

I continue to use of my SatNav to guide me along my journeys. The sailors used the sounding line to ascertain the depth of the water even in their storm. This sounding line was a long piece of rope with a weight attached at one end and having coloured strips tied every 6 feet. The sailor sounded at 120 feet it was still too deep and then they sounded again at 90 feet. The darkness may prevent or obscure your vision, the frightening howling winds may prevent or delay further sounding; you may be getting closer to 'shore' but you cannot definitely say how close, but you sense that there is 'a light at the end of the tunnel' 'a silver lining behind every dark cloud.'

You may be tempted to jump and abandon ship at the height of your desperation and fear. Maybe you have simply had enough or just simply 'flat out tired.' Like Paul, you might give or hear the words, 'Except these men abide on the ship they will perish!' I spoke about the need for discernment when to jump or when to remain. There are times when your survival depends on your faith to remain on board and ride out the storm.

Sadly, sometimes you may selfishly bail out and jump ship out of situations disregarding the impact it may have on yours or others' safety. You may have considered suicide, divorce, substance abuse or addictions as bail out strategies from your pain; but hold on, look how close you are to shore! And remember not a single soul will be lost. You may get there wet, cold, frightened, spent and on broken pieces but you survived! It is not so much how you got there, but *that* you got there!

At last, the Centurion listened to Paul and ordered everyone to remain. Sometimes you may have given instructions only for them to be rejected repeatedly. Possibly, like Paul, you may only gain some credibility and authenticity after much talking, pleading, admonishing and even prophesying or praying. Maybe they have observed your life, words, actions, gained confidence in you, and your word only after periods of unwavering, stable, consistent and faithful encouragement, not criticism and judgement. Perhaps your authenticity and credibility come after observing you in crises, after your words have been tested repeatedly and after you have been 'bitten'; and survived after shaking off some serpents in the presence of others. In *'Prayers that Heal the Heart'* Mark and Patti Virkler, write,

> *'I feel most healed when I am ministering God's grace to others, and I feel most fractured when I focus upon myself' (p.103).*

Perhaps you have a child who refuses to follow your instructions and lands into all manner of trouble. You may have to be the one to pick up the broken pieces later or put out fires you did not start! You may have to take in your daughter with that unplanned pregnancy, or bail out that wayward child from jail. You may have decided to keep that grown son or daughter in your house for much longer because they refused to listen and work hard in school, or failed to do sound financial planning now they have no savings or credit. You may decide to check that drug dependent child into rehab. The list goes on. Nevertheless, you have to believe that if you 'train up the child in the way he should go when he is old, he will not depart' (Proverbs 22:6). This does not mean he or she may not take a detour! Yet you trust God that eventually they will 'come to themselves' like the prodigal son and 'return home', and to self, purpose and destiny.

Reflection: What do others see or hear when you speak or act? What do you have to offer others in a storm?

Always keep your *sounding line* so that even in your darkest moments, you never lose sight of the 'shore': of hope, location direction or purpose. You may be in a dark and desolate place right now, but where are you going? Moreover, what is your current location in relation to your desired destination? You must see yourself coming out of this and embrace an expected end.

Be alert for even after you might clear the depths, there is still the risk of crashing on rocks and reefs closer to shore. There should never be a moment for complacency. The huge boisterous waves conceal the hidden dangers, the rock and the reefs. Even after a demanding and deadly journey through your storm, look out for these hidden dangers as you navigate your way to shore.

Although the ship crashed into them and was ripped to pieces by the savage winds, all made it safely to shore. So will you! You too must hold on to the debris or the broken pieces with jagged ends and painful splinters, of what you have left of your shattered dreams, heart and life, while the savage winds and boisterous waves push you to an unexpected destination. Mills (2017) asked,

> *'What about those routes that take us places we didn't want to go in the first place and there is no apparent purpose for the detour? Improvisation is necessary in arriving at our respective destinations' (pp145-147).*

This calls for trust and faith in God. Set your Satnav and trust the process even when they lead through unknown routes or diversions.

Summary List of Some Life Lessons
- Life's 'un-natural storms' and unexpected challenges will come.
- The thing that should carry you over could threaten to take you under.
- You will carry the thing that was carrying you.
- Use what you have left and not cry over what you have lost.
- Ride out your storms when you cannot make progress or gain ground.
- The darkest part of the night is just before dawn.
- A smooth sea does not make a skilful sailor.
- Minister in and through your pain as you develop an empathetic, credible and non-judgemental ministry.
- As you reach forward glance backwards - Use your painful life experiences to motivate, inspire, challenge and encourage others.
- Don't wait for perfection get started without it.
- Courage is not the absence of fear, but the conquering of it.
- Be adaptable and flexible, your imminent landing on shore may not be your final destination.
- Celebrate each stage of your achievement.
- Speak positively to and encourage yourself – Life and death are in the power of your tongue (Proverbs 18:21).
- Balance yourself against the compliments and criticisms of people.
- Be clear on your personal identity, your core beliefs and non-negotiable values.

- Divine revelation does not prevent storms or exempt you from trials, but gives a strategy in and through the storm.
- Cry if you must but move on.
- Be obedient.
- Don't live with regrets and dread the future.
- You may have to intercede for those who hurt you or cause your predicament.
- Remember the serum is in the venom; Use your pain to cure the brokenness – to inspire, cure, heal, encourage others.
- Take charge of your life – that was then this is now, Bind the devil in Jesus' name and move on to achieve your purpose.
- The oil of your anointing comes out of Gethsemane, a place of pressing and crushing.
- Brokenness is an opportunity to minister with power and passion.
- Know, accept and celebrate your abilities and capabilities: whether you can 'swim' unaided, on a plank or on broken pieces.
- Manage your associations: the closer you get to your destination you may need to narrow your circle.
- Life and death are in the power of your spoken words.
- If there is no enemy within, the enemy without can do you no harm.
- Greatness is incubated in the furnace of affliction.
- Positions and perspectives; mindsets and miseries are formulated by your attitude and responses to your trials.

- "Realistic goals may be achieved provided one has a dynamic sense of purpose that is far superior to all forces that constitute the odds" (O'Connor, 1984).

Final Word

You will make it safely through. Knowing your gifts, abilities and strength, you will use what you have and what you have left to make it safely through. You may go on, with or in spite of, but you will make it. You will confront, conquer and carry what once carried you even if it presents itself in another form that is different to the whole. You will make it safely through with the broken pieces. That is, you will realise that you are in fellowship with others, the comradery, partnerships and companionships. However, you are also in a relationship with the thing that carries you. Like Moses with the stick (his rod and staff); one with the plank, one with the scraps of wood as you cling desperately on for dear life amidst the raging sea. Though jagged, pointed and bruising maybe the ends, being brutally cut and hurt by the very thing you grasp to save you, yet therein lies your hope of survival and safe passage.

Dr Samuel Johnson reminds us that,

> 'Life affords no higher pleasure than that of surmounting difficulties, passing from one step of success to another, forming new wishes and seeing them gratified' *(The Complete Pocket Positives)*

You will make it safely through on broken pieces notwithstanding your *status quo*. Even if wholeness disappears, normal as you remember is no more, yet despite these changes: death of your dreams, hurts, pains, disappointments, regrets you will make it. You will adapt to a new way of speaking. Punctuate every utterance that could be negative with a 'but', 'yet', 'nevertheless' 'in spite of', 'however' or 'notwithstanding.'

I must admit in my humanity very few things annoy or distress me more than utterances that are wholly negative, toxic, unbalanced, filled with ingratitude or simply focus on all the bad things. Life's experiences can be bad undoubtedly; but there must be some good to identify, highlight, illuminate and focus on. Otherwise you could be a very sad individual and not very good company to be around, because that attitude of ingratitude will poison the atmosphere and depress others.

I find that these Scriptures are helpful and provide useful guides to how we can temper our conversations to reflect a balanced perspective, even in the midst of fervent brokenness; please note the use of *'yet', 'nevertheless'*, and *'but.'*

In Lamentations 3:19-24 (NIV) we read,

> *'I remember my afflictions, wanderings, bitterness, gall; downcast soul **yet**; I remember and have hope, purpose, sustenance, mercies, compassion, provision, patience and confidence in God.*

In Psalm 42:5 David also carefully punctuates his state of being cast down and disquieted with a well-placed, 'yet'. Similar to when he 'encouraged himself in the Lord', we see here where he also challenged himself and through rigorous reflection and self-interrogation asks:

> *'Why art thou cast down, O my soul? and why art thou disquieted in me? hope thou in God: for I shall **yet** praise him for the help of his countenance.*

It is quite interesting although he asks the tough questions in the same breath, he provided the answer. True, things are not going well but he recognises the source of his strength, and the strength of his life. Jesus also clearly models this principle in his moment of intense and excruciating pain,

> *Father, if thou be willing, remove this cup from me: **nevertheless,** not my will, but thine, be done' (Luke 22:42).*

In Job 13:15 he also realises after chapters of intense interrogation of God, finally accepts His sovereignty and having achieved a measure of closure declares,

> *'Though He slay me **yet** I will trust in Him'*

This book and lesson are focused on Paul and his use of the word 'but' even in the midst of his brokenness, perplexity, persecution, despair and potential destruction is worth noting. He writes,

> *'We are pressed on all sides, **but** not crushed; perplexed, **but** not in despair; persecuted, **but** not forsaken; struck down, **but** not destroyed' (2 Cor 4:8-9)*

Do not put a *full stop* where God puts a *Comma!* Remember these two scriptures I earlier mentioned, 'Life and death are in the power of your tongue' and 'you are snared by your own words' not those of others. Therefore, accentuate the positives, minimise or eradicate the negatives!

Hence, whether 'with', 'despite' or 'on' broken pieces you will make it safely through your broken, pieces, places or person, 'in spite' 'but' or 'nevertheless.' Through transition, changes, fear, tempestuous seas, hopelessness, isolation, redundancies, family problems, financial reversals, health issues, marital or relational problems, homelessness, death of loved ones, pandemic fears and cares, recession, depression or whatever the situation may be, you will make it. You will thrive and flourish where others falter.

'I will make it!'

Yes, that is how you speak.

Reflection: Whether you encountered: hospitality or hostility, warmth or cold, ridicule or judgement or snake bite; why did you make it through and for what?' Did you suffer in vain?

Closure…. of Sorts

It is said 'after a storm, there must be a calm.' This can be an interesting time, one which we all handle differently. For some, it is a time of stress, anxiety, sadness, bitterness, regrets and disappointments. Others could use this as a time for reflection and 'post-mortem' to glean life lessons for positive application. This does not mean they the latter might not experience some of the emotions of the former, or that the former failed to reflect and analyse. Life is far more complicated. Even for those who come through seemingly or relatively unscathed, it could still be a process to get to a place of closure. There should be some form of interrogation, investigation, review, analysis and evaluation of the process.

During the storm, you take your take test in silence, in quiet contemplation. This might require having a confidante to share the load. However, there is a need to use wisdom to determine what may or may not be appropriate to share how, when, where or why. It might be crucial that you narrow your circle the higher you climb. This is not about pride, arrogance or conceit; rather it is about wisdom and good judgement. This is about knowing who to take along with you on the journey after you have suffered a while. After your analysis, review, examination and evaluation of your process, you undoubtedly will emerge a different person! You should. You will emerge stronger, better, more resilient, determined, changed, powerful and passionate.

Not everyone will appreciate this new mindset or shift in paradigm. They may want to see you languishing in regrets and negativity, moaning and complaining endlessly. This is counterproductive and has no place in the company or association of one who had benefited from the process and wants to move to purpose, productivity, growth and effectiveness. Not everyone is called to go where you are going. You may be called to soar like eagles; others might be called to scratch for worms like chickens at a different level. None is better than the other, just different calling and purposes, as it is said, 'birds of a feather flock together.'

I mentioned the lesson we can learn from Joseph who shared his vision with his brothers prematurely. Nonetheless, it was all in the plan and purpose; through the problem, the process, the purpose was fulfilled and he eventually made it from the pit through the prison to the palace. His 'post mortem' led him to develop an attitude and character of humility, empathy, grace, poise, dignity and forgiveness despite his tremendous power:

> *'Don't worry about it'*

He comforted his brothers, who hurt him,

> *'You meant it for evil but God made it good!' (Genesis 50:20).*

> *You intended to harm me, but God intended it for good to accomplish what is now being done, the saving of many lives (Genesis 50:20 NIV).*

Admittedly, getting to this stage is not easy; don't misunderstand me. It will demand different times through different processes for different people. You will have to develop a strategy to cope that is wholesome, healthy, moral, legal or faith-based. You may have a tremendous support system of close friends to be there for you. On the contrary, you may find it quite difficult to find a friend to share your experiences with after your storm. There is a place for talking after the storm to share experiences, relive the pain and the process or even revisit the scene of the hurt as part of the healing, rather than suffering in silence.

A challenge for some could be to find a friend who genuinely empathises and listens non-judgementally; one who is not too busy to care, neither is intimated by nor is jealous of your success. Anyone who cannot make time for you, who is always 'busy' evidently does not value you or your experiences and is therefore not worthy of being taken to the next level in your life's process. True friendships require sacrifice, loyalty and commitment. Thus, it is difficult to have many close friends.

Managing relationships does take time, effort and commitment. Not everyone has or will share your propensity, passion, purpose, path or power to greatness. The fact is that not everyone is prepared to make the level of sacrifice that is required to be you or to achieve what you have achieved. In other words, not everyone is willing to pay the price, although they may want the glory without the story! Some people you have to simply accept and respect this is who they are.

Understanding the principle of levels of associations is crucial to the purpose. For instance, who to ask to 'leave the room' before performing your miracles (Mark 5:40). Others might have to be asked to 'remain with the donkey' while you 'go yonder to worship' (Genesis 22:5); who must remain 'a stone's throw' while you go yonder to pray alone (Luke 22:41), when to 'shake dust from your shoes' and move on (Matthew 10:14); or those you take with you to your 'Mount of Transfiguration' (Matthew 17). Do not 'cast your pearls to swines or that which is holy to the dogs' (Matthew 7:6) because not everyone will celebrate your achievements and safe passage through your storm, and value the magnitude of your sacrifices to gain your success.

Sometimes after your storm, you may need to go where you are celebrated and not remain where you are merely tolerated. You have a lot to offer after your storm. Take the time to locate the right nurturing environment and associations in which you can truly flourish and thrive. I am not talking here about pride, conceit, egoism, narcissism or arrogance. Sometimes you will stoop to conquer and with great humility endure the menial to scale to the mighty. Yet with great humility and resolve you serve when you get there, remembering the lowly path of sacrifice and brokenness that got you there. Nevertheless, you need to recognise what it took out of you to get there. This 'pearl', 'virtue', or 'excellence' is not cheap. It is not for sale. Where others do not value your experiences or respect your painful process; where they cannot celebrate your achievements and simply recognise greatness and achievement, then it might be time to re-evaluate your condition, location and position, in light of others' perception.

A crucial part of your healing process as mentioned may be to revisit the 'trauma site' as part of your stocktaking and post-mortem. This could mean confronting a painful experience, going back to the place of your 'shipwreck' literally or metaphorically. It could mean talking over an unresolved conflict or simply deciding that it is not worth regurgitating. This is difficult to discern and requires much wisdom especially when others are involved. Closure for you could mean re-hatching or stirring up old and painful wounds for another person. It is always wise to contemplate the impact and implications of sharing your painful experiences where others could be harmed emotionally or otherwise. Identifying and being mindful of ethical and safeguarding issues are crucial.

Nonetheless, after the storm, there should be a time and place, whether personally, with a trusted person or professionally, where you reflect and re-evaluate. From this process, you will use your pain to prepare and propel you into purpose; to achieve greatness and in the process, confound the bullies and naysayers. Remember, the greater your pain, the greater the anointing, the passion and the power. Furthermore, from your process you will gain new insights, illumination, mindsets and paradigms and even associations as you decide what to 'cast over board' and what to salvage from your 'shipwreck.'

The account after the Feeding of the Five Thousand as recorded in Matthew 14:20 (NIV) is very applicable to illustrate the principle of using what you have left in order to move on to future success and purpose.

> *'They all ate and were satisfied, and the disciples picked up twelve basketfuls of **broken pieces** that were left over.'*

Do not under estimate the power of the broken pieces. Jesus remained behind to dismiss the crowd but sent the disciples to go ahead of him to the other side. Jesus had given so much in ministry and what was more, His cousin John the Baptist was recently beheaded. Although Jesus went away alone to pray, He did not have sufficient time to grieve.

Alone by the mountainside in prayer, Jesus prayed well into the night. Sometimes you have to 'build up yourself in your most holy faith' and 'encourage yourself in the Lord!' The disciples on the boat were already a considerable distance from land, buffeted by the boisterous waves because the wind was against it. Then out of the blackness of night came Jesus, walking on the water. Oh, the fear and dread they experienced, thinking it was a ghost. Jesus calmed and re-assured them:

> *But Jesus immediately said to them: "Take courage! It is I. Don't be afraid" (Matthew 14:27).*

You can rest assured that Jesus will come to you even on your stormy seas. The sequence of events that followed with Peter walking on the water is well documented. However, there are a few principles I want to extrapolate from this part of the story. Jesus climbed into the boat with them and immediately the wind died down. In your storms when fear and panic set in, you may not recognise when your help comes. It may come in and through an unfamiliar way, person or experience. It may come through the strength and anointing of your unaided effort, through a plank or even a broken piece from your shattered wreck. However, your storm is a teaching moment to introduce or re-introduce you to solutions, strategies and to God. You may be tempted to lose faith and question the faithfulness of God, but look at the timing of His intervention!

Sometimes we have very short memories or selective amnesia. The disciples were with Jesus and saw him feed five thousand men, not to mention women and children just a few hours ago, using a boy's packed lunch. Yet in a moment of crisis, again they panicked.

Reflection: What did you learn from your previous experiences? How will you use the life lessons as coping strategies for future storms? Do you fall apart in panic and absolute dread and depression every time you face a new challenge?

After the multitude had eaten, Jesus told the disciples to gather the scraps, the fragments, the broken pieces; nothing should be wasted. May I suggest that nothing happens by chance in your life? The scraps, fragments or the broken pieces all were once a part of that which was whole, complete, valuable and nourishing. After every storm regardless of how you have been spent, save your fragments, scraps and broken pieces.

> *'But why, should I?'*

You may ask.

> *'Aren't those simply good for the junk yard, the scrap heap and the rubbish bins!'*

Yet, in His infinite wisdom, Jesus said,

> *'Gather the broken pieces, let nothing be wasted.'*

As the winds subsided when Jesus entered the boat, the disciples were completely amazed. However, this crucial verse illuminates an important point:

> *'...for they had not understood about the loaves; their hearts were hardened (Mark 6:52 NIV).*

Let us look at this verse from a few other translations in order to illuminate the magnitude of the revelation you can take away from this life lesson:

> *'For they still didn't understand the significance of the miracle of the loaves. Their hearts were too hard to take it in.' (NLT)*
>
> *'For they had not gained any insight from the incident of the loaves, but their heart was hardened (New American Standard Bible)*
>
> *'For they had not learned the lesson taught by the loaves (Weymouth New Testament);*
>
> *'They didn't understand what had happened with the loaves of bread. Instead, their minds were closed GOD'S WORD® Translation);*

This is so profound! I had to take the time to include these different translations of the same verse to highlight the importance of the lesson. What did the disciples learn from the miracle? They had been with Jesus; they had seen the miracle of the feeding over possibly over 12,000 people out of virtually nothing. Even so, they had 12 baskets of scraps, crumbs, fragments and broken pieces to collect! Let us consider why their hearts hardened, so hard they could not take in the miracle. Why were their minds closed and simply failed to learn the lesson?

I have been working in the field of Education for nearly forty years. Admittedly, it can be frustrating when you have explained, taught, explained again then 'test' and the concepts are not grasped. Most times, the lesson has to be repeated. It may require a different strategy or method but the lesson must be re-taught until the concepts are grasped; if the students are to be successful in their examinations in order to move to the next level.

Firstly, the disciples were hardened in their minds or failed to gain understanding and insights from the miracle because they could have been exhausted and burned out from the demands of ministry. The disciples had to make personal sacrifices in order to follow Jesus, when living under Roman Occupation. Furthermore, they could have been exhausted from the demands of feeding the multitude. Note that after the lengthy sermon and the interrogation by Jesus as to how the multitude would be fed, they had to arrange the thousands of people into groups of fifties! Well, that would take some time!

Secondly, the disciples failed to remember the broken pieces, leftovers and fragments in the boat with them that they had collected. Why carry around fragments, scraps and broken pieces? Why value the scars and tears, cares, incidents, accidents and traumas? Why build an altar or a memorial after your flood? To remind you from whence you came! To remind you of God's goodness and faithfulness! To remind you that it is the power of God through the lessons learnt in and from the experiences that give you the strength and resilience to face new challenges. Never despise your storms, stories, experiences, problems or processes. If Jesus could miraculously feed the multitude, He could save them too. He will do it again.

However, they were slow to perceive His power. The dullness or the hardened state of their hearts and minds could mean that they did not quickly learn from the miracle, as they ought to have done, only few hours prior. They failed to grasp that He had all power, and could therefore calm the storm. Use your scraps, leftovers and broken pieces to remind you of your past successes. God can use them as reminders as sources of your power and deliverance. Go ahead. Tell your future about your past. Prophesy to your problem out of your pain, based on your problems; develop your purpose and passion.

Yes, go ahead, gather the broken pieces, stack them away, load them up in your boat and never forget that they are there with you! For they are your source of reflection, memory and recollection of the miracles, favour, blessings and grace you received at the hands of a merciful and faithful God in previous storms. You learn from your experiences and use them as catalysts for upcoming storms. I am sure you can understand the frustrations Jesus no doubt felt. On another occasion He replied,

> 'Have I been with you all this time, Philip, and yet you still don't know who I am? Anyone who has seen me has seen the Father! So why are you asking me to show him to you? (John 14:9 NLT).

They had all missed the point of the lesson. Yes, He comforted and re-assured them however, it would have been great if the lesson had been learnt. Sometimes your storms are not to be taken at a literal level. Whilst Jesus was feeding the multitude, He was teaching a class. Your tenacity and resilience are in your broken pieces, your storms and rehearsals. So, at the appropriate time, cast away your broken pieces but treasure the memories; and discard your leftovers, scraps or fragments from your miracle, but learn the lesson, develop the right attitude, serve others and use the lessons learnt as points of faith reference for future storms.

Reflection: What is your perception, mindset of, and attitudes in your storm: Hardness of heart or flexibility, pliable and trusting? Are you angry and bitter, filled with resentment or regrets?

We have seen that it is possible to serve in any sphere of life with hardened hearts, wrong attitudes, missed opportunities; being burn out, overworked, resentful and failing to grasp the intended life lessons from the tests. For instance, I mentioned Martha who served Jesus with a resentful heart towards her sister Mary and the older brother in the story of the Prodigal son. Let us also not forget that you can be hurt while doing good as in the case of Paul who was bitten and shipwrecked.

Have you grasped the insights, lessons, understanding, miracles and favour from your teaching moments? Use your favour to offset your famine. Use your 'fat' years of 'favour' to invest and save for the 'lean' years of 'famine' whether financially, spiritually, emotionally or otherwise.

May I hasten to add however, when you land safely out of your storm then you will see the true purpose or reason for your storm.

> *'When they had crossed over, they landed at Gennesaret and anchored there. As soon as they got out of the boat, people recognised Jesus. They ran throughout that whole region and carried the sick on mats to wherever they heard he was.*
>
> *'And wherever he went—into villages, towns or countryside—they placed the sick in the marketplaces. They begged him to let them touch even the edge of his cloak, and all who touched it were healed.' (Mark 6: 53-56 NIV)*

For Paul, after his storm and shipwreck, it was the healing of Publius' father and all on Malta who came to him, that reflected how the bitten hand became the instrument of healing and of power. Learn from your bite, your storms and shipwreck. Gather the scraps, the fragments, the splinters and the broken pieces of your previously whole 'ship' or 'nourishing scrumptious meal' (whatever these are for you metaphorically speaking), and take them with you into your next challenge. Bearing in mind that there is a healthy time to release them and make way for new experiences of teachable moments. Your storm was planned and your fight was fixed. Your scars are stars, stumbling blocks, stepping stones, messes, messages, mirage, miracles, impediments, implements, obstacles opportunities

'It Again, Another'

As we come to the end of this book, let us consider Jeremiah the Prophet. An interesting account is outlined in Jeremiah 18 where he was instructed by the LORD to go down to the Potter's house and use that experience as a teaching moment. The lesson or the message was not intended to be a descriptive one where he simply observed the potter working at the wheel. Instead, the Lord gave Jeremiah a message that was far more analytical and applicable; one with tremendous theological, philosophical and inspirational significance.

As Jeremiah obeyed and went, he observed that the vessel the potter was shaping from the clay was marred (blemished, flawed, disfigured, spoiled ad tarnished), in his hands. The potter formed it again into 'another' pot. He shaped it, as it seemed best to Him. The King James Version puts it this way,

> And the vessel that he made of clay was marred in the hand of the potter: so, he **made it again another**

> *vessel, as seemed good to the potter to make it (Jeremiah 18:4).*

This is powerful. Jeremiah received the revelation as the Word of the Lord came to him. However, then came the interrogation:

> *Can I not do with you, Israel, as this potter does?*

Declares the Lord,

> *Like clay in the hand of the potter, so are you in my hand, Israel, (Jeremiah 18:6 NIV.)*

Even if you are broken or marred, remember that you are still in His hands. You may have been scarred, wounded, perplexed, discouraged, despondent, disappointed or depressed. Perhaps you were ostracised, rejected, overlooked, undermined or exploited. Possibly, you have suffered loss, death, unmet expectations, broken dreams and dashed hopes. It could be that your investments did not yield the anticipated returns or you harbour guilt over poor decisions and choices you have made outside of God's will.

The message today is you are still in the hand of the Potter! As long as you remain there, you are safe. You are safe because He is always able, willing and ready to re-mould, re-fashion and rebuild what is left of your shattered dreams and broken life. Only God can make 'it again, another!' The fact that the clay or the raw material was marred, flawed, disfigured or blemished did not intimidate the Potter. He simply moulded it again into another vessel, although it was from the same raw material. You are the same 'it' yet you are 'another!' Therefore, whether as clay in the hand of the potter or a broken piece of splintered wreck, use what you have to propel you into your purpose and destiny.

There will be changes as you emerge a new person from your 'spinning' on the Potter's wheel and the 'storms' on the raging sea. The storms could represent the challenging circumstances from without, that ferociously beat upon you with boisterous winds. You will experience 'internal storms', however, the 'spinning' is about you personally being on the Potter's wheel being spun at high speed with so many internal challenges assailing you simultaneously. If only you firmly embrace your broken pieces and endure the spinning, you will undoubtedly emerge victoriously.

You will have a new perspective, attitude, resilience, purpose and shift in paradigm. Embrace this transition and transformation with humility, remembering that you may have to narrow your circle of associations to those that are constructive, nurturing and of faith as you scale the heights of success. Yet, remember to reach forward but glance backwards. What do I mean by this? I simply mean that as you scale the heights of success in whatever area of life, never forget from whence you have come. It is important in order to remain empathetic and helpful to others and to be a source of comfort to those in similar positions and conditions to where you have been.

In conclusion, use what you have left and do not become fixated on what you have lost. There is hope for you regardless of your past and God is able to turn things around for your good, that of others and His glory. Your end is fixed from the beginning so regardless of what you go through, your victory is pre-determined. Even if you are 'shipwrecked' whether it was as a direct result of your poor decisions and choices or not, God can give you favour in the midst of the storm. You may have to be the one to be 'at the place' to hear from God in order to encourage, inspire, and uplift others while you are in your storms. You may have to be the one to receive that Word of encouragement and comfort to pass on to others (like Paul from the Angel or Jeremiah from the Lord through the Potter). You may have to be the nurturer to motivate, inspire, encourage and even challenge others to refresh themselves and eat something, even in the storms of life! You may feel isolated and under-appreciated because you are always the one giving and ministering. Nevertheless, you will be encouraged and undergirded by God's eternal hands. You will find favour, grace and mercy whosesoever you find yourself and these will be of great benefit to others.

Even after you are spent in service and ministry there is always more to do, however refresh and nurture yourself to avoid burn out. You may have to set yourself apart to be renewed, rejuvenated, empowered and refreshed; and apply principles of transformational leadership and emotional intelligence (congruence or genuineness, empathy, authenticity, self-awareness, social skills, self-regulation and motivation), to your leadership pursuits. It is possible that you will be 'bitten' while in the service of others. Even though bitten by venomous snakes, you can take decisive action to shake it off into the fire. Because of the anointing on your life, you will not necessarily be adversely affected by what may have hurt others. This means that whilst you recognise that there is a cross for everyone to bear, comparing yourself to others and becoming stressed in anticipation of misfortune is not helpful.

I pointed out a very important principle, which I want to emphasize: The bitten hand became the healing hand! So regardless, of how you were bitten, hurt, in a storm or in the spinning, you can emerge victoriously to use your pain or problem, through your processes to be empowered with passion for purpose. Your power is in your pain; never underestimate the value of your personal story! The man born blind who Jesus healed, following interrogation and being ostracised from the Temple maintained his personal testimony declaring confidently,

'... One thing I do know. I was blind but now I see!'

I wish you well as you navigate the stormy seas of life. May you be strengthened in your dark and lonely hours; as you endure the relentless spinning on the Potter's wheel or buffering on the stormy seas. Remember you are still in the Potter's hands and He will make 'it again another vessel', though the first was marred. (Jeremiah 18:4)

Finally remember you need not worry about what you have lost; instead reach out and grab a splintered piece from the shattered and broken piece of what was your life. It may hurt you as you embrace it and swim to shore, but rest assured you will make it safely through, even on broken pieces!!

> *"...And the rest, some on boards, and some on broken pieces of the ship. And so it came to pass, that they escaped all safe to land. (Acts 27:44)*

References

Acknerman, R. and Maslin-Ostrowski, P. The Wounded leader: How Real Leadership Emerges in Times of Crisis. San Francisco, CA: John Wiley & Sons.

Antonio, F., 2016, *Leadership by The Book: Scriptural leadership Principles for Contemporary Application*, USA.

Ashimolowo, M., 2002, *Breaking Barriers*, London: Mattyson Media.

Cerullo, D., *Take it back: Reclaim Everything the Enemy Has Stolen,* North Carolina, USA: Inspiration Ministries.

Colbert, D., 2005, *Stress Less*, Florida, USA: Siloam.

Day, A., 2003, If *Caterpillars Can Fly So Can I: Master the 7 Universal Laws to Achieve and Prosper*, Florida, USA: Million Mountain Press.

Day, C. (2004) A Passion for Teaching, London: Routledge Falmer

Drucker, P., 1998 Peter Drucker on the Profession of Management, Harvard business school publishing, Boston, USA

Franklin, J., 2013, *Limitless*, USA: Charisma House Book.

Goleman, D. (Best of HBR 1998) What Makes a Leader in Harvard Business Review.

Holy Bible, New International Version®, NIV® Copyright ©1973, 1978, 1984, 2011 by Biblica, Inc.®

Jakes, T., 2017, *Soar! Build your Vision from the Ground Up*, New York, USA: Hachette Book Group Inc.

Jakes, T., 1996, TD Jakes Speaks to Men! Oklahoma: Albury Publishing.

Martin, D., 2000, *The Force of Favor,* Florida, USA: Favor International.

Meyer, J 2015, *100 Ways to Simplify your Life,* New York, USA: Hachette Book Group, NY, USA

Mills, J., 2017, *Wounded Soldier: A Greater Purpose,* UK: Amazon.

Munroe, M., 2003, *The Principles and the Power of Vision – Keys to achieving personal and corporate Destiny,* Whittaker house, Bahamas

Munroe, M., 1991, *Understanding Your Potential,* Nassau, Bahamas: Destiny Image Publishers.

Murdock, M., 2001, *Seeds of Wisdom on the Word of God, Volume 15,* USA: Wisdom International.

Murdock, M., 2001, *The 3 Most Important Things in Your Life*, Texas, USA: The Wisdom Centre.

Obama, M., 2018, *Becoming Michelle Obama*, UK: Penguin Random House

O'Connor, P., 2015, 'The Sustaining of a Christian Teacher's Career in a Secularizing Context' in Bryan, H and Worsley, (eds.) 2015, in *Being Christian in Education: Reflecting on Christian Professional Practice in a Secular World,* London: Canterbury Press Norwich.

Pinkney, M. (2005), *The Complete Pocket Positives,* The Five Mile Press Pty Ltd.: Australia

Ratcliffe, S. (2012), (Ed) *Little Oxford Dictionary of Quotations*, United Kingdom: Oxford University Press.

Scott, R., 2013, *Christians in the Firing Line*, London: Wilberforce Publications.

Scott, S., 2013, *Unfinished,* Colorado, USA: Waterbrook Press.

Tew, M (2007) School Effectiveness: Supporting Success through Emotional Literacy. London: Paul Chapman Publishing

The New International Webster's Pocket Quotation Dictionary of the English Language (1997, Trident Press International: USA

Tomlinson H. (2004) Educational leadership: Personal Growth for Professional Development. London: Sage Publications Ltd.

Treat, C., *Renewing the Mind: The Key to Transformation*, Tulsa, Oklahoma, USA: Harrison house Inc.

Verkler, M. and P., 2001, *Prayers that Heal the Heart: Prayer Counselling that Breaks Every Yoke*, Florida: Bridge-logos.

Warren, R., 2002, *The Purpose Driven Life: What on Earth Am I Here For?* Grand Rapids, Michigan: Zondervan.

Websites

https://www.kingjamesbibleonline.org/Matthew

https://www.biblegateway.com/passage/?search=Exodus+18&version=NIV

https://www.nhs.uk/conditions/snake-bites/

https://www.who.int/snakebites/antivenoms/en/

https://www.britannica.com/biography/Saint-Paul-the-Apostle/Mission

https://jesusalive.cc/paulstrials.htm

https://www.britannica.com/technology/panning

https://www.inc.com/author/ilan-mochari

https://www.franklincovey.com/the-7-habits.html

https://www.inc.com/ilan-mochari/vacuum-innovation.html

https://www.inc.com/author/ilan-mochari

https://www.gosh.nhs.uk/our-people/staff-z/richard-scott

https://www.kentonline.co.uk/thanet/news/gp-cleared-after-complaint-about-praying-with-patients-218088/

https://www.linkedin.com/pulse/you-want-thing-bad-enough-les-brown-andre-rynhardt-barnard

https://biblehub.com/sermons/acts/27-1.htm

https://www.britannica.com/technology/panning

- **Youth Seminars/Conventions** (Finding purpose, Raising aspiration, Relationships, Faith and Life Choices)
- **Men's/ Women's Breakfast & Seminars** (Relevant issues & shared story)
- **Local and International Conferences** (*Academic:* Doctoral thesis on 'Principles, values and Christian beliefs in Professional Practice – Sensitive and Controversial Issues) and **Non-academic** (Emotional Intelligence in Leadership, Finding purpose, Using what you have left for success; Using your personal story to inspire others & Turing pain into passion, power and purpose.
- **Motivational/Inspirational speeches:** Motivate, Inspire, Challenge and Encourage
- **Mentoring and support through shared experiences** - Life and Academic

- **Inspiring and Challenging Sermons**: Non-denominational

- **School Assemblies and Prize-giving Ceremonies**

- **Schools, Universities, Churches, Charities, Health, Corporate organisations, Individual and group presentations**

Phillip addresses a range of relevant, applicable and thought-provoking topics and issues of an academic, relational, professional, personal, theological, philosophical, motivational and inspirational nature with a view to motivate, inspire, encourage, challenge and provoke meaningful paradigm shifts and change in mindsets. Engaging, in-depth & conceptual. Each address will encourage meaningful life changes, substantial & outstanding personal achievements of targets, goals, visions and purpose.

For any of these speaking opportunities, please contact Phillip:

Email: Phillip.speakingservices@gmail.com

Social Media:

Dr. Phillip J. O'Connor

Phillip is a sessional academic university lecturer and a teacher for the past 38 years in Jamaica, Cayman Islands and the UK, teaching a range of subjects including Music, Physical Education, Mathematics, Sociology, Psychology and Personal Social Health Education (PSHE) among others. He lectures on the Postgraduate in Diploma Education programme, training teachers at Master's degree level.

He was baptised as a teenager and started preaching and playing the guitar from an early age. Phillip continued in ministry in the Cayman Islands, teachings, preaching and serving as full time Youth Minister for 3 years in the local church, while producing and presenting a weekly 4-hour radio programme, 'Times of Refreshing' on ICCI-FM.

Born in Birmingham and as a British citizen, he returned to England in 2001 from the Cayman Islands and continued to teach, preach, inspire, motivate and facilitate Youth and Men's fellowship seminars. Phillip presents Papers at International academic conferences in Norway, Ireland and England, whilst teaching full time. Now semi-retired, Phillip launched his own Ministry and serves as an inspirational speaker in a number of organisations in England, USA, the Cayman Islands and Jamaica. He completed the BA (Professional Studies in Education), (First Class Honours and a

Masters in Leadership and Management (Distinction) in 2011. He embarked on and successfully completed the Doctorate in Education, Christianity and Faith in Education (2012-2017).

Dr O'Connor addresses a range of relevant, applicable and thought-provoking topics and issues of an academic, relational, professional, personal, theological, philosophical, motivational and inspirational nature with a view to motivate, inspire, encourage, empower, challenge and provoke meaningful paradigm shifts and change in mindsets. Engaging, in-depth & conceptual, each address will encourage meaningful life changes, substantial & outstanding personal achievements of targets, goals, visions and purpose.

He is married to Rhona O'Connor, a registered nurse.

Printed in Great Britain
by Amazon